W9-AYE-386

# Antique Trader®
# TOOLS
## PRICE GUIDE

Edited by
## Kyle Husfloen

Contributing Editor
## Clarence Blanchard

©2003 Krause Publications

Published by

**krause publications**

An F+W Publications Company

**700 East State Street • Iola, WI 54990-0001**
**715-445-2214 • 888-457-2873**
**www.krause.com**

Our toll-free number to place an order or
obtain a free catalog is 800-258-0929.

Library of Congress Catalog Number: 2003107933

ISBN: 0-87349-708-2

Edited by Kyle Husfloen

Designed by Sandra Morrison and Wendy Wendt

Printed in the United States of America

# TABLE OF CONTENTS

# A Word to the Reader

Here at Antique Trader Books we are always working to expand our range of books and price guides on various popular collecting fields. I'm pleased to present here our brand-new *Antique Trader Tools Price Guide.*

It has taken many long hours of work to put together the more than 2,100 entries here, and it would not have been possible without the invaluable assistance of Clarence Blanchard of Brown Auction Services, Pownal, Maine. Clarence was always available to consult with and answer the questions of a tool novice such as myself. With his guidance I feel we have put together an excellent guide to the broad and fascinating world of tool collecting. Another helpful inspiration was the pioneering reference, *The Antique Tool Collector's Guide to Value* by Ronald S. Barlow (Windmill Publishing Company, El Cajon, CA, 1985).

In addition to our many detailed listings we have also been able to illustrate here more than 500 individual tools of all types and are also including a special 16-page full-color supplement for your enjoyment. As Mr. Blanchard points out in the following feature on tool collecting, there are several factors that will determine the value of any particular tool. In our listings we have striven to provide all the details we can that will help you understand what influenced the value of that tool. As always, we ask you to use this book only as a *guide*, a resource to help you better understand this collecting area and the pieces you may come across.

Although we are including twelve specific categories of tools, you will note that the section on "Planes" is especially extensive. The simple reason for this is that in today's market more planes are bought and sold than any other specific type of tool. Here you'll find planes ranging in date from the 18th through the mid-20th century. As with many types of antiques, age alone is not always the major factor in determining collector value.

My staff and I have worked diligently to select the best range of tools possible and have carefully edited and proofed all the material included here. However, please note that although every effort has been made to ensure accuracy, neither the compilers, editors nor publisher can assume responsibility for any losses that might be incurred as a result of consulting this guide, or of errors, typographical or otherwise.

Now, sit back and enjoy perusing our comprehensive guide to the wonderful world of tools. I hope you'll find it an invaluable reference and a volume you can take along on all your collecting forays. If you have any comments or suggestions, you are welcome to write. We'll do our best to respond to your letters.

Kyle Husfloen, Editor

# An Introduction to Tool Collecting

## by Clarence Blanchard

Tool collecting is nearly as old as tools themselves. Certainly it was not long after Stone Age man used his first stone tool that he started watching for that special rock or piece of bone. Soon he would have been putting tools away just for the right time or project. The first tool collector was born!

Since earliest man started collecting tools just for the right time or project, many other reasons to collect have evolved. As man created one tool, he could then use that tool to make an even better tool. Very quickly toolmakers became extremely skilled at their craft, and that created a new collecting area – collecting the works of the very best makers. In time toolmakers realized that tools were being purchased on the bases of the quality of workmanship alone. With this realization an even more advanced collector was born as toolmakers began making top-of-the-line tools from special materials with fine detailing and engraving. These exquisite tools were never intended for use but were to be enjoyed and collected. Many of the finest tools were of such quality that they are considered works of art.

## Focusing a collection

So many tools exist in today's world that many tool collectors focus on one special category. Some of the most popular categories to collect fall into the following general areas.

### Function

Focusing on finding tools with a particular function is a very popular way to specialize a collection. Some collectors seek out wooden planes, for example, while others hunt down wrenches, and some look only for hammers.

### Craft or trade

Others collect tools of a certain craft or trade: cooper, tinsmith and wheelwright tools are popular examples of that type of collection. Many collectors in this group can be seen at demonstrations and craft fairs showing how their tools are used and demonstrating the methods used by the old time trade person.

### Personal connection

Many collectors look for tools with certain names or connected to certain locations. Among these subcategories are particular family names or groups of names with historical connections, and hometowns, states, counties or other special places. This group of collectors is quite large, with many having a "hometown" or "my name" collection in addition to their other areas of interest.

### Company or brand

Collecting tools made by a particular company or maker is very popular. Some makers have long since ceased production, while others are still making tools today. Stanley products make up one of the most sought after company brands, and collections consisting of thousands of tools have been assembled around the Stanley name alone.

### Patents

Yankee ingenuity thrived in the 19th century, and thousands of tool patents were issued. Some were successful, while others were never manufactured. A large group of collectors seek only patented tools. These collectors tend to be very specialized, and each addition to their collections must meet specific requirements. Some collect only one type of tool. Complete collections have been made up of only patented braces, for example, or just patented planes. Other collectors will only collect tools patented before a certain date. Still others are only interested in the patents of one company or individual.

### Investment

Collecting as a means of making money, historically, has not been of primary interest. As some of the early collections come to market, however, it is becoming obvious that tools can be a great investment. With an educated eye, miles of travel and hours of searching, some collectors have reaped excellent returns on they tool investments.

As collecting continues to grow and monetary values increase, the investment side of the hobby must be considered. Clearly, with today's higher initial cost per tool, one must at least think about the long-term value of each purchase. Over the past few years values have been steadily rising. All indicators are that interest is strong and tool prices will continue to increase.

## Values

What makes a tool valuable? A general answer is easy: quality. Most valuable tools will be of high quality. If a tool is well made from high-end materials, chances are it is worthy of investigation. **Materials** are easy to spot and well known to us all. Ebony is better than maple, ivory trimmings are better than brass. **Quality of manufacture** is a bit harder to decipher, but with a little effort you can learn what a better tool "feels" like. This will not tell you the value or keep you from missing tools that require special knowledge, but it should help spot the gems.

To answer the value question in detail requires a great deal of knowledge that can take years to amass. As with all collectible areas, three basic considerations are paramount among all determining factors: **rarity, desirability** and **condition**. These factors must be considered first individually and then combined to determine value. Rarity and condition are generally fixed, while demand can change from time to time. All three factors combine to determine the importance of each item. Rarity sets the level of interest, demand controls the amount of interest, and condition determines how hard a collector will go after any given item. Any single factor, when exceptional, can move a piece from obscurity to stardom. If all three factors come together on the same item, you have a superstar.

Like most antiques, tools make up a wide and varied field that takes years of experience to master. Without the time or desire to acquire that level of knowledge, one can consult a price guide such as *Antique Trader's Tool Price Guide*.

This book is very helpful because all the prices listed are for actual tools. That is important because the values listed in this book are often neither the price at which a tool was offered nor someone's idea of the value of a given tool, but represent what was *actually paid* for a particular tool.

While matching a tool to a listing in the book can tell you what a particular tool sold for, it may not tell you the value of *your* example. The details are what determine the actual value. What this book can do is give you a general idea and maybe keep you from making a big mistake. Once you have found an item that appears to be the same as yours, you can use that information to determine how much more effort needs to be invested in determining the value of your item. For example, if you have a badly rusted handsaw and find the exact same saw listed for $25, it might not be worth further effort. On the other hand, if a similar saw lists for $3,000, your saw certainly has some value and may be worth more study.

As you use the book, keep in mind that the listings are only guidelines. Detailed knowledge is required to determine the value of any antique.

## Trends

As in all collecting areas, trends come and go in tool collecting. In the 1950s blacksmith-made items were all the rage, in the '60s coopers' tools took the lead, in the '70s braces were hot, and the '80s became the age of the wooden plane. In recent years the most significant trend has been the focus on condition, no matter what the tool. Today tool collectors are more aware of condition then at any time in the past. Even an older common tool in "hardware store new" shape has more value today then it did a few years ago. Rare Stanley planes that are "Mint in Box," for example, have sold for 8-12 times the price of a used example with no box.

Today the fastest growing area of collecting is patented tools. Planes lead the way, with several selling for tens of thousands of dollars. Braces and wrenches are probably tied for second place.

Trends will change. The tool collecting hobby as it exists today is about 35 years old. Most areas of interest have become well established, and the factors determining value are known. So while fads may come and go, tool collecting is here to stay.

## Building a collection

As you build your collection, learn all you can. Study your area of interest from top to bottom. Every dollar spent on a book and every minute spent reading will reward you tenfold. Once you have covered your primary interest, do not stop studying. Learn all you can about other types of tools. As you search for items in your area of interest, you will see many tools in related areas. Often your knowledge in another area will result in a purchase that can be converted into cash to build your collection.

As your hunt continues, keep in mind the importance of condition. For common tools the only value may be exceptional condition. Remember, as many antique dealers have said, "Junk is always junk." Buy the best example you can afford in the best condition you can find.

The worst that can happen is that you will have a lot of fun, meet many great people and, with just a bit of luck, make a profit on your investment.

Clarence Blanchard,
Brown Auction Services
27 Fickett Road
Pownal, ME 04069B

# Braces & Bits

Braces are a form of hand-held boring device that is fitted with a metal corkscrew-shaped "bit" that actually does the drilling.

According to tool authority Ronald Barlow, the Chinese are credited with inventing the double-crank brace about 100 A.D. It appears the brace did not become available in Europe until much later, about the 15th century.

The earliest braces were crafted of fine hardwoods with only the bit being made of metal. By the 18th century some better braces were trimmed with brass reinforcing plates to make them stronger. The next major step in development came in 1850 when Mr. William Marples of Sheffield, England came out with his "ultimate" brace that had a cast-brass frame with exotic hardwood infill. This became known as the "Ultimatum" type. About this same time a number of all-metal braces were developed in the United States. Eventually the all-metal version replaced the type with wood infill and by the turn of the 20th century it had become the world standard.

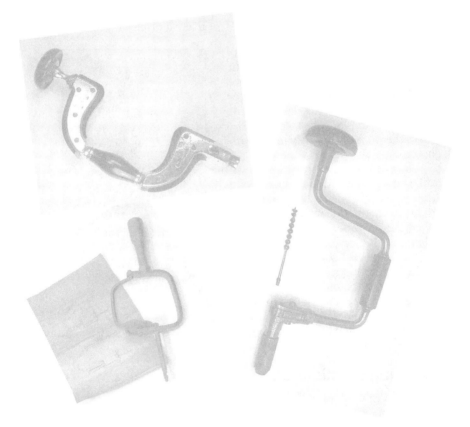

**Angular bit brace,** cast iron, marked "C.J. Haeberli & H.E.O. Schmidt. Pat. July 2, 1907," 90-degree handle detaches to make standard bit brace, fully convertible, rare & unusual, very good condition (removable arm a replacement) ........................ **$250**

**Auger bit,** cast iron, huge size, 4 1/4" wide at base, good condition ................................. **83**

**Auger bit,** cast iron, marked "Town Chaffe & Co. 6," single taper w/wooden tee handle, made in Sturbridge, Massachusetts, ca. 1849, uncommon maker, good condition ................................. **28**

**Auger bits,** cast iron, graduated set of 14 center bits, 10 countersinks of various types, three loose in bottom of case, four screw- and countersink-combination bits, all clean w/no rust, in fitted wooden case, good condition, the set ...................... **171**

**Auger bits,** cast iron, marked "Irwin," set of nine plus a screwdriver bit in wooden case, very good condition, 10 bits ............... **55**

**Auger bits,** cast iron, marked "Russell Jennings," set of 13 in tiered wooden case, very good condition, the set ...................... **85**

**Auger bits,** cast iron, marked "Russell Jennings," set of nine in tiered wooden case, very good condition, the set ...................... **55**

**Auger bits,** cast iron, Stanley No. 100, full set in three-tiered wooden box, Russell Jennings patent, like-new, the set ................... **176**

**Auger bits,** steel, marked "Job T. Pugh Phila.," all w/paper shank labels, some w/little use wear, in wooden case, set of 13 ...................... **95**

**Bit brace,** cast iron, Stanley No. 945-10 Inch, new in original box, fine condition ............................. **105**

**Bit brace,** cast iron w/hardwood handle, Stanley No. X3, w/6" sweep, does not seem to be listed in any of the references, good condition ......................................... **83**

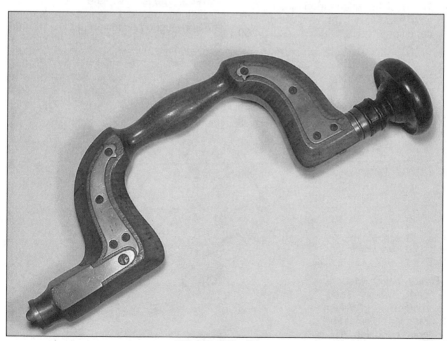

*Tillotson & Co. Brace*

**Bit braces,** cast iron, Stanley No. 945, two new tools in original box, fine condition ................................. **77**

**Bit braces,** nickel plated steel, Stanley No. 923, new in original box, fine condition, set of 2 (some minor storage stain, minor scuffs on box) ............................ **99**

**Brace,** all-brass, powder room-type, good patina, very good condition (a few dings) ........................ **28**

**Brace,** beech, friction fit pad w/pewter ferrule, early style, 5 1/2" sweep, fine condition, 14" h. without pad & bit ................... **130**

**Brace,** beech & plated metal, marked "Tillotson & Co.," slide chuck as most often found on Ultimatums, good condition, chip on edge of pad (ILLUS. on previous page) .............................. **176**

**Brace,** beech w/brass stem & fittings & ebony head, marked "Piklington, Pedigor & Co.," lever chuck, all the proper marks, good condition (handgrip repaired) ........................... **770**

**Brace,** beech w/ebony head, lady's style, uncommon small size, head very tight, very good condition ................................... **260**

**Brace,** beech w/ebony head, marked "Wm. Marples & Sons," brass pushbutton chuck, some original finish, very good condition ................................. **100**

**Brace,** beech w/lignum vitae head, plated brass stem, "Joseph Cooper. Patent" marked on brass plug cover, button chuck marked, very good condition ................................. **200**

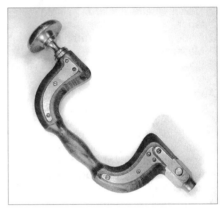

*"R. Sorby & Sons" Brace*

**Brace,** beech w/plated brass fittings, marked "R. Sorby & Sons," good condition (ILLUS.) ..... **149**

*Beech, Ebony & Ivory Brace*

**Brace,** beech w/ebony pad w/ivory ring, marked "William Marples Ultimatum," good condition (Illus. at right) .................. **468**

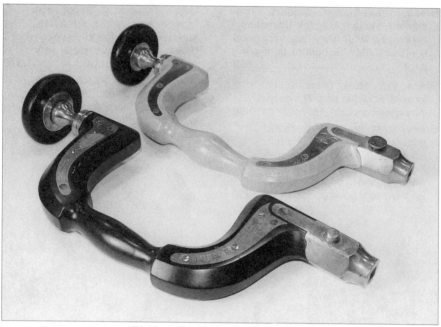

*"H. Hawke" & "Barton Brothers" braces*

**Brace,** birch, heart-shaped locking screw on pod, early, very good condition, 6" sweep, 15" h............................................ **209**

**Brace,** birch w/pewter ferrule, early form, very good condition, 9" sweep, 17" h...................................... **127**

**Brace,** boxwood w/ebony head, marked "H. Hawke" w/eagle trademark, brass head plug encircled w/ivory ring, chuck button marked, very good condition (ILLUS. top w/Barton Brothers brace) ...................... **440**

**Brace,** brass, ebony & beech, marked "C. & T. Pilkington. T. Tillotson & Co.," rare patented brace, brass stem, ebony pad & beech body, heavy brass plates, one crank some repair, good condition (ILLUS. below left)............ **743**

**Brace,** brass & steel w/rosewood head, marked "D. W. Goodell. Northampton, Mass. Patent No. 28, 1865.," brass & steel chuck w/locking jaws inside close as outside ring turned, mark weak & not readable, unusual brace, good condition...................................... **210**

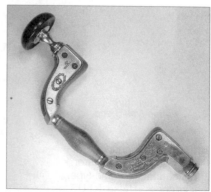

*Rare Patented Brace*                                    *Brass-framed Brace with Beech Infill*

**Brace,** brass-framed w/beech infill, marked "William Marples Ultimatum," ebony pad w/full ivory ring, very good condition. (ILLUS. bottom right prev. page) ......................................... **660**

**Brace,** burl head, brass & iron ferrules, screw-in pad, 7" sweep, very good condition, 16" h. ................... **90**

**Brace,** cast brass w/rosewood grip, marked "G. Horton, Sheffield," marked "Registered Nov. 8th, 1858. No. 2528," w/pushbutton spring chuck, English, very good condition........... **850**

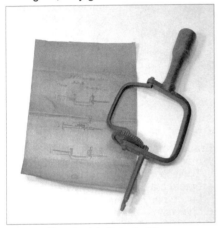

*Chamberlain Patented Brace*

**Brace,** cast iron, brass & wood, marked "Dexter H. Chamberlain, Patented Feb. 7, 1854," rare brace works on crank & double-gear design,

chuck rotates at about five times rate of handle, wood fine, surfaces as found w/even brown patina, brass gears, very good condition (ILLUS.)................ **1,375**

**Brace,** cast iron, graceful curve forms gentle sweep from chuck to wooden head, spring chuck w/file decorations, France, 18th c., very good condition ....................... **600**

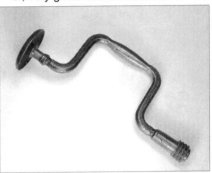

*"Stackpole" Brace*

**Brace,** cast iron, marked "Stackpole Patent. September 23, 1862. Portland, Maine," small size, split chuck locks w/a brass ring, very clean, 7" sweep, 12" h. (ILLUS.) ....................... **171**

**Brace,** chairmaker's style, maple w/screw-lock pod, 7" sweep, 14" l. (no bit in pod) ............................. **105**

**Brace,** chairmaker's type, hardwood, early style, good condition.................... **226**

**Brace,** chairmaker's type, hardwood, spring chuck w/three

*Ultimatum
Frame-type Brace*

**Brace,** ebony, marked "Alfred Ridge Manufacturer," Ultimatum frame-type, tight check in head (ILLUS. at right) ............................. **358**

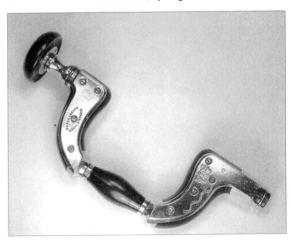

wooden pods, Dutch, ca. 1800, 5" sweep, fine condition, 11 1/2" l. .................................. **330**

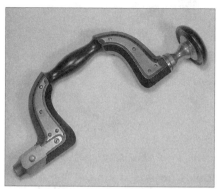

*Ebony Brace from Sheffield*

**Brace,** ebony, marked "Sheffield Plated," very showy, fine condition (ILLUS.) ......................... **418**

**Brace,** ebony w/brass plates & lignum vitae head, marked "Barton Brothers - Ultile duici - Imp'd. Patent Brace - Sheffield," w/patented spring chuck, England, very good condition, wood w/two shrinkage checks (ILLUS. top of p. 11 w/H. Hawke brace.) ......... **550**

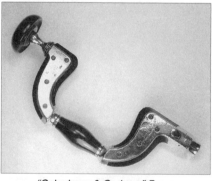

*"Colquhoun & Cadman" Brace*

**Brace,** ebony w/metal fittings, marked "Colquhoun & Cadman," framed Ultimatum type, lever locking device, scroll markings, rare brace by uncommon Sheffield, England maker, 19th c., good condition (ILLUS.) ..................................... **358**

**Brace,** ebony w/metal fittings, marked "William Marples," Ultimatum framed-type, very good condition (chip on wooden hand pad) .................................. **370**

**Brace,** gunmetal w/hardwood head, Armor's spark-proof type, w/pushbutton spring chuck, very good condition ........................... **160**

**Brace,** hand-wrought iron w/burl head, screw chuck, large, 9" sweep, 14" h. ............................. **95**

**Brace,** hardwood, brass, ebony & ivory, marked "Alfred Ridge Manufacturer, Metallic Frame Patent Brace," brass frame w/ebony infill, ivory ring, very good condition (wood w/couple age checks, ebony head tight hairline check) .................................... **380**

**Brace,** hardwood, marked "John S. Fray. Bridgeport, Conn. Spofford Patent. Nov. 1, 1859.," stamped "10" on underside of pad, brace patent later picked up by Stanley, good condition ......... **40**

**Brace,** hardwood w/brass chuck & chuck wrench, marked "Davis Level & Tool Co.," fine condition.... **220**

**Brace,** hardwood w/plated metal fittings, marked "T. Wells & Co.," spring chuck, good condition (pad loose, plug missing) ..................................... **65**

**Brace,** heavy brass frame w/ebony stuffing w/dark brown & black contrasting figure, marked "Henry Pasley's Own Manufacture. The Ne Plus Ultra Framed Brace," brass cap w/ivory ring, good condition (ring missing two sections, joints are loose) .................................... **375**

**Brace,** iron, Davis patented type, marked on the ratchet adjuster knob, early type (wrist pad w/a few nicks)..................................... **60**

**Brace,** iron w/55% plating, marked "Millers Falls," wood grip & top pad, 6" swing, good condition ..................................... **41**

**Brace,** iron w/75% plating, marked "Goodell Pratt Co.," patented ratchet mechanism w/half-round selector lever on bottom side of gear box, wood grip & top pad, good condition......... **31**

**Brace,** iron w/wooden knob handle, cage head-type, two-pole style, massive, early & hand-wrought, 12" sweep, 18" h........ **72**

**Brace,** maple, hand-made w/heart thumbscrew for locking pods into chuck, early & fine w/seven pods, very good condition, 18th c. ......... **638**

**Brace,** maple, miniature, 4" sweep, very good condition, 9" l. ......... **171**

**Brace,** maple w/boxwood head, one square pad is springlocked, early, graceful, good condition ..... **130**

**Brace,** possibly ash, miniature, 3" sweep, very good condition, 9" l. ......... **138**

*"Wm. Kent. Hibernia Works Sheffield" Brace*

**Brace,** rosewood w/metal trim & unusual brass chuck, marked "Wm. Kent. Hibernia Works Sheffield," chuck spring & button fine, England, very good condition (ILLUS.) ......... **550**

**Brace,** steel brace w/ebony head on brass stem, fine condition ......... **210**

**Brace,** Ultimatum type, metal w/ebony infill, marked "I. Sorby.

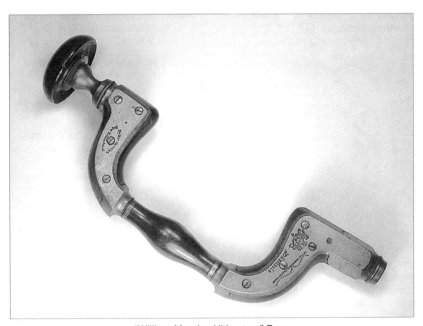

*"William Marples Ultimatum" Brace*

**Brace,** rosewood w/metal fittings, marked "William Marples Ultimatum," good condition, ivory ring missing, chip in edge of pad......... **880**

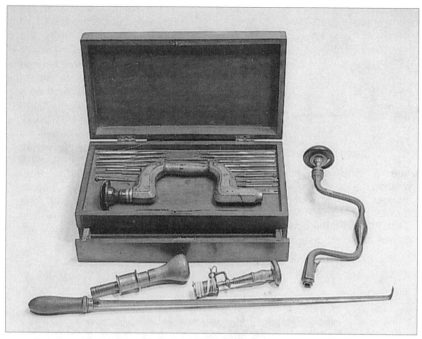

*Brace & Bit Sets & Drills*

**Brace & bit set:** brass & ebony Scottish style brace, eight center bits, six countersinks, three reamers, ten nose bits etc.; brass stem, ebony head, heart-shaped bit release, light surface rust, the set (ILLUS. right w/brace & bit set & drills).................................................................................................................**150**

Sheffield," ivory ring perfect, England, very good condition........ **440**

**Brace,** wagon maker's, elm or oak, 10 1/2" sweep, 18" h. (three old repair straps on bottom crank) ........................... **61**

**Brace,** wooden w/one pod, possibly maple, 18th c., good condition, 9" sweep, 14" h. ............. **132**

**Brace & bit set:** steel & walnut brace plated w/brass fittings, marked "Slater - Sheffield," twenty-two bits, including set of ten long spoon bits, in walnut box; box w/lift top & drawer below, dovetailed construction, England, good condition, box 5 3/4 x 10", 18" l. (ILLUS. top w/brace & bit set & drills) ................. **600**

*Self Acting Brace*

**Brace & bits,** beech w/plated metal fitting, marked "Tillotson. Rob't Marples. Self Acting Brace," slide chuck, lignum wood pad, complete w/16 early bits, mostly counter-sinks & reamers, good condition, the set (ILLUS.) ............................... **198**

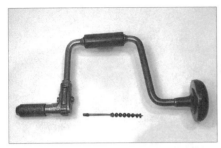

*Brace & Bit from Set*

**Brace & bits set,** cast iron w/wood grip & top handle, marked "Holt Mfg. Co. No. 10," ratchet mechanism patented Sept. 26, 1893, the odd holding device patented July 11, 1893 by H.V. Smith, in slightly dinged up wooed box & w/a box of 10 bits, very good condition, the set (ILLUS.) ........................................ **1,760**

**Brace & bits set,** probably birch w/iron rings, includes seven pods, 18th c., all mounted on a barnboard frame, good condition, the set (ILLUS. below) ........................................ **303**

**Braces,** lignum vitae & plated metal, marked "Wm. Bee" & "Henry Brown" w/"Wm. Bee" chuck, lignum vitae heads, good condition, the pair (one chuck spring broken, crack in one head) ........................................ **143**

*Early Brace & Bits Set*

**Chairmaker's brace,** hickory w/brass & iron ferrules, w/fixed bit about 1/8" diameter, 3" sweep, fine condition, 13" h. ............ **65**

**Corner brace,** cast iron, Stanley No. 984, in original box, fine condition ............................................ **220**

**Corner brace,** cast iron, Stanley No. 984, like new in original box, ca. 1950 .................................. **204**

**Corner brace,** cast iron w/97% finish, Stanley No. 984, fine condition ............................................ **132**

**Corner brace,** cast iron w/wood handles, traces of original paint, rare, good condition (traces of light pitting) ................................................ **45**

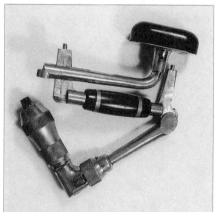

*Rare Stites Folding Bit Brace*

**Folding bit brace,** cast iron w/98% plating & hardwood, marked "Charles W. Stites Folding Bit Brace. Patented May 16, 1905," made by Fray for Stites or under agreement w/him, never appeared in catalog, may be only surviving one of its kind, fine condition (ILLUS.) .................. **7,000**

**Gang mortiser,** cast iron, unmarked, five bits cut a 3/4 x 4" lock pocket mortise, unusual, good condition .................................... **127**

**Mortise gang bit,** cast iron w/95% finishes, marked "Grand Rapids Sash Pulley Co.," three bits geared to rotate together to cut out a pocket mortise, looks to cut 1 x 2 1/2", fine condition .............. **75**

**Ship carpenter's auger bits,** iron, marked "The Ford Patent Auger Bit Co. Holyoke, Mass.," 13 single-twist bits, w/original wooden box w/95% label inside, rare set, fine condition, bits about 18" l., the set ............................ **250**

**Shipbuilder's brace,** oak w/walnut head, iron ferrule, hand-wrought w/tall head, alligator jaws, 8" sweep, fine condition, 19" h. ..................................... **160**

**Surgeon's brace,** stainless steel, marked "Zimmer," tall handle, fine condition .................................... **110**

**Sweep brace,** cast iron, adjustable, pad & chuck w/four set points for sweep, fully adjustable from 6" to 14", both parts can be removed or swung inside, unmarked by probably patented, clean w/good wood, rare, very good condition (no chuck jaws) ................................... **1,150**

**Twist bits,** steel, marked "Snell Mfg. Co.," fine condition, set of 13 in wooden case, the set ............... **65**

**Wibble braces,** plated metal, marked "John Fray," good plating & proper chuck screw, good condition, the pair ................... **105**

**Wimble,** cast iron w/25% plating, marked "John S. Fray," wood handle, good condition (minor pitting near chuck) ................................ **60**

# Drills

Drills also have ancient origins and are somewhat related to braces except that they tended to have more specialized uses and more modern types can be operated with one hand.

Probably the earliest type of drill is the *bow drill* that has probably been around for some 10,000 years. This style required a bow-shaped section that was pulled back and forth rapidly by hand to power the vertical drill tool. By Roman times *pump drills* had been developed and allowed the user to operate it with one hand. Much

later came *breast drills* that were fitted at the top with a curved brace against which the user could lean with his chest, thus enabling him to have the full force of his body to steady and push the drill.

It wasn't until the later 19th century that the more modern push-style drill was developed that eventually developed the double-spiral grooves on the shaft for easier hand-pumping action. Although still used well into this century, most people now depend on easy-to-use electric power models.

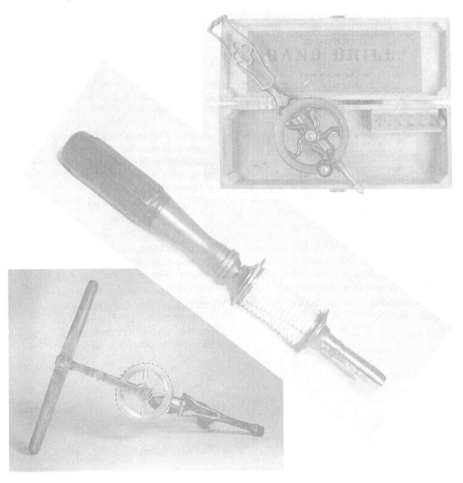

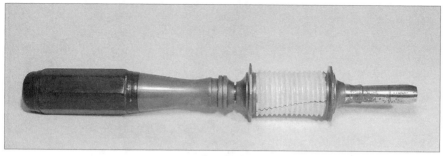

*Bow Drill*

**Bow drill,** octagonal rosewood handle w/ivory spindle, pianomaker's-type, marked "H.S. & Co. N.Y. No. 29," Hammacher & Schlemmer & Co., typical stress crack in ivory ................................................................................................................. **413**

**Auger handle,** iron & steel, hardwood T-handle ratchet, one handle can be removed & screwed into top end, mint, w/2" auger bit in new condition (ILLUS. p. 236 left w/mitre box).... **$110**

**Automatic drill,** iron w/turned wood handle, label reads "No. 2 Automatic Drill - Goodell Brothers Company, Greenfield, Mass. U.S.A.," in original metal box w/full paper label, fine condition ..................................................... **61**

**Beam drill,** wooden frame, marked "Star," fully adjustable front or back, hold-up & rack removal, one 2" auger, good condition ..................................................... **160**

**Bench drill,** cast iron, hand-crank w/feed advance wheel at the top, clamps to the bench, good condition (refinished in red & black)................................................. **66**

**Bench drill,** cast iron w/70% red & black paint, marked "Goodell-Pratt Co.," auto-advance lowers bit as it turns, good condition, 5 1/2" table, 20" h................................ **50**

**Bow drill,** brass drum w/maple head, steel chuck, original spring steel bow, rare w/old bow, good condition (two pieces ILLUS. bottom left, w/braces & bits & hand drill, p. 15) ..................... **200**

**Bow drill,** brass w/rosewood knob handle & iron spindle, good condition, 9" h........................... **110**

*Bow Drill with Bow*

**Bow drill w/bow,** brass & iron w/rosewood, very clean, very rare w/bow, very good condition................................................................................................................ **605**

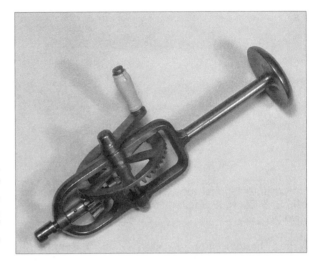

*Brass and Ivory Frame Drill*

**Frame drill,** brass & ivory, all-brass except for chuck & ivory handle , open 6-spoke wheel, mushroom pad, very showy, fine condition, 10" l. ........................ **193**

**Bow drill,** cast iron w/upright turned wood handle, marked "Pat'd May 7, 78," heavy iron flywheel w/ratchet mechanism so drill rotates in only one direction, good condition (chip on drive wheel & chuck) .................. **220**

**Breast auger,** wrought iron, very early hand-wrought type w/octagonal body w/tee handle, possibly 18th c. or earlier, good condition (bit slightly pitted) ............. **75**

**Breast drill,** cast iron w/50% finishes, marked "Winchester No. 8733," two speeds achieved by moving gear & crank up or down a notch, level built into body, good condition........ **85**

**Breast drill,** cast iron & wood, marked "CC (star) 10," drive mechanism is gear & pierced wheel, four rings of holes for four speeds, 20% paint, wood fine, unusual, good condition .......... **75**

**Breast drill,** gunmetal & rosewood, marked "S.A. Case.," gunmetal drive wheel & gear, drive wheel cast w/arm to increase leverage, rosewood handle, unusual, good condition, w/6" wheel, 13" l. ........... **110**

**Breast drill,** iron w/30% japanning, Millers Falls two-hand style, hard to find, good condition (dirty)................... **240**

**Breast drill,** steel, marked "Ruger Breast Drill Model 595A," pistol-shaped hand drill considered uncommon to rare, drill in design of Marples Game Getter, paint near perfect w/bit of flaking on drive wheel, original box w/full label, box good, tool near new ....................................... **900**

**Combination breast drill & mowing machine blade sharpener,** cast iron w/wooden handles, marked "Ayers Pat. June 23. 1868.," large wheel drive, retains mowing tooth grindstone, good condition............ **110**

**Hammer drill,** cast iron, marked "Patent 276598??," turn crank & bit rotates & hammers at the same time, good condition (surface pits, hard to read)............. **413**

**Hand drill,** brass-framed nickel-plated iron w/95% plating, turned ebony handles, unusual, very good condition (handle w/old shrinkage check) ...................... **160**

**Hand drill,** brass-framed w/cast iron wheel & crank & turned burl handles, small size, clean, very good condition .................................... **165**

**Hand drill,** cast brass-framed w/rosewood head w/steel crank, 6" geared wheel, extra heavy & large, very good condition................................... **220**

**Hand drill,** cast iron, marked "Jellinghaus & Co.," w/crank set at 45 degree angle, perhaps designed for drilling next to vertical surfaces, turned wood handle, unique design, good condition ........................................... **310**

**Hand drill,** cast iron, marked "Yankee No. 1545, North Bros. Mfg. Co.," deluxe model w/right & left ratchet movement, pre-Stanley, in original box, tool & box near new, fine condition.......... **280**

**Hand drill,** cast iron, marked "Yankee Radio Hand Drill No. 1431A - North Bros. Mfg. Co.," in original box, tool new & mint, fine condition (box a bit dirty w/some wear, but has full labels)...................................... **110**

**Hand drill,** cast iron w/50% japanning, Stanley No. 610 Pistol Grip Hand Drill, Sweet Hart logo, snap lock bit caddy on side, a few paint spots, good condition ......................................... **190**

**Hand drill,** cast iron w/50% japanning, Stanley No. 610 Pistol Hand Drill, Sweet Hart logo, snap lock bit caddy on side, good condition............................ **200**

**Hand drill,** cast iron/w90% plating, marked "Goodell-Pratt Co. Greenfield, Mass.," three jaw chuck w/several patent dates, plating on knobs & handle fine, rare boring tool, very good condition, 7 1/2" h. (plating in gear wheel flaking)........ **140**

**Hand drill,** iron, unusual long straight spiral-type, large brass center handle moves up & down, good condition, 16" h............ **25**

**Hand drill,** unplated brass w/maple handle, marked "Auto Hand Drill - Best Tool Co. Boston. Patent June 11, 95," pull cord works drill bit, fully operational, pull cord & ring are replacements (ILLUS. center w/bow drill & braces & bits, p. 15)............................ **110**

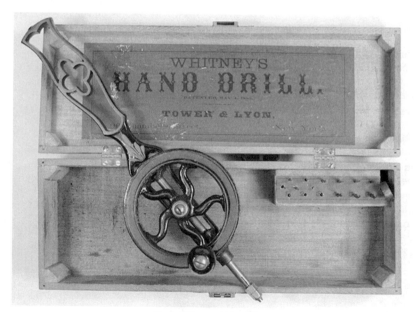

*Early Patented Hand Drill*

**Hand drill,** cast iron w/nearly perfect black japanning w/red & gold trim, marked "Whitney's Hand Drill Patented May 4, 1886. Tower & Lyon," in original box w/15 drills & a chuck wrench, fine condition ......................... **1,650**

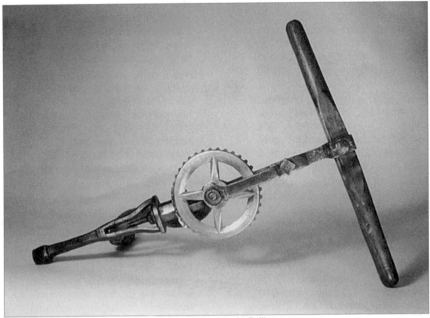

*Early Handmade Drill*

**Hand drill,** hand wrought iron w/cast brass gears, all handmade including hand-cut bolts, 18" l. wooden T handle, 18th c. or earlier, very good condition, 22" l. (ILLUS.)................................................................................................ **715**

**Jeweler's drill,** cast iron w/85% japanning, marked " Millers Falls Jeweler's Drill.," black japanning w/about 85% original red & gold pin stripping, fine example, very fine condition.......... **140**

**Jeweler's hand drill,** cast iron body w/100% japanning, brass gear, frame, chuck & head, unusual, fine condition...................... **165**

**Pipe auger,** cast iron w/wooden tee handle, 1 1/4" diameter, 11 1/2' l. fixed shaft, good condition....................................... **75**

**Pipe auger,** cast iron w/wooden tee handle, 2" diameter, 9' l., good condition ..................................... **55**

**Pipe log augers,** cast iron, for drilling wood pipes, sizes 2 1/2" to 4 1/4", fine condition, set of 4.... **297**

**Pod augers,** cast iron, marked "Zimmermann," set of 8 in graduated sizes, early & hand made, only one marked, varying lengths & shaped tangs appear to be a set, sizes 3/16 to 3/4", lengths from 14"-21", good condition, the set.............................. **100**

**Push drill,** cast iron w/ivory forward hand grip, marked "A.H. Reid. Phil'ada. Pat. Dec. 12, 1882.," traditional Reid design, front grip old appears to be original, unusual & unique, good condition.............................. **380**

# Edged Tools

In this section we are including a variety of tools that rely on sharpened edges to produce the required results. The most common tool of this type is the ax, with its smaller cousin, the hatchet. Narrow-bladed hand adzes are used to chip out narrow grooves in wood as are various types of chisels and draw knives. Draw knives have long, narrow and gently curved metal blades with wooden angled handles at the ends. They derive their name from the fact that the user "drew" or pulled them towards his body when using them for trimming work on narrow boards or spindles.

In prehistoric times the earliest axes were chipped from stone and eventually were tied to wooden handles. Metal heads came along during the Bronze Age, and just a few years ago the earliest such tool was discovered among the objects belonging to the famous "Ice Man," whose body turned up near the border of Austria and Italy. This discovery has enabled scientists to push the start of the Bronze Age back at least 1,000 years.

Eventually iron became the material of choice for all such tools, and hand-wrought axes of all types were made right into the early 19th century. There are many varieties of ax with the most common being those used to fell or hew trees, but special styles evolved into battle axes, mortising axes and the gruesome beheading ax. One variety, called the "goosewing-style," gets its name from the long gently curved "wing-like" blade.

The first American factory for "mass-producing" hand-wrought axes was opened in the 1820s. By the mid-19th century more refined machine-made axes and hatchets gradually replaced the handcrafted types and quality steel put an end to the ancient iron ax.

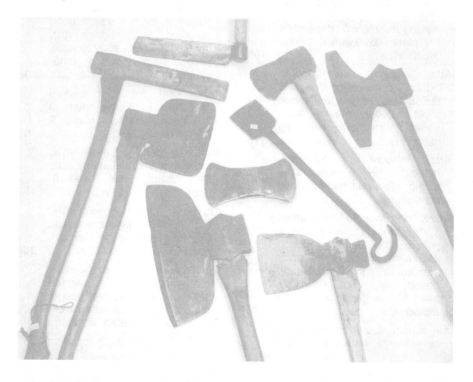

**Adz,** cast iron, hand-type, Connecticut style, shaped handle, 4" l. blade, good condition ........................................ **$94**

**Adz,** cooper's-type, wrought iron head, white bone handle, good condition, head 7" wide, overall 8" l. ..................................................... **220**

**Adz,** hand or sculptor's-type, wrought iron, old wood handle, small size, good condition, edge 1 1/2" w. ........................................... **60**

**Adz,** hand-wrought iron, marked "Gutter," small size, great wood handle, head 2 1/4" w., 5 1/2" l. ...... **94**

**Adz,** iron w/old wood handle, cooper's double-type, flat edge on one end, curved on the other, very early & hand-wrought, good condition, 12" l. ...... **94**

**Adz,** iron w/wood handle, cooper's howel-type, slightly round blade, short handle, very good condition ................................ **72**

**Adz,** iron w/wood handle, marked "Anton Baro," double-bitted, unusual curved cutting ends, English catalog notes use for making milkmaids' yokes, "N"s in mark backwards, good condition ........................................ **165**

**Adz,** wrought iron, marked "Kieffer," combination straight & radius cuts, early & well-made w/old wooden handle, well-known Pennsylvania maker, tip to tip 7" l. ........................................ **176**

**Adz,** wrought-iron pole-type, marked "IR" w/decorative stamp, old wood handle, good condition ........................................ **50**

**Adze,** hand wrought iron, marked "JV" w/cross above diamond, polled, w/early punch decoration in vine & dot motif, appears to be from Indian trade period, very good condition, head 8" l., edge 4" w. (handle replaced) ........................................ **100**

**Ax,** aluminum, ceremonial, used by the fraternal order Woodsmen of the World, in the style of a three-pound pole ax, "WOW" cast into the head, wooden handle, very good condition ................................... **50**

**Ax,** cast iron, embossed mark "L.G.B. Cincinnati," no handle, good condition ................................ **90**

**Ax,** cast iron, marked "Collins," double-bitted camp size, original handle & leather case, good condition, head 6" deep, edge 2 1/2" w. ............................ **140**

**Ax,** cast iron, marked "Fulton Special Extra Quality Fully Warrented," w/stars, leaves & designs, deep embossing, nearly new, leather blade edge protector, good wooden handle, fine condition ................................ **248**

**Ax,** cast iron, marked "Our Best. Snow & Nealley. Bangor, Maine," Sleeper-style, ca. 1900, good condition (handle old but replacement) ................................ **50**

**Ax,** cast iron, marked w/embossed "Raven," embossing fine, old wood handle, larger size, good condition, light surface rust, head 8" l. (ILLUS. p. 32 top row, second from right with other axes) ................................................... **95**

**Ax,** cast iron, marked "Winchester," double bitted, 3 lb., good condition (case & handle new) ................................... **60**

**Ax,** early iron goosewing-style, old wooden handle, many early Pennsylvania lines, head 9" deep, edge 13 1/2" w. ................... **187**

**Ax,** early iron goosewing-style, old wooden handle, marked "IK," long slipper edge, German, head 6" deep, edge 16" w. ........... **358**

**Ax,** early iron goosewing-style, old wooden handle, marked "J.B. Stohler," applied edge, unusual poll, Schaefferstown, Pennsylvania, head 8" deep, edge 12 1/2" w. .............................. **303**

**Ax,** wrought iron, chopping-type, touchmarks, applied bit & quite early, handle nice replacement, good condition ............................... **175**

**Ax,** wrought iron, Gabriel w/horn touchmark, goosewing-style, original handle, good condition, head 9" deep, edge 13" w. ........... **484**

**Ax,** wrought iron, goosewing-style, bearded but better described as a hood, good condition, applied edge 5" w. (handle a poor replacement) ........ **150**

**Ax,** wrought iron, goosewing-style, canted socket, small eye, triple line rib & applied edge, typical Pennsylvania Dutch-type, replaced wooden handle, good condition, head 8 1/2" deep, edge 13" w. ........................ **275**

**Ax,** wrought iron, goosewing-style, European touchmarks, old wood handle, good condition, head 7" h., edge 13" w. .............................................. **140**

**Ax,** wrought iron, goosewing-style, large left-handed type, applied edge, old wooden handle, good condition (some pitting & crack at one end, wormholes in handle) ................... **220**

**Ax,** wrought iron, goosewing-style, mark unreadable, applied edge, handle poor replacement, head 8" deep, edge 13 1/2" w. (surfaces as found) ....................... **225**

**Ax,** wrought iron, goosewing-style, marked w/a touchmarks of a pine tree, three stars, "52," & another pine tree & three stars, large-eyed model, good condition, head 9" deep, edge 15" w. ............................................. **165**

**Ax,** wrought iron, goosewing-style, small size, highly decorated, old handle, very good condition, head 6 1/4" deep, edge 12" w. ........................ **242**

**Ax,** wrought iron, goosewing-style, unmarked, decorated in line & dot motif, applied edge, old handle, good condition, head 7 1/4" deep, edge 16" w. .... **450**

**Ax,** wrought iron, goosewing-style w/wooden handle, marked but only number "30" legible,

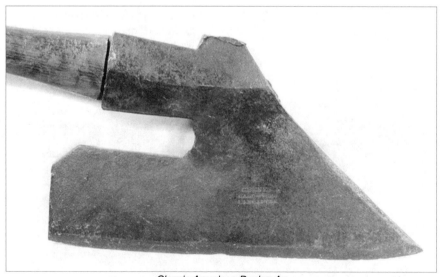

*Classic American Design Ax*

**Ax,** wrought iron, goosewing-type, marked "G.Sener.," classic American design, old handle, Lancaster, Pennsylvania, very good condition, edge 13 1/2", 8 1/2" l.
.................................................................................................... **413**

Europe, 8 x 21", edge 25" w. (old weld on blade edge, some pitting) .............................................. **358**

**Ax,** wrought iron, goosewing-type, touchmarks include six stars & two slashed lines, very good condition, head 8 1/2" deep edge 16" w. .................................... **300**

**Ax,** wrought iron, goosewing-type, traditional style, good condition, head 6 1/2" deep, edge 12" w. (old handle w/many worm holes, some pitting) ....................... **200**

**Ax,** wrought iron, goosewing-type, unmarked, very narrow poll, old handle, good condition, head 7 3/4" deep, edge 14" w. (even coat of pitting) ................................. **200**

**Ax,** wrought iron, illegible mark w/crescent moon & six circles, goosewing-style, small eye, upturned socket, Pennsylvania Dutch-style, old wooden handle, very good condition, head 8" deep, edge 12 1/2" w...... **330**

**Ax,** wrought iron, iron felling-type, early style w/applied edge & poll, very thin, head 9" deep, blade 10" w., good condition........ **138**

**Ax,** wrought iron, long narrow blade marked w/a sunburst & stylized tree touchmark in center, old wood handle, very unusual shape, good condition, head 9" deep, edge 13" w. (ILLUS. p. 32 top row, far right with other axes) ............................... **31**

**Ax,** wrought iron, marked "Busstafe. Seebach," goosewing-style, very good condition, head 7" deep, edge 12" w. (blade concave from use) ......................... **145**

**Ax,** wrought iron, marked "C. Silvius," goosewing-style, early classic form, old wood handle, blacksmith-made, Lancaster, Pennsylvania, head 7 1/2" deep, edge 12 1/2" w. (weak mark, some pitting) ....................... **220**

**Ax,** wrought iron, marked "D. Lichty," goosewing-style, early classic form, old wood handle, clear mark w/four stars, Pennsylvania, very good condition, head 7 1/2" deep, edge 14" w. .................................... **330**

**Ax,** wrought iron, marked "IP" w/touchmarks, goosewing-style, small eye, canted socket, applied edge, Pennsylvania-style, good condition, head 6 1/2" deep, edge 15" w............... **193**

**Ax,** wrought iron, marked "J. Fink. G. Sener," goosewing-style, old wood handle, Lancaster,

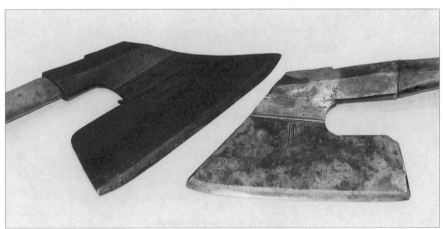

*Two American Goosewing Axes*

**Ax,** wrought iron, marked "D. Ermold," goosewing-style, tight eye, applied edge, canted socket w/original straight wooden handle, Pennsylvania, very good condition, head 8 1/4" deep, edge 12 3/4" w. (ILLUS. right w/other goosewing ax)
.................................................................................................................................... **550**

Pennsylvania, head 7 1/2 deep, edge 12" w. .................................... **303**

**Ax,** wrought iron, marked "J. Lauri," goosewing-style, canted socket, small eye, applied edge, old wood handle, Pennsylvania, 7" deep, blade 12" w. (some pitting) ............................................ **275**

**Ax,** wrought iron, marked "J.R. Stohler," goosewing-style, left-handed, old wood handle, Pennsylvania, good condition, head 7" deep, edge 14" w. ............ **220**

**Ax,** wrought iron, marked "KD," goosewing-style, name cut or stamped on back side, original handle, surface clean w/very little rust, very good condition, head 9" deep, edge 12 1/2" w...... **250**

**Ax,** wrought iron, marked "L. Muller," goosewing-style, European, surface clean & no rust, great form, fine condition, head 7" deep, edge 20" w. ............ **908**

**Ax,** wrought iron, marked "Philip His.," goosewing-style, distinctive ogee at the back edge, marked w/week name stamp & letters "I+P," Berks County, Pennsylvania, very good condition, head 8" deep, edge 14" w................................. **1,375**

**Ax,** wrought iron, marked "Snyder," goosewing-style, canted socket, small rib, applied edge w/almost no eye, strong mark, old wood handle, American, head 8 1/4" deep, edge 12" w. .................................... **303**

**Ax,** wrought iron, marked "Staller. Vien," goosewing-style w/vine & dot decoration, offset handle stained red, European, unusual, good condition, head 9 3/4" deep, applied edge 11 1/2" w....... **240**

**Ax,** wrought iron, marked "TS," goosewing-style, canted eye, applied edge, old wood handle,

head 7" deep, edge 11" w. (several in-the-making cracks in the head)........................................ **193**

**Ax,** wrought iron, marked w/"IHS" under a cross & touchmark w/early "UHZ" owner marks, goosewing-type, very good condition, head 7" deep, bit 14" w. (new handle) ..................... **275**

**Ax,** wrought iron, marked w/touchmarks, early form, head 8 1/2" deep, edge 12" w. .............. **132**

**Ax,** wrought iron, marked w/touchmarks & "HF," goosewing-style, left hand type, handle old & may be original, good condition, head 8" deep, edge 13" w..................................... **950**

**Ax,** wrought iron, medium-width gently curved blade, decorated w/a punch-decorated shield, applied edge, old wood handle, some pitting, good condition, head 8" deep, edge 12" w. (ILLUS. p. 30 bottom row, center, with clapboard slick) ........... **83**

**Ax,** wrought iron, "Rohrbach" triple stamped on blade w/three sunbursts above, goosewing-style w/narrow eye, small nib between blade & socket, canted original wooden handle, very good condition, head 8" deep, edge 14 1/2" w. (ILLUS. p. 26 left w/other goosewing ax) ........ **1,045**

**Ax,** wrought iron, touchmarks "IB" w/stars, goosewing-type, pointed type, 18th c. style, very good condition, polled head 9 1/2" deep, edge 17" w................ **375**

**Ax,** wrought iron, triple-stamped "H. Stahler," goosewing-style w/canted socket & very small eye, nib on top side of old wooden handle, applied edge, early Pennsylvania maker, good condition, head 8 1/2" deep, edge 14" w. (overall pitting) .......... **550**

*Old Ax Head by Scarce Maker*

**Ax head,** cast iron, marked "B. Kelley & Co. Belfast, Maine. Genuine Extra Hand Hammered," marked head w/original paper label, short-lived late 19th c. company, rare, fine condition (ILLUS.)...................... **50**

**Ax head,** wrought iron, marked "Cayuga - Baker, Rose & Kimball Inc.," double-bitted style, Indian chief head embossed on one side of head, very clean, strong embossing, good condition (ILLUS. p. 32 bottom row center, with other axes) ................................................ **100**

**Bark spud,** early hand-wrought iron, spade-type, old wood handle, very good condition .......... **61**

**Barking spud,** wrought iron, long narrow rectangular blade w/ornate turned-down ears on the handle, very early & unusual, 18th c., good condition .. **165**

**Battle ax,** wrought iron, ornately scroll-cut sides & cut-out trefoil in the center of the head, overall etching on both sides of head, surfaces fine w/minimal pitting, wood handle, early & important, good condition ................................ **260**

**Beheading ax,** wrought iron, rare, France, 18th c., good condition, head 14" deep, edge 12" w. (surface w/light pitting) ...... **550**

**Broad ax,** cast steel, marked "J.R. Whiting. Belfast [Maine]. Cast Steel.," stamp tipped & clear only in center, old handle, ca. mid-1850s, good condition, , head 8" deep, edge 6 1/2" w. ......... **75**

**Broad ax,** wrought iron, "J.P. Billings. Clinton, Maine," early applied edge, strong mark, ca. 1830, good condition (handle new but great hand-made example)............................................ **50**

**Broad ax,** wrought iron, marked "B. Kelley & Co. Belfast [Maine]," one of only two known axes w/Belfast location stamp, second half 19th c., good condition, head 10" l., edge 6 1/2" w. ....................... **55**

**Broad ax,** wrought iron, marked "Evansville Tool Works," long blade w/arched top & flat edge, old wood handle, good condition, edge 7" w. (ILLUS. p. 30 bottom far left with clapboard slick) ................................................ **110**

**Broad ax,** wrought iron, marked "Vaughan & Pardoe.

*Dated Basketmaker's Shave*

**Basketmaker's shave,** cast iron, initialed & dated on side "1842," hand-cut bolts hold blade, good condition, some wormholes ............................................. **440**

*Dated Chisel*

**Chisel,** handforged iron, impressed w/"1848" & "Melchi Scott" & decorative whitesmithing, old wooden handle appears to be original, good condition, 3" w. x 11 1/2" l. (ILLUS.) ............ **275**

Warranted. Union [Maine].," rare mark, old handle, good condition, edge 6" w. (poll peened over a bit but mark still readable) ........................................ **55**

**Broad ax,** wrought iron, marked "W. Brown," old wood handle, head 11" deep, edge 9" w. ............ **33**

**Butt chisels,** cast iron, Buck Brothers, wooden handles, in owner-made box, sizes from 1/4 to 1 1/2 inch, all about 9" l., very good condition, set of 8 (one w/replaced handle)............ **160**

**Camp ax,** cast iron, Keen Kutter, head & button on leather case marked w/"KK" logo, handle old but not original, edge fine, good condition ......................................... **55**

**Carving tools,** cast iron, marked "S.J. Addis," brass ferrules & turned rosewood mushroom-top handles, fine condition, set of 15 ................................................ **418**

**Carving tools,** cast iron w/rosewood handles, marked "Millers Falls," set of six in original slide-top box w/original label on bottom, fine condition, small 5" l. chisels, the set ............ **110**

**Chamfer shave,** cast iron w/95% japanning, Stanley No. 65, complete, fine condition ................. **83**

**Chamfer shave,** cast iron w/95% japanning, Stanley No. 65, second Sweet Hart logo vintage, fine condition.................... **132**

**Chamfer shave,** cast iron w/95% japanning, Stanley No. 65, Type 1 w/"Stanley Rule & Level" & patent date in circular logo on blade, very good condition (hang hole) ....................................... **90**

**Chamfer shave,** cast iron w/98% japanning, Stanley No. 65, Sweet Hart vintage, fine condition ......................................... **193**

**Chisel,** cast iron, marked "Samson. Union Hardware Co.," slick-type, fine condition, 3 1/2" l. (minor surface stains) ..... **132**

**Chisel,** cast iron, marked "T.H. Witherby," slick-type, wooden handle w/much original finish, fine condition, 3"............................. **286**

**Chisels,** iron, marked "Winsted," 3/8" size, in original box, fine condition, remaining set of 5 ................................................ **105**

**Chisels,** iron w/turned boxwood handles, marked "Hearnshaw," long paring gouges, clean & fine condition, set of 5 ......................... **193**

**Chisels,** iron w/turned wood handles, paper label reads "'Addis' - Ward & Payne, Sheffield....," various sizes in original fitted box, England, 19th c., very good condition, set of 19 ................................................ **440**

**Clapboard slick,** all hand-wrought iron w/tee handle & applied edge, long flat shovel-like blade, extra large, good condition, 4 1/2" w. front edge ...... **61**

**Clapboard slick,** hand-wrought iron w/applied edge, marked "M.A. Noyes," w/"D" style handle, very good condition, edge 3 1/4" w. (surface rust) ......... **55**

**Clapboard slick,** wrought iron, all iron, small flat squared blade on long flat iron handle w/long hook at the end, applied edge, good condition, 22" l., edge 4" w. (ILLUS. p. 32 center row, right, with other axes) ..................... **55**

**Clapboard slick,** wrought iron, long narrow blade w/short angled handle grip at one end & wide rectangular section at the other end, illegible deep stamped mark, rare w/iron handle, pitting, good condition (ILLUS. below, top with group of axes) ..................... **72**

**Clapboard slick,** wrought iron, marked "D. R. Barton & Co., Rochester, N.Y.," large rectangular flat iron blade w/beveled edges, long flat iron handle w/wooden handle grip, weak stamped mark tipped when struck, fine quality tool, fine condition, edge 3 1/2"w. ....... **500**

**Cleaver,** cast iron, marked "Wm. Beatty & Son. Chester. 6," w/standing cow logo, large rectangular head, old wood handle, clean & basically rust-free, 13" l. edge .............................. **50**

**Cleaver,** wrought iron, marked "L. & I.J. White 1837," No. 8 size, very clean w/about 90% of handle decal, very good condition, edge 8" w. ...................... **70**

**Coach maker's ax,** wrought iron, marked "Balaton Tekord.," old handle, Europe, good condition, head 10" deep, edge 10" w. .......... **94**

**Coach maker's ax,** wrought iron, marked "G" w/anchor trademark, clean & without rust, old handle, good condition, head 10" deep, edge 11" w. ......... **259**

**Cooper's shave,** cast iron missing most of japanning, marked "Bailey. Boston," unusual design w/two screws acting as hold-downs for cutter, mark w/large Boston stamp different than more commonly seen mark, good condition, 2 9/16" cutter, 18 1/4" l. (pitting) ...... **150**

**Cooper's shave,** cast iron w/55% japanning, Stanley No. 56 1/2, 4" marked blade, hard to find, good condition .............................. **160**

*Clapboard Slick, Broad Ax, Ax and Turf Ax*

**Cooper's shave,** cast iron w/70% japanning, Stanley No. 56, good condition (no screw for cap) .......... **60**

**Cooper's shave,** heavy cast iron, Stanley, Vee-logo, 2 9/16" cutter, overall 16 3/4" l. ................. **105**

**Cooper's side ax,** wrought iron, marked but unclear, old handle, fine condition, head 8" d., curved edge 12" l. , ...................... **135**

**Cooper's side ax,** wrought iron, marked "D. R. Barton, Rochester.," handle old probably not original, good condition, overall clean & nice, head 7" deep, edge 9 1/2" w. (some pitting), ................................. **65**

**Corner chisel,** cast iron w/100% original gold paint on inside of shank, marked "James Swan," in original wooden box w/60% label, fine condition ...................... **149**

**Corner chisels,** cast iron, marked "James Swan," 5/8" size, two still unwrapped, in original wooden box w/97% label, tools like new, fine condition, set of 4... **352**

**Crank chisels,** cast iron, marked "Buck Brothers," flats in 1/2", 3/4" & 1 1/4" sizes, three 1" gouges in different radius, all w/original Buck handles, very good condition, set of 6 ............................................ **198**

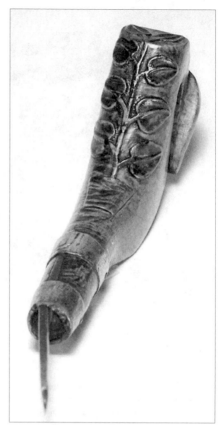

*Carved Burl Crooked Knife*

**Crooked knife,** wrought iron w/wooden handle, canted burl handle carved w/a horseshoe w/anchor & potted plant, hammered brass bands, early & very nice, fine condition (ILLUS. above) ...................................... **770**

*Chip Carved Crooked Knife*

**Crooked knife,** wrought iron, canted handle w/chip-carved dog, ax, & Masonic emblem, very detailed, very good condition .......................................................... **715**

*Axes and Other Edged Tools*

**Crooked knife,** wrought iron narrow angled blade set into wire- and cord-wrapped curved wooden handle, old blade, very good condition ............................... **120**

**Crooked knife,** wrought iron w/chip-carved wooden handle & great pewter ferrule running up the handle, not highly decorated, very well made, very good condition ............................... **200**

**Crooked knife,** wrought iron w/curved wood handle hand-carved w/heart on end, checked decoration w/six pointed star, cross, arrows & compass rose, owner's initials "HP," odd decoration for New England knife, very good condition ............. **275**

**Cutter & chisel grinder,** cast iron, Stanley No. 200, in original box complete w/envelope & instructions, tool looks unused, fine condition .................................. **143**

**Draw knife,** chairmaker's, iron w/long turned rosewood end handles, pommel-type, delicate design, good edge, very good condition ........................................ **210**

**Draw knife,** hand-wrought iron w/applied 3" w. edge, good condition,29" from center to center of handles, blade 17" l...... **190**

**Draw knife,** iron w/mahogany handle, fine condition, blade 4" l. ................................................. **150**

**Draw shave,** hand-wrought iron, curved blade w/vine & dot decoration along top, original handles, fine condition.................. **105**

**Draw shave,** iron w/brass handle washers, marked "Buck Brothers," miniature size w/4" blade, very good condition............. **88**

**Draw shave,** wrought iron, small size, very well made, very good condition, blade 4 1/2" w.............. **110**

**Draw shave,** wrought iron w/big-eared steer & tree touchmarks, hand-forged & early, good condition .......................................... **44**

**Felling ax,** iron, double-bitted Western or Puget Sound-type, marked only "W40," nearly 12" tall w/very narrow 3 3/4" edges...... **22**

**Felling ax,** wrought iron, marked "IC," France, ca. 1820, 7" w., 6 1/2" w. edge.................................. **39**

**Felling ax,** wrought iron w/applied edge & pole, old wood handle w/worn holes, head pitted, Pennsylvania, unusual style, 7" w. head, 8 1/2" edge................... **61**

**Firmer chisels,** cast iron, Buck Brothers-type, matching applewood handles, sized 3/8 to 2 inch, near-new condition, all about 16" l., set of 10 .............. **725**

**Froe,** wrought iron, illegible mark, w/handle & clug 14" l., good condition .......................................... **55**

**Froe,** wrought iron, old wood handle, very clean, very good condition, 11" l. (ILLUS. p. 32 top center w/axes) ......................... **75**

**Gouges,** cast iron, marked "Buck Brothers," crank neck-type, matched marked handles, sizes 1/8" to 3/4", largest is 13" l., includes straight flat & gouge, very good condition, set of 6 .......... **198**

**Gouges,** cast steel, marked "Wells & Wilcox. Cast Steel.," matching handles, good edges, very good condition, set of 7 ........ **165**

**Grooving tool,** iron w/turned wood handle, Stanley, unlisted & exact purpose unknown, possibly for cutting shallow grooves in carvings, fine condition ........................................ **237**

**Hand adze,** wrought iron, Connecticut style, early w/burl handle, applied edge, good condition ........................................ **154**

**Hand beader,** cast iron & ebonized wood, marked "Windsor" w/both patent dates, wood side handles, good condition (ILLUS. below, top w/razor edge shave & radius shave) ............................................. **303**

**Hand saw,** steel blade w/carved rosewood handle, marked "The Simonds Saw. No. 7A.," 4 1/2-

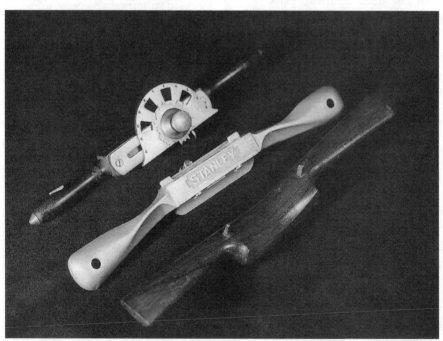

*Hand Beader, Razor Edge Shave & Radius Shave*

point, w/handle protector, clean & near mint.................................... **220**

**Hand saw,** steel, marked "Geo. H. Bishop & Co. 7," applewood handle, eight points, very clean, very good condition ........................ **66**

**Hatchet,** cast iron, marked "American Beauty" embossed logo w/full stem rose, original handle, rare mark, fine condition, head 7" deep, edge 3 1/2" w. ......................................... **85**

**Hatchet,** cast iron, marked "Black Raven. Kelley Axe Mfg. Co.," embossed head w/90% original gold paint, old handle, rare to see this logo w/gold paint, good condition, head 6 1/2" deep, edge 3 1/4" w. , ............................ **105**

**Hatchet,** cast iron, marked "Buhlson Co. Detroit, Mich.," camp-type w/embossed label, old handle, good condition ............ **65**

**Hatchet,** cast iron, marked "Morley Bros. Wedgeway. Hand Made. Unsurpassed.," board - type, embossed label, old handle, good condition, blade 4 1/2" w. ......................................... **65**

**Hatchet,** cast iron, marked "Western Clipper. McGregor-Noe Hdwe Co. Springfield, MO.," shingling-type w/stamped in logo, new handle, good condition ......................................... **65**

**Hatchet,** cast iron, marked "Winchester," w/nail puller, original handle, good condition, head 5" deep, edge 3" w. .............. **45**

**Hatchet,** cast iron w/90% plating, marked "E.C. Simmons Keen. Kutter USA," w/strong embossed label, good condition, head 3 1/4" deep, edge 1 3/4" w............................. **140**

**Hatchet,** iron, marked "Marbles No. 5," wooden handle, good condition (poll rolled over a bit, replaced handle) ............................ **36**

**Hatchet head,** cast iron, marked "American Beauty," w/embossed rose logo, rose retains much of the original color, no handle, good condition ................................. **95**

**Hay knife,** wrought iron, miniature salesman's sample, wooden handles w/50% red paint, good condition, 14" l. ............................ **253**

**Hewing ax,** iron, marked "...Ballston, NY," great finish, old wood handle, very good condition, 12" w. blade ................... **83**

**Hewing ax,** wrought iron, long head w/rounded top edges, old wood handle, good condition, head 9 1/2" deep, edge 14 3/4" l. (ILLUS. p. 32 bottom row left, with other axes) ................ **37**

**Ice chopper,** wrought iron, wide flat four-pront blade, long handle w/loop grip, lightweight, very good condition, 26" l. ........... **143**

**Knife,** wrought iron, marked "C.S. Osborne," wide flat crescent-shaped blade w/turned wood handle at top center, very clean blade, very good condition, edge 10" w. ....................................... **60**

**Marking knife,** brass & ebony, full blade length remains, extra long, thin size, 7/16" cutter, fine condition, 6" l. ................................. **80**

**Mast ax,** wrought iron, marked "R. King," clean, very good condition, replacement handle (ILLUS. p. 32 bottom row right, with other axes) ............................... **21**

**Miner's track hatchet,** cast iron, used in coal mines for repairing track & making adjustments, old wooden handle, eight-sided poll & edge both 3 1/2" w., rare, good condition, overall 10" l. (overall pitting) ............................. **120**

**Mitre trimmer,** cast iron, marked "C.P. Batchelder - Franklin, N.H.," double acting w/two fences, cuts both sides or corner, rack and pinion arrangement moves two cutters, flower design cast in cutter board & open work base, cast iron w/green finish, rare, good condition (paint about 50%, old repair on handle) ........... **500**

**Mortise ax,** cast iron, very clean w/probably original wood handle, very good condition, head 16" l., edge 3" w. (ILLUS. p. 32 top row far left with axes).... **170**

**Mortise ax,** wrought iron, marked "G. Sener. Lancaster, PA.," spread-winged eagle over name, Sener made edged tools until 1848, good condition, head 9" deep, edge 1 3/4" w. ................... **90**

**Mortise ax,** wrought iron, single-but type, old wood handle, good condition, 10" w. head..................... **39**

**Pattern maker's shaves set:** brass, one large hollow shave, two smaller round shaves, one flat shave, two double-enders, two side-by-side rabbet shaves, two miniature round shave, good condition, set of 10.............. **220**

**Peat or sod ax,** wrought iron, illegible mark, large rectangular head w/rounded corners, old wood handle, good condition, head 10" deep, edge 9" w. (ILLUS. p. 32 center row, left, with other axes) ............................... **65**

**Peavey,** wrought iron, miniature size, most likely salesman's sample, long turned wood handle, very good condition, overall 27" l. .................................. **253**

**Putty knife,** rosewood handle & beryllium blade, Stanley No. B38, rare marked Stanley beryllium tool, fine condition (a few scratches)................................ **310**

**Rabbet shave,** bronze, Stanley No. 71, second Sweet Hart logo, in original box w/full label, box a bit worn w/some repair (ILLUS. below)........................... **1,300**

**Rabbet shave,** gunmetal, Stanley No. 71 Gunmetal Shave, Sweet Hart logo on blade, rabbet w/fence, never used, mint condition ........................................ **550**

**Radius shave,** rosewood w/iron cutter, marked "Wm. Johnson. Newark, NJ," 2 1/2" cutter w/slight curve, good condition,

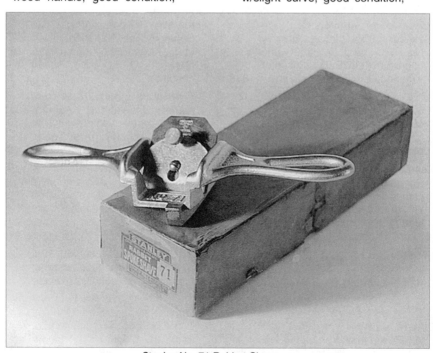

*Stanley No. 71 Rabbet Shave*

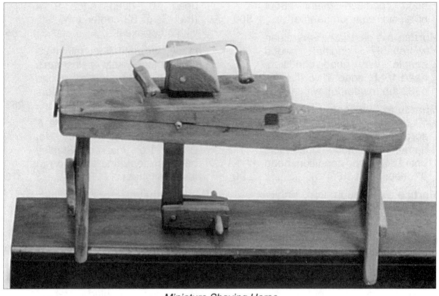

*Miniature Shaving Horse*

**Shaving horse,** hardwood, miniature size modeled after full-size cousin, complete w/small draw knife, fine condition, 8" h., 13" l. ............................ **90**

handle w/one edge chip (ILLUS. p. 33 bottom w/hand beader & razor edge shave)............................ **94**

**Razor edge shave,** cast iron w/near 100% plating, Stanley No. 76, hard to find, fine condition (ILLUS. p. 33 center w/hand beader & radius shave)... **633**

**Saddle maker's spoke shave,** rosewood w/brass wear plate & cutter adjusting nuts, marked "Dixon & Sons," adjustable, fine condition......................................... **80**

**Scythe,** iron, marked "Bute Bohneid Balbe Arbeit," full four-color twin cow trademark w/wheat & roses, golden tone blade never mounted in haft, Austria, fine condition.................... **130**

**Shave,** iron, unmarked shave, cutter marked "L. Bailey," cap is a Bailey w/the loop eye, but shave not listed as Bailey design, good condition ................... **31**

**Shears,** tailor's type, cast iron w/50% japanning on handgrips, marked "Ph. Weber. Cin'o.,"

brass center nut for tensioning, large size w/8" edges ..................... **55**

**Shingling hatchet,** cast iron, marked "Kees Mfg. Co. Beatrice, Neb.," attachment on end of head sets depth, head marked "OVB," rare, good condition ......................................... **80**

**Shipwright's gouge,** cast iron, marked "Leighton, Auburn, N.H.," handle w/old screw at top, 3" blade, rare, good condition ....................................... **130**

**Side ax,** wrought iron, sunburst & other touchmarks, early style w/triangular head, old wood handle, good condition, 7" w., 8" w. edge...................................... **116**

**Slicing tool,** wrought iron, long tapering blade w/curved end w/socket for poll-type wooden handle, good condition, blade 22" l. .................................................. **55**

**Slick,** cast iron, marked "Douglas Mfg. Co.," good wooden handle, good condition, 4" l. (some deep pitting on edge)...................... **60**

**Slick,** cast iron, marked "P. Merrill" very thin blade w/applied edge, Hinsdale, N.H. maker, rare, good condition, 4" .. **135**

**Splitting ax,** wrought iron, burl handle, good age, Japanese, great form, very good condition, head 5" deep, edge 4 1/2" w. ....... **220**

**Spoke shave,** boxwood w/40% plating on blade, Stanley No. 84 razor edge, Sweet Hart logo, good condition, 2" w. blade ............ **72**

**Spoke shave,** boxwood w/60% plating on blade, Stanley No. 85 razor edge, good condition, 2 1/2" w. blade ................................. **72**

**Spoke shave,** cast iron, Stanley No. 60, Sweet Hart vintage, one shave in box that held six, tool new, box fine w/light dirt ............... **205**

**Spoke shave,** cast iron, Stanley No. 67 Universal, complete w/both bottoms & fence, w/original box w/good label, used, good condition .................... **143**

**Spoke shave,** cast iron w/100% plating, marked "Murray No. 2 Patent July 30, 01," adjustable, fine condition ................................. **248**

**Spoke shave,** cast iron w/100% plating, marked "Preston. Patent," oval handle, unused condition ......................................... **230**

**Spoke shave,** cast iron w/100% plating, Stanley No. 67 Universal, early type w/rosewood left & right handles, both bottoms & fence, ca. 1915, mint.................................................. **155**

**Spoke shave,** cast iron w/40% japanning, Stanley No. 62, reversible, B casting, good condition ......................................... **99**

**Spoke shave,** cast iron w/90% plating, Stanley No. 67, Universal w/both bottoms & fence, good condition .................... **154**

**Spoke shave,** cast iron w/92% plating, Stanley No. 75 razor edge, hard to find, fine condition, 2" w. blade .................... **578**

**Spoke shave,** cast iron w/95% japanning, Stanley No. 151R, Sweet Hart logo, some original bluing on adjuster screws, very rare, fine condition ........................ **210**

**Spoke shave,** cast iron w/98% plating, Stanley No. 76 razor edge, rare, fine condition, 2 1/2" w. blade ............................... **660**

**Spoke shave,** cast iron w/traces of japanning, marked "Bailey Tool Co. - Patented July 26, 1870," lever lock-style, brass pressure plate w/patent date, rare cam-action lever type, good condition ............................... **127**

**Spoke shave,** cast iron w/worn japanning, marked "L. Bailey. Boston," hollow face, good condition ........................................... **37**

**Spoke shave,** iron w/beech handles, marked "D. Flather & Sons, Sheffield, England, Irving Hdw. Co Ltd. 12 Warren St., New York City.," & "Celebrated Joiners Tools" etched on bottom side of cutter, near new, near perfect wood, ends of handles never finished, fine condition, cutter 3" w. .................... **100**

**Spoke shave,** iron w/boxwood handles, Stanley No. 85, good condition (hang hole in handle)...... **83**

**Spoke shave,** nickel plated, marked "L. Bailey. Patent June 19, 1866," manufactured by Stanley Rule & Level, rare in that Stanley would plate certain tools only for special orders or presentations, this shave is only known example of No. 60 plated, exceptional condition........ **170**

**Spoke shave,** rosewood & cast iron w/90% plating, Stanley No. 67 Universal, Sweet Hart vintage, early type with left/right handles, flat bottom, good condition (one ferrule cracked) ...... **55**

**Spoke shave,** rosewood w/60% plating on blade, Stanley No. 81 razor edge, very good condition, 2" w. blade .................... **330**

**Stair rail shaves,** beech bodies w/iron blades, marked "F.J. Gouch. Worcester, MA.," blades held in place w/heavy iron plates that match sole contour, w/irons w/heart-shaped tops, uncommon maker, fine condition, left & right pair ...................................... **400**

**Sugar ax,** cast iron, fine condition, head 8 1/4" l., edge 2 1/2" w. (handle old but not original).......... **140**

**Timber scribe,** wrought iron w/hardwood block handle, early rectangular block style w/removable folding metal arm, good sharp cutting edges, uncommon style, very good condition ........................................ **120**

**Timber scribe,** wrought iron w/hardwood handle, early style w/folding arm, file decoration, good sharp cutting edges, swing arm folds into handle, very good condition ...................... **120**

**Timber scribe,** wrought iron w/rosewood handle, point & two cutting edges, good condition ........ **41**

**Turf ax,** wrought iron, marked "Horton and Arnold," hand-forged large flattened pear-shaped head, wood handle w/fine smooth patina, New York state maker, 1850s, very good condition (ILLUS. p. 30 bottom right with clapboard slick) ........... **275**

**Twybill,** wrought iron, touchmarks, small size w/long narrow head w/narrow blade edge, no doubt American, some decoration where shank meets head, old handle, good condition, 16" l. .............................. **260**

**Wheelwright's side ax,** cast iron, Europe, 18th c., good condition, head 14" l., edge 7" w. ................. **170**

**Wood shave,** wrought-iron w/hardwood double handles, marked "S. Lar??ion.," carved mouth & top, hand cut bolts, 18th c. or earlier, good condition, blade 4 1/2" , overall 14" l. ................................................ **150**

# Hammers

Hammers closely followed the evolution of edged tools such as the ax, and some examples had dual purposes, one end for hammering, the other for chopping.

Again, by the 18th century, hammers had developed into a multitude of specialized forms and were used by a wide variety of craftsmen, not just woodworkers.

The most familiar type today is the *claw* hammer with the forked claw opposite the flat hammer face. The *ball peen* hammer featured a rounded knob opposite the hammering face.

Although most old hammers had iron heads and later, steel heads, there are types that were all-wood for doing lighter work.

As with most tools, mass-production did not get under way until the 19th century and cast steel hammers only became widely available and affordable after the Civil War.

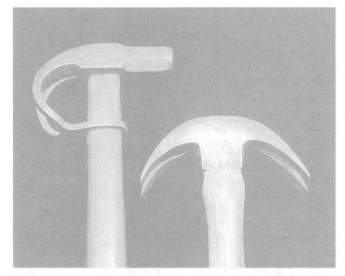

**Adz-head hammer,** cast iron, marked "Chisel Claw Hammer Co.," overall clean w/original wood handle, very good condition (some surface rust)..... **$120**

**Ball peen hammer,** beryllium copper w/95% green accent paint, Stanley No. B4, extremely rare marked Stanley beryllium tool, fine condition......... **525**

**Beetle,** burled walnut head, large cylindrical head centered by a long straight wood handle, good condition, head 10" d., 7" h. ........... **99**

**Bill-poster's hammer,** cast iron head, marked "Keen Kutter," in two sections, nail & poster clips fine, w/store code & $3 price penciled on handle, rare, fine condition ........................................ **260**

**Bill-poster's hammer,** cast iron, three-section style w/brass joints, unusual, unmarked, good condition ........................................ **155**

**Box opening & nail pulling hammer,** cast iron w/wooden handle, marked "Gilfillan Scale & Hdw. Co. Chicago. Pat. Pend.," as handle is tilted backward, jaws of nail puller close on head of nail, very delicate, good condition (face lightly peened over) ...................... **300**

**Boxmaker's hammer,** cast iron, strap-type w/one long claw, marked w/the Masonic emblem, old wooden handle, good condition ........................................ **90**

**Bung extracting hammer,** cooper's-type, cast iron & wood, patented, barred tip drives into bung for easy removal, when extracted, wing nut turns down shank & pushes extracted bung off hammer head, handle old & may be original, good condition... **625**

**Carver's mallet,** lignum vitae, good condition, 10" l. (one tight check) ................................................. **31**

**Carver's mallet,** possibly maple, good condition, 12" l. ....................... **23**

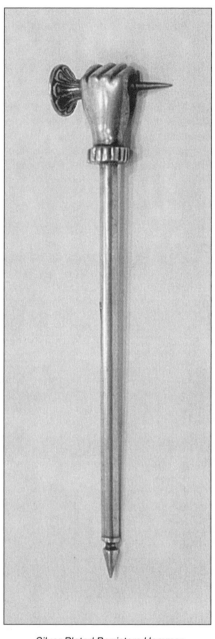

*Silver Plated Barristers Hammer*

**Barrister's hammer,** silver plated w/97% plating, breaks wax seals on envelopes, very ornate w/hand gripping torch like poll & pick, appears to be silver plated, fine condition (ILLUS.) ......................... **600**

**Chisel-claw hammer,** cast iron w/wooden handle w/95% black paint, marked "Chisel Claw Hammer Co. H.A. Ayvad. Pat. Apd. For. Hoboken, N.J.," Type 1 before patent was issued on Aug. 26, 1930, rare, retains 40% of original paper label on handle, fine condition .................. **175**

**Claw hammer,** cast iron, marked "Pat'd Nov. 4, 02," double claw style, George Voight patent-type, handle probably original but w/chip off tail end, properly stored & very good condition (ILLUS. p. 44 right w/triple-claw hammer) ........................................ **210**

**Claw hammer,** cast iron, Selsor Patent-type, double polls, face rounded, old but probably not original wood handle, good condition ......................................... **36**

**Claw hammer,** presentation-type, gold-plated iron, mounted on a wooden board w/metal plaque inscribed "Estwing Gold Hammer Award for 50 years Service to the Hardware Industry. L.C. Seufert.," originally awarded to Mr. Seufert who operated a hardware store in Pierce City,

Missouri, handle w/leather grips, "L.C. Seufert" on handle in gold letters, complete w/hammer & wall holder, fine condition ........................................ **170**

**Claw hammer,** wrought iron, marked "I. Warner," hand-made by early New Hampshire maker, good condition ................................. **28**

**Claw hammer head,** cast iron, special award, marked "Stanley Atha 1875-1975, 100 Years.," hammer head cut in half & mounted on a rectangular wooden plaque, very good condition ......................................... **65**

**Claw hammer & wrench combination,** cast iron, marked "Anchor Plumb," head in fine condition w/old wooden handle, overall good condition .................. **130**

**Combined hammer & lifter,** cast iron & hardwood, marked "J. Lindley. Pat. Dec. 2, 1890," head rotates & claws act as stove-lid lifter, original handle, rare hammer, good condition ....... **330**

**Cooper's bung hammer,** cast iron, marked "Fleischmann's Two Stamped Dry Gins" on one side, "Two Stamped Magnolia

*Rare Double-face Hammer*

**Double face hammer,** cast iron & hardwood, marked "D. Maydole," hits on both forward & backward stoke, mark strong & clear, old & possible original handle, rare, very good condition ................................................................................................. **600**

Whiskey" on other, very good condition ...................................... **165**

**Double-claw hammer,** cast iron w/95+% original black finish, marked "Pat'd Nov. 1902," mark double struck, near mint (paper label missing from handle) .......... **275**

**Fulcrum-claw hammer,** cast iron, heavy rhino horn claw for extra leverage when pulling nails, old handle, fewer than five known to exist, very good condition ...................................... **225**

**Hammer,** cast iron, marked "A.T. Nelson Pat'd July 28, 1908. Wilton, Iowa.," patented cutting edge on front of head acts as scraping tool, very uncommon hammer, old handle, fine condition ...................................... **105**

**Hammer,** cast iron, marked "Cheny," 28 oz. w/nail holding device, unusual weight, good condition .......................................... **85**

**Hammer,** cast iron, marked "Fish," guaranteed original, one of only two known, handle old & appears to be original, very good condition ........................... **1,225**

**Hammer,** cast iron, marked "Winchester September to October Special," part of Winchester series of tools that were on special each month, original handle, very good condition, 16 oz. ........................... **100**

**Hammer,** cast iron w/90% japanning, Stanley No. 52 1/2, 10 oz., original label on wooden

*Wrap-around Claw & Double Claw Hammers*

**Hammer,** cast-iron head w/wooden handle, double claws, no face, sometimes referred to as "wrecking" hammer, fine condition, replaced handle (ILLUS. right w/wrap-around claw hammer) .............................................................................. **225**

**Hammer,** cast-iron head w/wood handle, marked "Solomon Anderson. Aug. 20, 1845," first U.S. hammer patent, wrap-around claw added support while helping hold head in place, rare in this fine, marked condition (ILLUS. left w/double-claw hammer) ...................................................................................................................... **1,000**

handle, clean & nice, fine condition .......................................... **65**

**Hammer combination tool,** cast iron, odd design w/small hammer & what appears to be a scraping edge tool, good condition, only 1 1/2" h. ................. **46**

*Engraved Presentation Mallet*

**Mallet,** presentation-type, sterling silver shield fastened to burl head, ivory handle w/sterling end cap, engraved on shield "Presented to Sir Wm. Dunn Bart. M.P. by Jas. Dunlop - Joiner Contractor on the occasion of his laying the foundation stone of The Paisley Grammar School - Wm. B. Barbour Academy - 25th May 1896," head 3 3/4" d., overall 8" l. (ILLUS.)... **350**

**Nail hammer,** cast iron, Stanley No. 11 1/2 100 Plus, looks new & unused, in original box, fine condition (box w/one bad corner & broken spot on top) ..... **193**

**Saddler's hammer,** cast iron, marked "Patented Dec. 10, 1867 - Feb. 3, 1863," a Stanley Conklin patent model, marks weak, very rare marked example, good wood handle, overall good condition ................... **95**

**Saddler's hammer,** strap-type w/side claws for tacks, good condition (face rounded a bit) ...... **33**

**Saw maker's hammer,** cast iron head, old handle, head w/slight bend, very good condition (old but not original handle) ............................................. **65**

**Staple-pulling hammer,** cast iron, marked "John McCormick Patent.," design patented March 28, 1899, rhino horn design head, old replacement handle, rare & unusual, good condition ........................................ **200**

**Stone bushing hammer,** iron, wedge locked teeth, large, good condition, teeth 9 1/2" l., overall 22" l. ................................... **135**

**Strap hammer,** wrought iron, marked "E. Ingall," great iron head enhanced by tiger maple handle hand-carved w/deer foot end, handle may not be terribly old, fine condition ............ **300**

**Strap hammer,** wrought iron, small size, delicately made, original handle shows heavy use, very good condition ............. **150**

**Tack hammer,** cast iron, slender head w/offset nail puller, large size, old wood handle, good condition, overall 8" l. ................... **85**

*Double & Triple Claw Hammers*

**Triple claw hammer,** cast iron, solid cast iron head w/three nearly equal size claws, design similar to C.I. Yonge patent of June 11, 1901, this hammer is a true triple claw, perhaps only example of its type known, surface has some pitting & face a couple minor chips, handle appears original, great style & certainly one of the rarest of all hammers, 5" h., good (ILLUS. left w/double claw hammer)...... **1,200**

# Levels

Most people familiar with levels today may not realize that the earlier type didn't feature a "bubble" in a tube to operate.

As far back as ancient Egypt builders used a wooden A-shaped frame that suspended a weight on a cord from the top of the "A." When placed on a level surface, the weight would hang perfectly perpendicular to the frame. This general style of level was used into the 17th century, and early American carpenters often made an L-square frame that suspended a plumb bob that worked on the same principle as the A-frame type.

It wasn't until the end of the 17th century that the new "spirit" level (i.e. - with a bubble tube) first came on the scene, but this version did not come into widespread use for 200 years. Since the early 19th century spirit levels have been made, using either a wooden board to enclose the bubble tube or even ornately cast iron frames. It is these handcrafted and decorative levels that are of greatest interest to modern collectors. More common examples can sell for under $100 while the choicest models can bring several thousand.

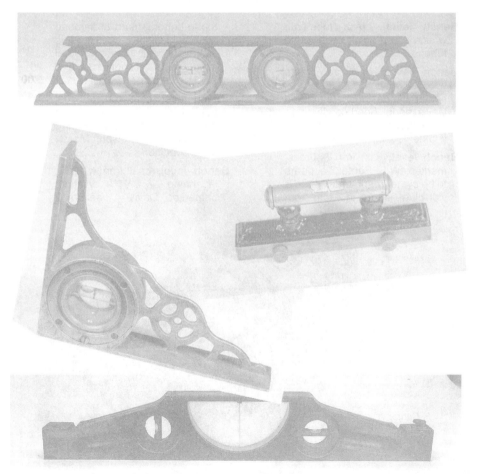

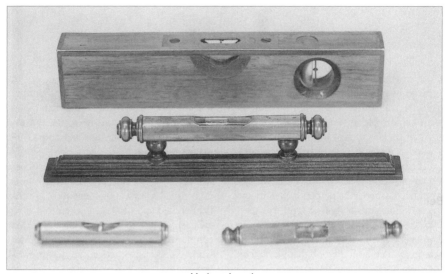

*Various Levels*

**Bench level,** brass tube-type w/nice acorn finials, odd round tube .................................................. **$72**

**Bench level,** cast iron base w/55% plating, plated vial holder w/brass ends, unmarked Davis model, good condition, 8" base (ILLUS. above, middle row w/other levels) ................................ **450**

**Bench level,** cast iron & brass, marked "W.F. Senter," appears to be owner mark, brass plate & vial plug, tapers in width from top to bottom, heart & diamond cut-out designs, end reading vial, very well made, w/wood case, fine condition, 6" l. (ILLUS. below) ............................... **578**

**Bench level,** cast iron, unusual truss design, brass name plate on top, Universal Boring Machine Co., Hudson, Mass., good condition ............................... **230**

**Bench level,** cast iron w/100% japanning & 97% plating, unmarked Davis 4" bench &

*W.F. Senter*
*Bench Level*

square, both original screws, fine condition (ILLUS. below) ....... **303**

**Bench level,** cast iron w/50% finishes, 4" pedestal type, unmarked Davis, plated tube, very good condition ..................... **180**

**Bench level,** cast iron w/70% japanning, green paper label behind glass vial reads "W.T. Nicholson. Maker. Providence, R.I.," brass top plate, forerunner to Stanley No. 43, rare, good condition ......................................... **350**

**Bench level,** cast iron w/95% nickel plating, marked "Goodell Pratt No. 822," w/ground & graduated vial, in original wooden box w/65% label, fine condition, 12" l. .......................... **165**

**Bench level,** cast iron w/95% plating, marked "Miller Level & Hardware Co. Unionville, Conn. - Pat. Apl'd For," in original box w/incomplete label, unusual, very good condition ..................... **125**

**Bench level,** ebony w/brass plates, very decorative w/cut-out top, end & side plates, good condition ......................................... **193**

**Bench level,** hardwood w/nearly perfect gold pinstriping & black japanning, marked "Queen & Co. Phil'a.," brass edges,

complete w/original wooden case, fine condition, 8" l. ........... **1,265**

**Bench level,** wood & brass, arched mantel clock style, unusual low profile, japanning worn, brass top plate, manufactured level, good condition ......................................... **198**

**Bit & square level,** cast iron, Stanley, new in original green box w/some wear & fading, 20th c. ......................................... **94**

**Bit & square level,** cast iron, Stanley No. 44, in original box, fine condition (box worn but fully readable) ......................................... **143**

**Bit & square level,** cast iron, Stanley No. 44, new, in original worn green box w/label, fine condition ......................................... **220**

**Combination bench level & square,** cast iron, w/75% red japanning, early & rare, good condition ......................................... **525**

**Combined level & grade finder,** brass-trimmed hardwood, marked "American Combined Level and Grade Finder - Patented and Manufactured by Edward Helb - Railroad, PA.," includes plumb, level, compass, inclinometer, etc., wood w/coat of new finish, good condition ........ **190**

*Davis Bench Level*

*Electric Level*

*Rare Corner Level*

**Corner level,** cast iron w/98% japanning, marked "Millers Falls Co. No. 20," 4" sides w/90 degree corner, can read plumb & level w/one vial, rare due to limited sales, fine condition (ILLUS.) ........................................ **1,760**

*Corner Level*

**Corner level,** filigree-cast aluminum w/single vial, marked "Davis & Cook. Watertown, N.Y. Patented Dec. 7, 1886. Aluminum," plating 95%,

extremely rare, very good condition (ILLUS.) ..................... **1,980**

**Electric level,** hardwood w/brass slide switch on side, marked "Stetson's Patent Electric Level No. 110," marked w/Stratton patent dates & "Pat. Pending," battery in base lights up plumb & level vials, portholes highlighted in silver paint for illumination, manufactured by Stratton from No. 1B type levels, very rare, mint (ILLUS. above) ....................................... **3,080**

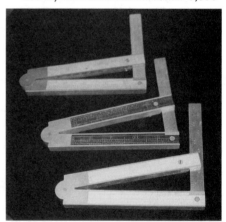

*Three Inclinometers*

**Inclinometer,** boxwood & brass, marked "The C-S Co. - Pine Meadow, Conn. - U.S.A.," combination rule, level, protractor, pitch gauge, etc., very good clean condition (ILLUS. top w/other inclinometers).................... **242**

**Inclinometer,** brass & wood w/95% original paint, marked "Chamberlain - Jan. 1, 1867," arm pivots as degrees are read from protractor hinged to level

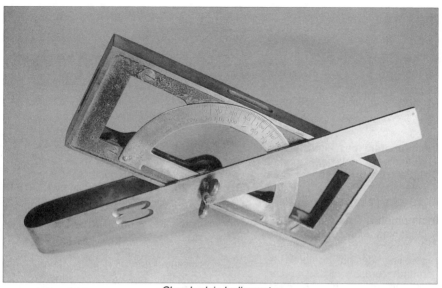

*Chamberlain Inclinometer*

base, plumb & level bubbles, rare, fine condition (ILLUS. above) .......................................... **1,210**

*Inclinometers & Level*

**Inclinometer,** cast iron arched mantel clock-style w/large brass center dial, marked "L.L. Davis," gold-painted side brackets w/80% paint, two-threaded hole in base, good condition (ILLUS. at left, center w/other inclinometer & level) ............................................... **412**

**Inclinometer,** cast iron w/85% japanning, marked "Davis Level & Tool Co.," ornate pierced scrolling design, very good condition, 18" l., 2 7/8" h. .............. **165**

**Inclinometer,** cast iron w/90% japanning, marked "Davis Tool & Level Co.," ornate pierced scrolling design, very good condition, 24" l., 2 13/16" h. .......... **468**

**Inclinometer,** cast iron w/95% gold leafing, marked "L.L. Davis' Adjustable Spirit Level," ornate pierced scrolling design, top & bottom retain most original finish markings, fine condition, 12" l. ........................... **1,155**

*L.L. Davis Inclinometer*

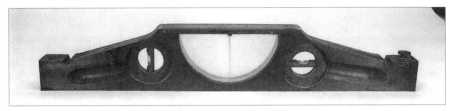

*Hight Micrometer Level Inclinometer*

**Inclinometer,** cast iron w/95% japanning & gold leaf, marked "L.L. Davis," very good condition, 12" l. (ILLUS. bottom previous page)............................... **275**

**Inclinometer,** cast iron w/95% japanning, marked "Davis Level & Tool Co.," ornate pierced scrolling design centered by round brass dial, original machine marks on top & bottom rails, very good condition, 7" l. (ILLUS. p. 49, bottom w/other inclinometer & level) ..................... **440**

**Inclinometer,** cast metal w/100% gold leafing & japanning, marked "L.L. Davis," arched mantel clock-shaped, complete w/original worn box & set of instructions, very rare, fine condition (ILLUS.) ...................... **3,410**

**Inclinometer,** cherry beam w/brass dial w/pivoting arm, unmarked but appears to be a P. Hodge & Co. product, adjust-level vial type, arm can be set to desired pitch, good condition, 30" l. (missing locking screw) ....... **633**

**Inclinometer,** cherry & mahogany laminate, marked "Hight Micrometer Level - Toledo, Ohio," plumb, level, inclinometer & pitch level, glazed center window w/mirrored pendulum-type inclinometer w/semicircular scale, one end equipped w/screw-type pitch adjuster, w/adjustable plumb & level vials, paper label inside window w/instructions on how to adjust, hard to find, very good condition (ILLUS. above) .............................. **800**

**Inclinometer,** cast iron w/nearly 100% japanning, marked "Davis Level & Tool Co.," ornate pierced scrolling design, near mint, 24" l., 2 13/16" h. ................. **330**

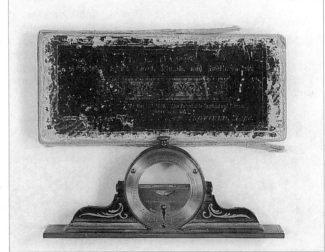

*Rare Davis Inclinometer with box*

*Bradford Union Inclinometer*

**Inclinometer,** cherry, marked "Bradford Union," semicircular glass tube w/dial for direct reading of angle, aluminum top & bottom rails, marked only "C.S. Powell" in arc on face plate, very clean & nice, fine condition 24" l. (ILLUS. above) .. **1,100**

**Inclinometer,** cherry stock w/inset brass fittings, marked "T.F. Deck Gravity Level Co. Patented Dec. 15, 1896. Feb. 14, 1905. Toledo, Ohio," large dial, early type, very clean & working, fine condition, 30" l., 4 1/4" h. ...................................... **1,210**

**Inclinometer,** cherry w/aluminum top & bottom rails, marked "The Semi-Circular Level Co. Kane, PA. Pat. April 5, 1904," circular vile-type w/vial forming full half-circle, rare, very good condition, 24" l. ............................................. **1,540**

**Inclinometer,** cherry w/boxwood dial inclinometer, marked "C.S. Co.," very good condition, 28" l. .... **28**

**Inclinometer,** cherry w/boxwood dial, marked "C.S. Co.," dial-type w/dial sets degree of pitch, good condition (couple of dark stains)............................................... **72**

**Inclinometer,** chestnut, marked "The Downey Level. Orr & Lockett Hardw. Co. Chicago. Pat'd Sept. 29, 1891," pendulum-type w/printed face & brass & glass porthole, very good condition, 30" l. ................ **2,090**

**Inclinometer,** ebony & brass, marked "W. & S. Jones. Holborn, London.," full quarter circle arc, hinged in middle,

*Ebony and Brass Inclinometer*

*Rare McDowell Radial Inclinometer*

swings for readings 0 to 90 degrees, ebony body hinged w/level in one leg, holding bottom leg w/work & leveling top leg angle can be direct read, backside of arc marked, "Devised by Wm. Chapman, Esq. Civil Engineer. Inches Base to a Foot in Height Applicable to Walls of Masonry to Earth Work to Piles &c. Inches Rise on a Yard Base.," folds to fit in pocket, ca. pre-1850 production, fine condition, 6" legs, (ILLUS. bottom of previous page)............................ **1,400**

**Inclinometer,** ebony w/German silver fittings, marked "Stephens Co. - Patented Jan. 12, 1858," combination rule, level, protractor, pitch gauge, etc., rarest of the three types of Chapin Stephens inclinometers, very good condition (ILLUS. p. 48 center w/other inclinometers)............................ **10,120**

**Inclinometer,** hardwood arched at the top center, marked "Pat. Apld. For," brass inset dial adjusts for pitch similar to a Davis model w/a locking screw built into the rotating ring, vee-groove in bottom, good condition (body well used)............ **725**

**Inclinometer,** hardwood & brass, marked "A.F. McDowell Radial. Pat. Dec. 12, 05.," long brass arm rotates to set pitch of level vial, rare inclinometers used Stratton No. 1 levels as bodies for McDowell patent arm, shows use, rare, good condition (ILLUS. above) .......................... **1,100**

**Inclinometer,** hardwood, long narrow form w/arched center section enclosing double hinged vials used to set pitch on a single-quarter arch, arched bolt locks vial at setting, good condition, 30" l. .............................. **209**

**Inclinometer,** hardwood, marked "Pat'd By T.F. Deck Dec. 5, 96. Toledo Gravity Level Co. Toledo, Ohio," inset round dial w/pendulum mechanism, first type w/4" d. dial, silvered degree ring, brass disk on back w/same information as on dial, sheet steel tips, good condition, 24" l. (steel tips pitted).............. **2,970**

**Inclinometer,** hardwood w/inset brass dial, marked "The Deck Gravity Level Co. Pat'd Dec. 5, 96 and Feb. 4, 05. Toledo, Ohio.," dial-type w/pendulum mechanism, rare & desirable, very good condition, 24" l. ........ **2,200**

*Melick Inclinometer*

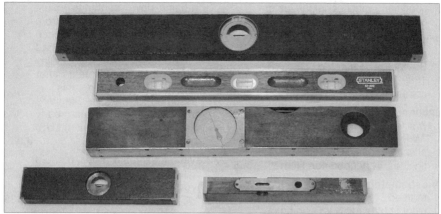

*Early Inclinometers & Levels*

**Inclinometer,** iron arched openwork mantel clock-style, marked "The Melick Clinometer Co. Patented Dec. 3rd, 1889. St. Louis," 80% japanning, gold leaf & red paint 80%, rare style, good condition (ILLUS. bottom of previous page) ....................... **2,860**

**Inclinometer,** ivory, marked "Stephens & Co. Patented Jan. 12, 1858," two-fold w/level, protractor, scales, etc., marked w/"15" on one leg, light tobacco yellow color, good condition w/one chip & several stress cracks, 12" l. (ILLUS. p. 205 center w/various measuring tools) .... **1,155**

**Inclinometer,** ivory w/German silver fittings, marked "Stephens Co. - Patented Jan. 12, 1858, No. 38," combination rule, level, protractor, pitch gauge, etc., very good condition, two tight hairlines (ILLUS. p. 48 bottom w/other inclinometers) ............................. **2,310**

**Inclinometer,** mahogany, marked "Davis Level & Tool Co.

Adjustable Spirit Level," shows some use, uncommon, good condition, 12" l. (ILLUS. above, bottom left, with other levels) ....... **358**

**Inclinometer,** mahogany, marked "Gibson Plumb & Level Mfg. Co. Lahoma, Okla. U.S. Patent June 25, 31907.," center glass dial w/pendulum-type needle, reads in degrees around a full circle, plated nameplate on top side, clean & rare, very good condition, 26" l. (ILLUS. below).... **358**

**Inclinometer,** mahogany, marked "L.L. Davis," brass trim & round center inset, dark & heavy, good condition, 30" l., 3 5/8" h. (ILLUS. above, top with other levels) ............................................... **990**

**Inclinometer,** mahogany w/brass end tips, marked "L.L. Davis," patented adjustable dial in center, good condition, 12" l. (bulb broken) ................................. **413**

**Inclinometer,** mahogany w/brass trim, marked "L.L. Davis," dark heavy wood, level in top

*Inclinometer by Gibson Plumb & Level*

condition, much original luster on brass, 24" l., 3 1/2" h.............. **3,080**

**Inclinometer,** wood w/inset metal-framed dial, marked "W. B. Melick Patented Dec. 3, 1889," dial finished 80%, good condition, 18" l. ............................... **286**

**Inclinometer,** wooden body w/silvered 2" d. dial, marked "W.B. Melick," dial rotates as pitch changes, 90% red & silver finishes, very good condition........ **385**

**Inclinometer & level,** boxwood, marked "Stephens & Co.," w/fold-out blade & level in base, only known unbound example of the No. 036 rule & believed to be the first type quickly replaced w/bound version, very good condition .............................. **425**

**Inclinometer level,** cast iron w/100% japanning, mantel clock shaped, unmarked, graduated dial w/set points on both sides of circle to allow settings of 360 degrees, fine condition ..................................... **1,375**

**Inclinometer & level,** mahogany & brass, marked "L. Brooks. Patent of Aug. 29, 1854," two-piece body construction w/rod running down center to adjust vial for various pitches from zero to 1" per foot, w/pitch adjuster in one end, never had paper label applied by Stanley who purchased patent after Brooks' death, so this is assumed to predate Stanley's purchase or be an early Stanley, fine condition (ILLUS. below)......................................... **3,080**

**Level,** aluminum & brass, marked "The Chapin-Stephens Co.," Vogel patent, good condition, 24" l. .................................................. **65**

**Level,** aluminum, marked "Empire Levels Milwaukee, Wis.," patented adjustable holder, produced using screws, ca. 1930, together w/1921 advertisement for the level, fine condition ....................................... **100**

**Level,** aluminum, marked "L.S. Starrett Co. No. 192," one pair of vials set at 45 degrees, quite rare, new condition, 24" l. ............. **150**

**Level,** birch w/brass fittings, marked "American Combined Level and Grade Finder," commonly known as the Helb Railroad Level, combines compass, inclinometer, plumb &

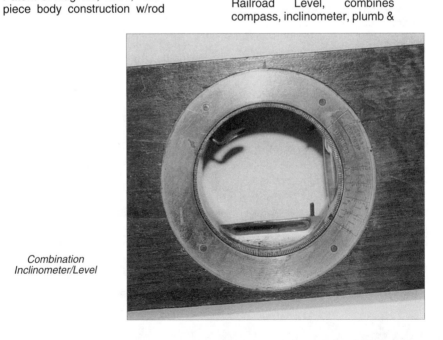

*Combination Inclinometer/Level*

horizontal bubbles as well as sighting level, original paper label, very good condition (ILLUS. p. 53 third from top with other levels) ................................. **248**

**Level,** brass -bound mahogany, Stanley No. 95, w/full decal, ca. 1925, unused condition, 24" l. ...... **440**

**Level,** brass- bound rosewood, marked "Millers Falls Co. Millers Falls, Mass. No. 10," double stamped, rosewood Millers Falls No. 10 levels rare since made after Stratton patents ran out, short-lived production, extremely rare size, good condition, 6 1/2" l. ...................... **800**

**Level,** brass-bound mahogany, marked "EAIA 50th Birthday. 1933-1983," special commemorative Stanley No. 324 model w/EAIA medallion, new in box (ILLUS. p. 53 second from top with other levels)......................... **330**

**Level,** brass-bound mahogany, marked "Goodell-Pratt Company," decal & original finish about 85%, fine condition, 2" h., 20" l....................................... **75**

**Level,** brass-bound mahogany, marked "Goodell-Pratt Company," original decal 95%, fine condition, 3 x 26".......................... **138**

**Level,** brass-bound mahogany, marked "Goodell-Pratt Company," w/traces of original finish, decal label, good condition, 2 1/4" h., 30" l. ............................... **45**

**Level,** brass-bound mahogany, marked "Stratton Bros. No. 1," very good condition (few scrapes on wood)........................... **66**

**Level,** brass-bound mahogany, Stanley No. 1093, marked "L.S.K. & Co.," on top edge, good condition, 30" l. (uncommon length for this model).............................................. **120**

**Level,** brass-bound mahogany, Stanley No. 42-320, 1983 commemorative level for the

50-year anniversary of EAIA, rare .................................................. **105**

**Level,** brass-bound mahogany, Stanley No. 98, first Sweet Hart trademark, very hard-to-find trademark, near mint, 12" l. (brass polished)............................. **300**

**Level,** brass-bound rosewood, marked "Goodell-Pratt Co. No. 4030," retains 99% of finish & complete decal, 30" l., 2 1/2" h. .... **468**

**Level,** brass-bound rosewood, marked "Stratton Bros. Greenfield, Mass. 10," good condition, 2" h., 24" l. .................... **200**

**Level,** brass-bound rosewood, marked "Stratton Brothers," great grain pattern w/traces of original finish, very good condition, 26" l. .............................. **193**

**Level,** brass-bound rosewood, marked "Stratton Brothers, Greenfield, MA," 8" w/end plumb, wood near perfect, fine condition ....................................... **275**

**Level,** brass-bound rosewood, marked "Stratton Brothers. Greenfield, Mass, Patented Mch. 1 1870.," wood fine & brass untouched, very good condition, 8" l. (lines scratched at level bulb).................................... **190**

**Level,** brass-bound rosewood, marked "Stratton Brothers. Greenfield, Mass. Patented Mch. 1, 1870. No. 10," w/side view plumb vial, very good condition, 8" l. (wood grainy & dark, brass as found).................... **190**

**Level,** brass-bound rosewood, marked "Stratton Brothers. Greenfield, Mass.," w/end plumb, wood perfect, brass polished, fine condition................. **200**

**Level,** brass-bound rosewood, marked "Stratton Brothers. Greenfield, Mass. Patented Mch. 1, 1870," clean, well done, very good condition, 6 1/2" l. ........ **300**

**Level,** brass-bound rosewood, marked "Stratton Brothers.

Greenfield, Mass.," w/late mark intended for metal levels only, rare as only three wooden levels w/this mark are known, near mint (ILLUS. p. 46 top row w/other levels) ............................... **500**

**Level,** brass-bound rosewood, marked "Stratton Brothers. Greenfield, Mass.," nicely cleaned, fine condition, 6 1/2" l.... **700**

**Level,** brass-bound rosewood, marked "Stratton Brothers. No. 1," polished, in cloth bag, very good condition, 30" l. ..................... **171**

**Level,** brass-bound rosewood, marked "Stratton Brothers No. 10," rare type w/porthole plumb vial, very good condition, 8" l. ..... **330**

**Level,** brass-bound rosewood, marked "Stratton Brothers No. 10," rare type w/porthole plumb vial, like new, 8" l. ......................... **385**

**Level,** brass-bound rosewood, marked "Stratton Brothers. Patented July 16, 1872. Oct. 4, 1887. May 22, 1888. No. 1.," wood fine w/great grain pattern, very good condition, 30" l. ........... **105**

**Level,** brass-bound rosewood, marked "Stratton Brothers. Patented Mch. 1, 1870," Type 2 w/end vial & side view ports, very good condition, 8" l. ............. **209**

**Level,** brass-bound rosewood, marked "Stratton Brothers. Patented Mch. 1, 1870," Type 1 w/end vial & no side view ports, much original finish, fine condition ....................................... **468**

**Level,** brass-bound rosewood, marked "Tower & Lyon," very good condition, 6 1/2" l. (mark weak, often the case w/levels

Stratton made for other companies) ..................................... **220**

**Level,** brass-bound rosewood, Stanley No. 98, good condition, 12" l. ...................................................... **220**

**Level,** brass-bound rosewood, Stanley No. 98, much original finish, fine condition, 18" l. (minor dings) .................................. **248**

**Level,** brass-bound rosewood, Stanley No. 98, Sweet Hart logo, hard to find size, good condition, 9" l. .............................. **550**

**Level,** brass-bound rosewood, Stanley No. 98, w/nearly all original finish, fine condition, 12" l. ... **450**

**Level,** brass-bound wood, marked "The American Combined Level and Grade Finder - Edward Helb - Railroad, PA," used to design, plumb, level, grade, sight & includes a compass, clean w/perfect paper label, 24" l. ................................. **248**

**Level,** brass-trimmed hardwood, marked "Davis & Cook," double porthole model, good condition (missing on cap) ............................... **22**

**Level,** cast iron base & brass level tube w/rotating protector, both unfinished without japanning, Stanley No. 34, World War II-type, probably produced when black paint was spared for war effort, good condition, 8" l. .............. **35**

**Level,** cast iron, marked "American Level Co. Detroit Mich.," nonadjustable frame, vials set in gold-painted holders, fine condition .................... **50**

**Level,** cast iron, marked "Davis & Cook," pinwheel open filigree

*Pinwheel Open Filigree Work Level*

*Rare Odd Fellows Cast Iron Level*

design, sometimes called pretzel level because of pinwheel shape, needs cleaning, very good condition (ILLUS. bottom of previous page)............................ **1,045**

**Level,** cast iron, marked "Disston & Morris Tool Works - Philada.," hinged handle w/ornate cast leafy scrolls & company name in side plates, vials filled w/red alcohol, fancy, good condition, 28" l............ **396**

**Level,** cast iron painted black w/gold highlights, decorated w/various openwork motifs of the Odd Fellows cast into the body, only one of three Odd Fellows cast-iron levels known w/level vial mounted in pedestal tube, 19th c., casting perfect, finishes nearly 100% (ILLUS. above)........................................ **1,700**

**Level,** cast iron, Stanley No. 36G 12-Inch, tool about new, in original box w/85% paper label, fine condition (box w/water stain) .............................................. **110**

**Level,** cast iron w/100% plating, marked "Athol Machine Co.," fine condition, 12" l. ........................ **65**

**Level,** cast iron w/30% finish, marked "W.T. Nicholson Pat'd May 1st., 1860. Prov. R.I. No. 15," manufactured by Stanley Rule & Level Co., good condition, 24" l. .............................. **130**

**Level,** cast iron w/40% japanning, marked "Davis Level & Tool Co.," arched mantel clock-style, good condition (both ends cut off)....................................................... **85**

**Level,** cast iron w/60% japanning, marked "Standard Tool Co.," diamond cut-out decoration, good condition, 6" l. ...................... **175**

**Level,** cast iron w/60% japanning, marked "W.T. Nicholson," made by Stanley Rule & Level Co., good condition, 14" l. ..................... **121**

**Level,** cast iron w/60% plating, marked "Davis Patent No. 9. M.W. Robinson Co.," good condition, 24" l. (rails need cleaning) ........................................... **70**

**Level,** cast iron w/80% japanning & 80% gold pinstriping, marked "L.L. Davis Adjustable Spirit Level," center bubble adjusts to

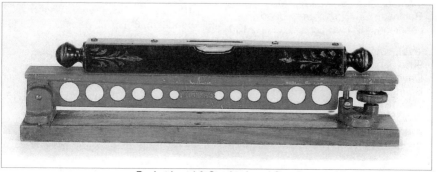

*Pocket Level & Stanley Level Stand*

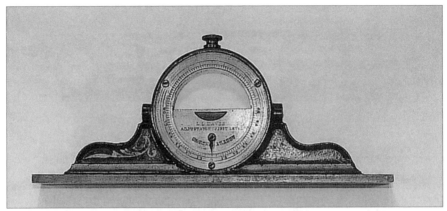

*L.L. Davis Mantel Clock Style Level*

set angle, uncommon 18" model, very good condition .......... **625**

**Level,** cast iron w/90% japanning & 75% gold leaf, marked "Davis Level & Tool Co.," w/center inclinometer, in wooden case, very good condition, 2 1/4 h., 12" l. ................................................. **385**

**Level,** cast iron w/90% japanning & about 80% of the original gold pinstriping, marked "Manufactured by L.L. Davis. Springfield, Mass.," pocket-type, No. 39, rare, very good condition, 8" l. (ILLUS. bottom of previous page, top, w/Stanley level stand).................................... **1,400**

**Level,** cast iron w/90% japanning, marked "Davis Level & Tool Co.," tall version, very good condition, 24" l. ............................... **385**

**Level,** cast iron w/90% japanning, marked "Davis Patent M.W. Robinson Co. No. 8," very good condition, 18" l. ............................... **130**

**Leevel,** cast iron w/90% plating & 90% japanning, marked "The Davis Level & Tool Co. Springfield, Mass. Pat'd May 29, 1877, 1883.," iron level w/plated vial holder, one level & two plumb vials, reasonably bright, good condition, 6" l. ........... **575**

**Level,** cast iron w/93% japanning, marked "W.T. Nicholson - Pat. May 1, 1860," also marked "Stanley Rule and Level," very clean & near mint, w/original wooden case, 20" l. ........................ **330**

**Level,** cast iron w/95% japanning & gold pinstriping, marked "Davis Level & Tool Co. Pat. Sep. 17, 1867," No. 2 size, ornate pierced scroll design, fine condition, 12" l. ........................ **750**

**Level,** cast iron w/95% japanning, marked "Davis Level & Tool Co.," ornate pierced scrolling design centered by inset level ring, fine condition (light dirt) ........ **300**

**Level,** cast iron w/high percentage of original japanning under newer polish, marked "Davis Pat. M.W.R. Co.," level & two plumb vials in brass plated tubes w/nearly 100% plating, very good condition, 6" l. ................................. **175**

**Level,** cast iron w/near 100% japanning & near perfect gold pinstriping, marked "L.L. Davis," mantel clock-style, fine condition (ILLUS. above) .......... **1,155**

**Level,** cast iron w/near perfect japanning, Stanley Rule & Level Co., marked "Nicholson's

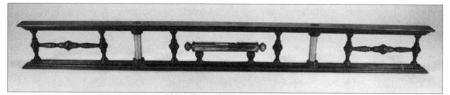

*Very Rare Cast-Iron Level*

Patent May 1, 1860," fine condition, 14" l. .................... **350**

**Level,** cast iron w/nearly 100% japanning & traces of bluing on screws, marked "Davis Level & Tool Co.," in wooden case, fine condition, 12" l. .................... **358**

**Level,** cast iron w/open framework & 90% gold highlights, marked "Davis Spindle," rarest of Davis skeleton types, very good condition, 24" l. (ILLUS. above) .......................... **4,730**

**Level,** cast iron w/worn japanning & slight traces of gold paint, marked "L.L. Davis," mantel clock style, good condition ......... **220**

**Level,** cherry, brass portholes, top & end plates all nearly 3/8" above wood surface, fancy brass w/Gothic arch brass end fittings, good condition ................ **230**

**Level,** cherry, marked on a brass plate "Wood's Patent Tower & Lyon," pop-up sights, very good condition, 24" l. .................... **70**

**Level,** cherry, marked "Winchester" No. 9806-16, good condition (nicks) .................... **40**

**Level** cherry w/black handy hold, Stanley Four Square, Box 3 style original box w/three colors, hard to find, box & level good condition .................... **250**

**Level,** ebony & brass, marked "Buist. Edin'r.," very decorative brass top & end plates, wood fine, unusual Scottish level, good condition .................... **121**

**Level,** ebony, brass & wood, marked "E. Preston & Sons," ebony w/brass top plate & ends, marked "Wood Pat. Cats Eye

Level Tube," leather case, very good condition, 10" l. .................... **55**

**Level,** ebony w/brass trim, marked "E. Preston & Sons.," brass top plate & tips, wood fine, very good condition, 6" l. ........ **70**

**Level,** ebony w/brass trim, marked "Warranted," "D. Urire" carved on side, top plate & tip's end w/fancy heart decoration, good condition .................... **75**

**Level,** hardwood, marked "Hight Micrometer Level. Pat. Apl'd For. Toledo, O.," w/pendulum-type inclinometer, plumb, level & pitch gauge, traces of original finish, rare, very good condition **1,000**

**Level,** hardwood, marked "Mason's," breaks down into three sections, suitcase clips & mortise & tenon joint holds each section together, level vial & provision for plumb bob, fine condition, 4' l. .................... **72**

**Level,** hardwood, marked "Peterson's Patent," patentée from Menominee, Wisconsin, top portion of wooden stock curves in long arc, level vial set into a cutout in side w/top part of stock forming a handle over top of bubble, brass sole & tips, rare & unusual, very good condition .................... **165**

**Level,** hardwood, marked "Winchester" No. 9825, both bubbles are good cat's eye vials, good condition (wood has some dings).................... **40**

**Level,** hardwood telescoping-type, two interlocking dovetailed extensions on each end expand this 26" level out to 49", two screws w/brass wingnut heads hold it closed, reportedly a Harrisburg, Pennsylvania patent type, very good condition .. **358**

**Level,** hardwood w/plated metal fittings, marked "American Combined Level. Helb.," combination-type w/grade finder, compass, etc., wood fine, paper labels clear & strong, very good condition (worn plating) ................................. **170**

**Level,** light wood w/grain pattern, possibly striped mahogany, marked "C.S. Co. Pine Meadow, Conn.," w/brass plates & ends, adjustable, good condition, 26" l. ................................. **75**

**Level,** mahogany, marked "B.F. Criley. Isabella. Chester Co., PA," double level vials, no plumb, name & location visible behind glass vials, unusual, good condition, 44" l. ..................... **176**

**Level,** mahogany, marked "Tower & Lyon No. 15," Wood's Patent-type w/pop-up sights, marked in the wood, uncommon, very good condition, 18" l. ..................... **150**

**Level,** mahogany outside & rosewood center, marked "John Rabone & Sons. Makers. Birmingham," brass tips & center wear plate, triple stock, adjustable, English, unused condition, 24" l. ............................. **220**

**Level,** mahogany w/95% of original paper label, marked "Manufactured by L.L. Davis. No. 22," traces of original finish, very good condition, 30" l. ............ **418**

**Level,** mahogany w/brass tips, marked "H. Chapin. Union Factory. 296," rare & early, good condition, 15" l. ...................... **65**

**Level,** mahogany w/brass tips, marked "No. 25," early adjustable-type w/a brass porthole, only marked w/the model number, very good condition, 27" l. ............................. **215**

**Level,** mahogany w/brass tips, Stanley Rule & Level mark w/ eagle trademark, Type 1, very good condition, 30" l. (couple of dings) ............................... **220**

**Level,** mahogany w/brass top plate, marked "Patten. Wash., DC," name is on top plate in fine script, vial backed w/green paper that generally indicates an early level, fine condition, 1 x 1 1/4 x 9" .................................. **100**

**Level,** pocket-sized, slender iron six-sided rod w/fancy turned brass ends, marked "Davis Level & Tool Co.," 97% plating, rarest Davis level, 3 3/4" l. (ILLUS. p. 49 top w/inclinometers)......... **1,320**

**Level,** rosewood & brass, marked "Stratton Brothers. Patent Mch. 1, 1870.," end plumb vial, great owner stamp for "E.F. Hamilton" w/hobo & over-the-shoulder pack, stamp w/much detail, brass lightly cleaned, very good condition, 8" l. ................................ **330**

**Level,** rosewood, marked "Hall & Knapp" w/eagle trademark, traces of original finish, very good condition, 30" l. ..................... **528**

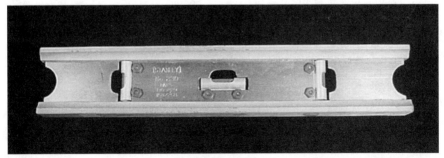

*Stanley No. 230 Level*

*Label from Level Set*

**Level,** steel web & aluminum flanges, Stanley No. 230, I-beam construction, adjustable vial, extremely rare, did not make it into full production, fine condition, 12" l. (ILLUS. bottom previous page) .............................. **550**

**Level,** wood, marked "Woods Pat. June 14, 1887. Ma'f'd By Tower & Lyon.," spring-loaded pop-up sights, 40% original paper label remains, fine condition, 24" l. (storage dings, & nicks) ............... **275**

**Level,** wood, unmarked appears to be a Jennings, fine condition, 18" l., 2" h. ...................................... **418**

**Level,** wood w/brass tips, marked "The American Combined Level and Grade Finder - Edward Helb - Railroad, PA," dark original finish, very clean w/near perfect paper label, very good condition, 24" l. .............................. **248**

**Level adjusting stand,** cast iron w/98% japanning, Stanley No. 178, new & near mint, 32" model .............................................. **715**

**Level & inclinometer,** mahogany w/brass tips, marked "L.L. Davis Adjustable Spirit Level" equivalent to No. 4 but tall version, single locking screws on top & bottom without brass plate, rare, good condition, 3 5/8" h., 24" l. (wood w/plug at bottom edge) ............................. **1,000**

**Level & plumb,** brass-bound rosewood, Stanley No. 98, early style w/pins holding edge plates

in place, very good condition, 12" l. ................................................ **325**

**Level & plumb,** brass-trimmed mahogany, marked "Lambert, Mulliken & Stackpole. Boston, Mass.," brass tips, good condition, 28 3/4" l. (few dings on wood) ......................................... **23**

**Level & plumb,** cherry w/95% finishes, marked "Beverly Hardware Co. No. 644 - Henry Disston & Sons," Disston keystone decal, in original box, fine condition, 16" l. (box repaired) ......................................... **140**

**Level set:** cherry & mahogany, Stanley Model Shop Tools, first of laminated cherry & mahogany, marked "Akron Eclipse No. 6 1/2 Pat. 12-20-04" level, 30" l.; second mahogany, marked "Stratton Brothers No. 2," patent dated 1872 & 1888, marked w/Stanley model shop number "1137"; third brass-bound mahogany, marked "Stratton Brothers No. 1," patent dated 1872 & 1888, also carries Stanley model shop tag reading "5/27/42 - Model 10721 Level Wood Stratton #1-28" - From G. Egers office" w/back marked "This is a model and must be returned to Dept. 58 Stanley Tools"; all three levels fitted into custom-made mahogany velvet-lined box of recent manufacture, fine condition (ILLUS. of label above) ............... **880**

*E. King Level & Square*

**Level & square,** brass, marked "Improved Reflecting Spirit - Level & Square - Wilbar's Level Square - Mafuf'd By E. King. Dunton, Mass. - Patented April 20, 1852," a 3" brass cube fitted w/90-degree level vials on top & side mirrors on two opposing faces, only known example, fine condition (ILLUS.) ...................... **6,600**

**Level stand,** cast iron w/97% red japanning, mounted on mahogany base, marked "Stanley" in center, never offered in catalogs, may have been intended as salesman's sample, only 9" size of three known to exist (ILLUS. bottom of p. 57, bottom, w/pocket level) ........................... **1,050**

**Level with inclinometer,** cast iron w/97% japanning & 95% gold leaf, marked "Davis Level & Tool Co.," center inclinometer, fancy pierced scrollwork design, good condition, 18" l., 2 3/4" h. (ILLUS. top of next page.) ............. **605**

**Machinist's level,** cast iron, Stanley No. 39 1/2, Sweet Hart logo, in original box, tool like new, box shows some wear, very good condition ......................... **66**

**Mining clinometer,** cast metal, marked "M. Attwood's Mining Clinometer A. Lietz Co.," all-in-one pocket instrument w/compass, pitch indicator, double levels & 90 degree sighting device, clean & fine,

*Porter Plumb & Level Indicator*

*Davis Level with Inclinometer*

very good condition (lens for one dial loose but repairable)....... **110**

**Pitch adjuster for wood levels,** cast iron, Stanley No. 5, bright & shiny, original dark box w/full label, fine condition........................ **242**

**Pitch level,** cast iron w/100% japanning, marked "L.S. Starrett No. 133 B," adjustable level vial set pitch, 15" l. ................................. **66**

**Plumb & level inclinometer,** walnut & glass, marked "R. Porter. Patent Applied For.," pendulum-type inclinometer, walnut picture-frame-like design holds pendulum needle that rotates full 360 degrees, etching shows two men laying up a brick wall w/aid of Porter Indicator, Porter was an American pre-industrial inventor & artist, first half 19th c., near perfect w/original glass, fine condition, 9 1/2" square (ILLUS. bottom of previous page)........................... **8,800**

**Pocket level,** brass, marked "Acme Patent. March 31, 1891," designed to be used as independent tool or as attachment to rule, square or auger bit, this brass type w/solid ring is one of three types made, fine condition, 2 x 2" ....................................... **95**

**Pocket level,** brass, marked "Acme Patent March 31, 1891," designed to be used as independent tool or as attachment to rule, square or auger bit, acts as inclinometer by adjusting to direct reading scale from 0 to 90 degrees, fine condition, 2 x 2"...... **105**

**Pocket level,** cast iron w/80% plating, marked "Stratton Bros." in semicircle w/"Greenfield, Mass." straight across, cylindrical shape on flat base, very rare style for Stratton, 2 3/4" l. (ILLUS. p. 46 bottom row left w/other levels)............................ **1,100**

**Pocket level,** cast iron w/near 98% plating, marked "Davis Level & Tool Co. Springfield, Mass.," brass ends, rare, not shown in catalogs, fine condition, 3 3/4" l. (ILLUS. below)..... **1,300**

**Pocket level,** plated cast iron w/brass ends, marked "Davis Level & Tool Co. - Springfield, Mass.," cylindrical, rare, never advertised in catalogs, plating near worn, good condition, 3 3/4" l. (ILLUS. p. 46 bottom row right w/other levels) ............... **475**

**Railroad track level & gauge,** cast iron, marked "Wooding &

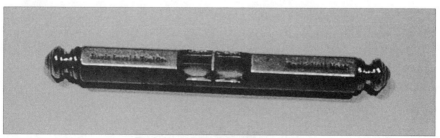

*Davis Level & Tool Co. Pocket Level*

Verona Tool Works, Verona, PA.," narrow gauge, level & adjustable gauges for pitch & width, monogram mark often called "machinist's flyball governor logo," much original finish & 85% paper label, fine condition ........................................ **200**

**Shaft liner & leveler,** nickel-plated brass w/90% finishes, marked "F.A. Bernier, Son & Co. Shaft Liner and Leveler," patent dated "July 31, 1917," unusual, very good condition ....... **110**

**Sighting level,** boxwood & metal, lift-up sights, boxwood graduated w/unusual scale, well-made plane table sighting level, good condition ........................ **61**

**Sighting level,** brass-trimmed mahogany, marked "F.J. Gouch," Worcester, Massachusetts, presentation-type w/inscription on side brass plate "L.Y. Steele, Hudson, N.H.," large vial adjusters Hall & Knapp style, both ends w/slide-up sights lock in place w/small turn knob, first marked Gouch level known, w/fitted wood storage case, very good condition, 1 1/2 x 3 3/8", 28" l. ...................... **550**

**Sighting level,** cast iron w/90% japanning, marked "Warwick Tool Co. - Patent Applied For - Patented June 23, 1868," brass fine, untouched, near mint ........... **121**

**Sighting level,** mahogany w/brass fittings, marked "Pat. Applied For," sight down into top & line of sight directed out through the end, unknown maker but paper label marked, very good condition, 12" l. (ILLUS. p. 53 bottom right with other levels)................................... **72**

**Sighting level,** rosewood or mahogany w/heavy brass plates protecting edges, pop-up sights at each end held in place w/nicely finished cap screws, w/plumb, very good condition....... **700**

**Square level,** cast iron w/50% japanning, marked "L.L. Davis No. 37 1/2," proper screw, good condition ........................................ **160**

**Telescopic hand level,** brass, marked "W. & L. Gurley Co.," patent dated "Apr. 5, 1887," hand-held binocular design, sight through one side at target while other eyepiece displays level bubble, w/fully working optics, very rare, very good condition ........................................ **300**

**Wye level,** brass w/80% Moroco finish, marked "W. & L.E. Gurley. Troy, NY. L. No. 29769.," telescope w/side mount object & eye piece focus, w/mahogany box, tripod, very good condition, spirit level 7 1/2" l., overall 19 1/2" l. .............. **425**

# Machinery

In this section we are including a variety of large mechanical devices that were developed during the 19th century in order to perform specialized tasks. Most are floor-model styles, with the earliest one being powered by foot-operated treadles that were later evolved into steam- or gas-driven motor-operated types. Finally by the early 20th century electric motors provided steady and efficient operation.

Although not many collectors have room to display some of these larger machines, they do offer interesting insights into the Industrial Revolution of the 19th century.

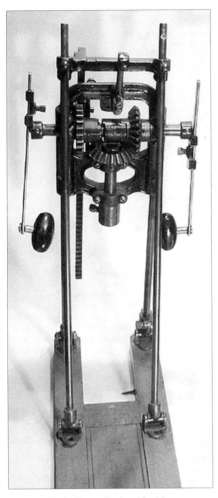

*Early Beam Boring Machine*

*Early R. Ball Beam Boring Machine*

**Beam boring machine,** cast iron, marked "Millers Falls," fully adjustable metal frame w/advance & retract gearing, w/original wooden shipping crate, light use, very good condition (ILLUS.) .............................. **$660**

**Beam boring machine,** cast iron, marked "R. Ball & Co. Worcester, Mass. Patented July 2, 1868.," wooden base w/metal column for drill, 180-degree vertical adjustment, rack & pinion adjusting, geared advance & retract, traces of red paint, rare, good condition (ILLUS.) ...................................................... **660**

*Boss Buckeye Beam Boring Machine*

**Beam boring machine,** cast iron, marked "The Boss Buckeye Machine. Patent Dec. 19, 1882," all-metal base & vertical support w/wooden seat, embossed eagle, fine finishes, complete w/wrench & bit, uncommon, very good condition (ILLUS.)..................................................... **550**

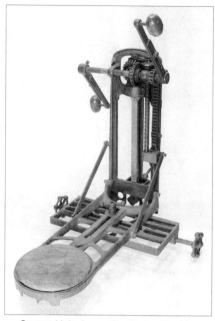

*Square Hole Auger Co. Boring Machine*

**Boring machine,** cast iron w/50% original red finish, marked "The Square Hole Auger Company,

*Early Model
Boring Machine*

**Boring machine,** cast iron & wood, marked "Riley Smith of Patent, Feb. 10, 1843," early model boring machine, rectangular wooden supports hold drill gears & vertical retraction mechanism, four handles w/screws fasten machine to work, bit retraction by lever arm & pulley arrangement, early & most unusual, good condition .........**2,200**

*Table Model Burnisher*

Wooster, Ohio." square-hole beam drill, James Oppenheimer's Patents of "Oct. 21, 1885, Sept. 22, 1885 and April 6, 1886," iron frame clamps to beam & cuts w/oscillating chisel head that slowly advances depth of cut w/each pass, quite the design, & test cuts show it works, extremely rare & an amazing tool from height of American Industrial Age, fine condition (ILLUS. top right previous page) .................................... **3,300**

**Burnisher,** cast iron w/94% finishes & pinstriping, marked "Entrekin Swing-Back Burnish-er. Pat'd. Dec. 2, 1873 ...," wooden grip on crank handle, large table model, very good condition (ILLUS. above) ................ **127**

**Dowel maker,** cast iron w/95% japanning, Stanley No. 77, complete w/nine cutter heads, great walnut display & storage stand, rare complete set, very good condition ..................................... **880**

**Dowel making machine,** cast iron w/new blue finish, Stanley No. 77, 1/4" cutter looks to be original, fine condition (polished surfaces have developed an even brown patina) ............................. **340**

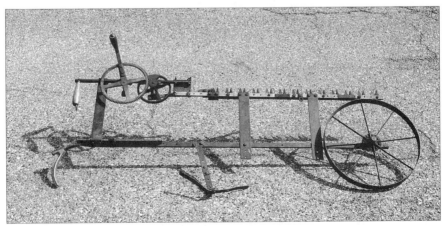

*Walk-Along Hedge Trimmer*

*W. Mills Rose Engine*

**Hedge trimmer,** cast iron, long walk-along hand-crank trimmer, sickle bar-type, 30" cutter, 15" wheel rides along ground to steady machine, good condition (ILLUS. bottom of previous page)......................................................... **230**

**Jigsaw,** iron, treadle-type, marked "Empire. Seneca Falls Mfg. Co. Seneca Falls, N.Y.," professional model, completely restored w/black, red & gold paint & refinished wood trim, large-sized, 19th c. ............................ **605**

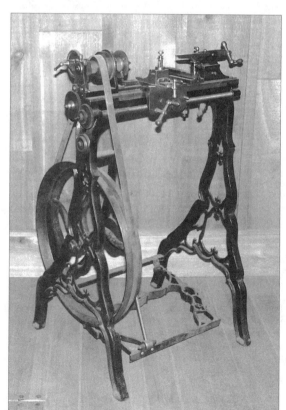

*Treadle-model Lathe*

**Lathe,** iron treadle-model, unmarked but high quality w/tool rest & tail stock, plus a gear-driven tool rest for screw cutting, restored, near perfect, 19th c., very good condition (Illus.) **..743**

**Lathe,** cast-iron, marked "W. Mills. 9 Woodbridge Str. Cleckenwell, London.," rose engine-type, turns spiral patterns in various objects of all materials & shapes, best know examples found on pocketwatch cases, working lathe w/rosette barrel containing 13 rosettes, slide rest, additional rest, touch, cast-iron fly wheel, rocking spring attachment, traversing attachment, etc., high quality machine by one of the finest makers, ca. 1830, very good condition (ILLUS. top of previous page) .................................. **8,250**

**Lathe,** oak frame w/sliding tailstock, 13" centers, 6" swing, very well made w/beaded edge decorations, very good condition ................................................ **220**

**Mortise machine,** cast iron, marked "W. F. & J. B. Rockford, Ill.," foot-powered, lion paw feet, nine bits in graduated set nearly impossible to find, retains much of original gray finish w/red & black pin stripping, good working order, very good condition (ILLUS. below) .............. **1,050**

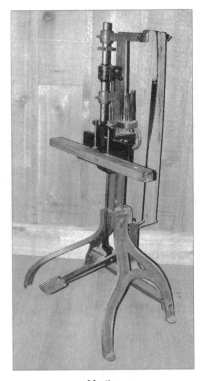

*Mortiser*

**Mortiser,** cast iron, foot-powered, marked "Gould. Newark, N. J.,"

*Mortise Machine with Lion Paw Feet*

*Early Treadle Combination Machine*

upright design w/adjustable table & five cutters, completely restored w/fine green paint & refinished wood trim, 19th c. (ILLUS. top of previous page)...... **165**

**Treadle lathe, grinder & jigsaw,** cast iron w/90% japanning, marked "Goodell's Improved Treadle Lathe, Grinder and Jig Saw," complete w/no breaks or repairs, leather belt fits properly, very good condition, only missing one jigsaw blade (ILLUS. left) .......................................... **220**

**Treadle machine,** cast iron, marked "The Companion," combination foot powered lathe, table & fret saws, sharpening stone & drill on end of drive shaft, paint near 100% w/all original red pinstriping, no blower for the jig saw , very fine condition (ILLUS. below) ............... **550**

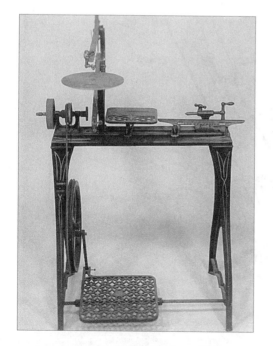

*"The Companion" Treadle Machine*

# Planes & Scrapers

In today's tool collecting market, older planes are probably the most popular collecting specialty. There are a wide variety of planes and related tools with blades used for trimming and shaping wood, and we include a wide selection here.

There is some debate among historians as to who first developed the woodworking plane, but it certainly dates to centuries before the Christian era. The plane first appeared in the Eastern Mediterranean region and by Roman times iron plated planes with wooden cores as well as cast iron planes were being made.

In Colonial America most woodworkers used English-made hardwood planes fitted with iron blades. It was in the first decades of the 19th century that a number of American plane makers started making and marketing their products, and by the 1840s and 1850s the first plane making factories arrived.

Some of these early English and American wooden planes were true works of art, being crafted with the finest materials including rosewood mahogany, ivory and brass. Today the choicest of these can sell for tens of thousands of dollars. Much more abundant wooden planes of simpler hardwoods can be purchased for a fraction of those prices.

The end of the wooden plane era began in the 1870s when the Stanley Rule and Level Company began mass-production of iron-bodied planes, a type developed by Leonard Bailey. By 1900 the "Bailey" planes by Stanley had eclipsed all other types. Stanley remains a leading manufacturer of tools today, and there are collectors who specialize in the tools of this famous firm.

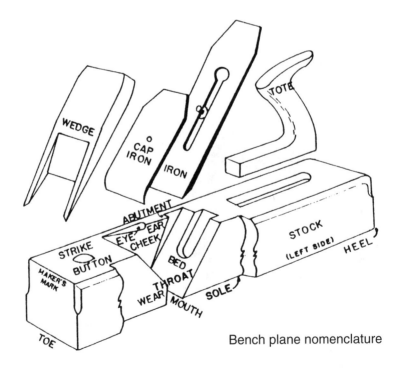

Bench plane nomenclature

# STANLEY TOOLS

### PRICES OF PLANE PARTS
## STANLEY "BAILEY" IRON PLANES

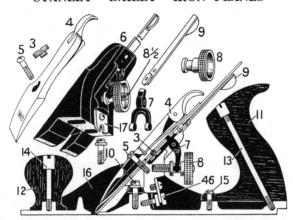

*Old Style Frog*

*New Style Frog*

| No. | Name of Part | No. of Plane | 1 2 2C | 3 3C | S1 A1 4 1C | 1½ 4½C | S5 A5 5 5C | 5¼ 5¼C | 5½ 5½C | A6 6 6C | 7 7C | 8 8C |
|---|---|---|---|---|---|---|---|---|---|---|---|---|
| 3 | Cap Screw | $ .10 | | | | | | | | | | |
| 4 | Lever | .50 | | | | | | | | | | |
| 5 | "  Screw | .10 | | | | | | | | | | |
| 6 | Frog Complete - specify new or old | .70 | | | | | | | | | | |
| 7 | "Y" Adjusting Lever | .10 | | | | | | | | | | |
| 8 | Adjusting Nut | .20 | | | The price is the same for all numbers. | | | | | | | |
| 8½ | Cutter Adjusting Screw | .10 | | | | | | | | | | |
| 9 | Lateral Adjusting Lever | .20 | | | | | | | | | | |
| 10 | Frog Screw | .10 | $ .10 | $ .10 | $ .10 | $ .10 | $ .10 | $ .10 | $ .10 | $ .10 | $ .10 | $ .10 |
| 11 | Rosewood Plane Handle | .50 | | | | | | | | | | |
| | Aluminum Plane Handles | .80 | | | | | | | | | | |
| | No. 3X Fits Planes 3, 4, 5¼ | | | | | | | | | | | |
| | No. 5X Fits Planes 4½, 5, 6, 7, 8 | | | | | | | | | | | |
| 12 | Plane Knob | .30 | | | | | | | | | | |
| 13 | Handle Bolt and Nut | .20 | | | | | | | | | | |
| 14 | Knob  "  "  " | .20 | | | | | | | | | | |
| 15 | Handle Toe Screw | .... | .... | .... | .10 | .10 | .10 | .10 | .10 | .10 | .10 |
| 16 | Plane Bottom | 1.70 | 2.00 | 2.00 | 2.40 | 2.40 | 2.40 | 2.40 | 3.30 | 4.70 | 5.70 |
| 16 | Frog Adjusting Screw | .10 | .10 | .10 | .10 | .10 | .10 | .10 | .10 | .10 | .10 |

Add 10 per cent. for Corrugated Bottoms.
Add 30 per cent. for Bottoms and Frogs for Planes A4, A5, A6.
Add 10 per cent. for Bottoms and Frogs for Planes S4 and S5.

In ordering be sure to specify **number and name of Part** and number of Plane, thus: No. 4 Lever for No. **5** Plane. It will also help us if you will include with your order a rough sketch or tracing of the part desired.

*Barrel Plane*

**Barrel plane,** cast iron w/95% japanning, marked "The Chapin-Stephens Co.," possibly patented & used in a turning lathe, unusual, like new (ILLUS.)............... **$550**

**Beader,** cast iron, Stanley No. 66, Type 1, w/tall screw, w/cutters & both stops, in original green box & copy of the 1886 pocket catalog, very good condition (box & catalog well worn, box end label missing).................................... **143**

**Beading plane,** carriage maker's tailed-type, maple, cast iron & bone, carved form of silhouetted bird, steel fence & bone wear surface for boxing, good condition (wedge not original) ................. **200**

**Beading plane,** cast iron, Stanley No. 69, single hand-type, very light use, original box w/good label, fine condition............................... **743**

**Beading plane,** cast iron w/90% japanning, Stanley No. 66, Type 1 w/tall fence screw, seven cutters, both fences, oval fence held on w/spare screw only came w/one tall screws, rare w/cutters & both fences, very good condition ..................................... **190**

**Beading plane,** cast iron w/97% japanning, Stanley No. 2, w/corrugated bottom, ca. 1925 w/1892 blade, wooden handle & knob hand grip fine w/much of original finish, overall fine condition, ............ **525**

**Beading plane,** cast iron w/wooden handles, marked "Windsor Hand Beader. Poole Williams & Co.," near new w/brown finish & full label, in original faded box, very good condition............................ **385**

**Beading plane,** hardwood, marked "I. Teal," English maker who immigrated to the U.S., good condition, 7/8" w........................ **50**

**Belt maker's plane,** cast iron w/92% japanning, Stanley No. 11, Sweet Hart logo, rosewood handle, ca. 1920s............................... **77**

**Bench jointer plane,** cast iron, marked "Sandusky Tool Co. Established 1868. No. 19 SC.," w/patented adjuster & corrugated bottom, semi-steel bodies w/Oct. 14, 1925 patented adjustment mechanism, produced very short time & considered rare, maple handle & knob hand grip retain 90% original finish, paint 98%, polished surfaces factory fresh, like new, fine condition ................................................ **800**

**Bench plane,** all-steel, Stanley No. S4, w/rivets showing on top side, wooden handle, good condition (paint well worn) ..................... **135**

*Stanley Bed Rock No. 606 Plane*

**Bench plane,** brass Stanley Bed Rock No. 606, one-off casting, wood handles okay, very heavy & well done, good condition (ILLUS.) ................................................ **121**

**Bench plane,** cast iron, marked "Bailey Vertical Post No. 3," large brass adjuster wheel marked "L. Bailey. Boston. Patent Aug. 7, 55. Aug. 31, 58," Moulson Brothers iron, wooden handle & knob grip, solid black lever cap, rare, fine condition (ILLUS. top of next page) .......... **5,700**

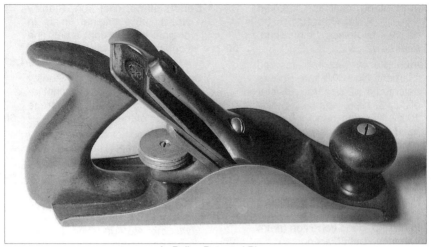

*L. Bailey Patented Plane*

*Fine Gage Tool Co. Bench Plane*

**Bench plane,** cast iron, marked "Gage Tool Co. Vineland, NJ. Patented Apr. 15, 1913.," w/lowest blade angle possible, cutter marked, fine condition (ILLUS.)............................................ **3,520**

**Bench plane,** cast iron, marked "L. Bailey Patent Vertical Post Plane.," No. 7 size, Moulson Brothers iron, transitional plane between Bailey split frame & adjustable frog patent, nice example of rare plane, very good condition cutter 2 3/8", 21 1/2" l., (ILLUS. below left w/other Bailey plane)...................................... **2,800**

**Bench plane,** cast iron, marked "L. Bailey Vertical Post Bench," No. 3 size, iron stamped "Bailey Woods & Co.," thin nontapered cutter iron, rare plane w/very rare iron, good condition (lever cap old but probably not original)................................................. **5,500**

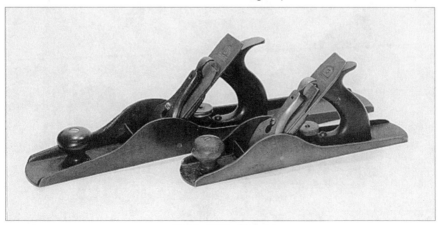

*Two L. Bailey Planes*

**Bench plane,** cast iron, marked "Millers Falls No. 10," extra heavy, two-piece lever cap, near new............................................ **50**

**Bench plane,** cast iron, marked "Sargent No. 10," w/a Shaw's patented 4 1/2 size frog adjuster of July 3, 1906, japanning nearly 100%, wooden handle & knob hand grip, extremely rare, fine condition (tote w/couple storage scrapes & nick off top edge) .......... **450**

**Bench plane,** cast iron, marked "Sargent No. 714 Auto Set Plane.," blade proper & marked "No. 714," wood handle & knob hand grip, good condition (paint enhanced but 80% original) ............. **85**

**Bench plane,** cast iron, marked "Steers 304," rosewood strips in sole, good condition (few nicks & bangs)............................................ **275**

**Bench plane,** cast iron, marked "Union No. 5," tool new & mint, original box w/full picture label, Union tools in box are rare (box w/some wear)................................. **290**

**Bench plane,** cast iron & rosewood, marked "Birdsill Holly Bench," Dwights & French iron, 2" w. cutter, smooth sole, rosewood tote dovetailed to body, Seneca Falls, 1850, rare size, fine condition, 9" l. (ILLUS. below) ..................................... **2,860**

**Bench plane,** cast iron, Stanley No. 1, 96% original finish, in original box w/script label, fine condition (tool w/light use, box w/wear & taping) ............................. **1,870**

**Bench plane,** cast iron, Stanley No. 2, in original box w/script label, fine condition (light storage stain on plane)....................................... **605**

**Bench plane,** cast iron, Stanley No. 2, Sweet Hart logo, tool mint, in original box, ca. 1920s, (some box edge wear) ...................... **605**

**Bench plane,** cast iron, Stanley No. 2-C, corrugated bottom, in original box, fine condition (tool w/some storage stain & light use, box dark).................................... **1,375**

**Bench plane,** cast iron, Stanley No. 3 C, corrugated bottom, new, in original box w/edge wear, fine condition ............................. **248**

**Bench plane,** cast iron, Stanley No. 3, in original worn box, very good condition (storage stain on plane, some paint & tape on box label)................................................ **88**

**Bench plane,** cast iron, Stanley No. 4 1/2 C, corrugated bottom, in original box (light use)................. **264**

**Bench plane,** cast iron, Stanley No. 4 1/2" H., Sweet Hart logo on cutter, never listed in Stanley catalog, produced without frog adjuster even after its introduc-

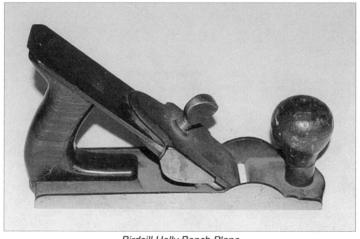

*Birdsill Holly Bench Plane*

*Ohio Tool Co.*
*No. 01 Bench Plane*

**Bench plane,** cast iron w/100% japanning, marked "Ohio Tool Co. No. 01," very rare, wooden handle & knob hand grip perfect, fine condition ...................... **4,180**

tion in 1910, absolutely mint, very fine condition ........................... **2,300**

**Bench plane,** cast iron, Stanley No. 4 1/2, near new, in original worn box w/90% label ...................... **149**

**Bench plane,** cast iron, Stanley No. 4 C, corrugated bottom, 95% original finish, in original worn box w/full label, very good condition ..................... **132**

**Bench plane,** cast iron, Stanley No. 4, near new, in original box, fine condition ............................. **83**

**Bench plane,** cast iron, Stanley No. 5 1/2 C, corrugated bottom, new, in original box w/good label, fine condition ................................ **198**

**Bench plane,** cast iron, Stanley No. 5 1/4 C, corrugated bottom, original well-worn box w/label, fine condition (tool w/light storage stain on one side) ...................... **688**

**Bench plane,** cast iron, Stanley No. 5 1/4, new & shiny, in original box ....................................... **160**

**Bench plane,** cast iron, Stanley No. 5 C, corrugated bottom, 96% original finish, in original worn box w/script logo, very good condition ...................................... **83**

**Bench plane,** cast iron, Stanley No. 5, new, in original box ................. **83**

**Bench plane,** cast iron, Stanley No. 6 C, corrugated bottom, in

original box w/label, fine condition (tool w/light use, box taped on one corner) ........................................ **220**

**Bench plane,** cast iron, Stanley No. 7 C, corrugated sole, tool near-new, war-type, in original box w/75% label, fine condition (box w/taped corners) ......................... **193**

**Bench plane,** cast iron, Stanley No. 7, new & never used, in original box w/full label & only minor edge wear, fine condition .... **182**

**Bench plane,** cast iron, Stanley No. 8 C, tool new & mint, corrugated bottom, in original box w/full label, fine condition ............... **275**

**Bench plane,** cast iron, Stanley No. A5, Sweet Hart logo, lightly used, in original early style box, fine condition, ca. 1920s ................... **413**

**Bench plane,** cast iron, Stanley No. G36, wood bottom, handle & knob hand grip, dark finish, uncommon size, good condition .... **330**

**Bench plane,** cast iron w/ 90% japanning, Stanley Bed Rock No. 605 1/2, Type 4, wooden handle ...................................................... **171**

**Bench plane,** cast iron w/ 98% japanning, Stanley Bed Rock No. 608, Type 6, wooden knob handle, very good condition ................... **528**

**Bench plane,** cast iron w/35% japanning, Stanley Bed Rock No.

605 1/2, Type 4 cap, wooden handle & knob hand grip, good condition ............... **138**

**Bench plane,** cast iron w/50% japanning, marked "L. Bailey. Victor. Patented Aug. 23, 1867 and Dec. 12, 1876. No. 4.," parts all proper & working, hardwood handle & knob hand grip, very fine example, good condition, 2" cutter, 9" l. ............... **525**

**Bench plane,** cast iron w/50% japanning, Stanley Bed Rock No. 604 1/2, Type 6/7, smooth bottom, wooden handle & knob hand grip, good condition ............... **214**

**Bench plane,** cast iron w/50% japanning, Stanley No 2 Pre-lateral, Type 2 w/I-beam receiver & solid back lever cap, adjuster nut recessed, cutter worn out & replaced about turn of century, used Type 4 adjuster, hardwood handle & knob hand grip, rare #2, good condition ............... **350**

**Bench plane,** cast iron w/65% japanning, Stanley Bed Rock No. 602, Type 7, very good condition (wooden tote w/base crack, body w/light pitting) ............... **468**

**Bench plane,** cast iron w/65% japanning , Stanley Bed Rock No. 604, Type 4, wooden handle, good condition ............... **61**

**Bench plane,** cast iron w/65% japanning, Stanley Bed Rock No. 607, Type 6, corrugated, wooden handle & knob hand grip, good condition ............... **165**

**Bench plane,** cast iron w/65% japanning, Stanley No. 8, Type 4 pre-lateral, wooden handle & knob grip, all parts appear proper, good condition ............... **99**

**Bench plane,** cast iron w/70% japanning, marked "Union X No. 0.," number one size plane, vertical post adjustment mechanism, original blade marked "Union Mfg. Co. New Britain. Ct., USA.," extremely rare, hardwood handle & knob hand grip, good condition (tote w/very tight hairline crack) ............... **2,700**

**Bench plane,** cast iron w/70% japanning, Stanley Bed Rock No. 608, Type 5, corrugated, wooden handle & knob hand grip, good condition ............... **308**

**Bench plane,** cast iron w/75% japanning, Stanley 4 1/2 Heavy, wooden handle & knob hand grip, good condition, ca. 1905 (tight crack in knob) ............... **1,045**

**Bench plane,** cast iron w/75% japanning, Stanley Bed Rock No. 605, Type 5 w/4B cutter, corrugated, wooden handle & knob hand grip, very good condition ............... **110**

**Bench plane,** cast iron w/75% japanning, Stanley No. 2, corrugated, wooden knob handle, good condition ............... **495**

**Bench plane,** cast iron w/80% japanning, Stanley No. 4 1/2, first one w/Sweet Hart logo, wooden handle, corrugated, red logo on

**Bench plane,** cast iron w/85% japanning, miniature, marked "Blandin No. 1," adjuster knob stamped "Blandin," w/rocking type cutter adjustment, ebony knob grips, one of only nine No. 1 Blandin planes known to exist, 5 1/2" l ..... **17,500**

*Blandin No. 1 Miniature Plane*

lever cap, made in Canada markings, ca. 1920s........................... **110**

**Bench plane,** cast iron w/85% japanning, Stanley Bed Rock No. 602 Corrugated, Type 6, wood handle & knob hand grip, very good condition ................................... **1,760**

**Bench plane,** cast iron w/85% japanning, Stanley Bed Rock No. 603, Type 4, corrugated, wooden handle, very good condition ... **275**

**Bench plane,** cast iron w/85% japanning, Stanley Bed Rock No. 603, Type 4, wooden handle, good condition ..................................... **176**

**Bench plane,** cast iron w/85% japanning, Stanley Bed Rock No. 605 1/2, Type 4, corrugated, wooden handle, good condition (small chip in tote, hairline crack in knob handle)..................................... **165**

**Bench plane,** cast iron w/85% japanning, Stanley Bed Rock No. 605, Type 4, corrugated, wooden handle, good condition ................. **88**

**Bench plane,** cast iron w/85% japanning, Stanley Bed Rock No. 607, Type 4, wooden handle......... **138**

**Bench plane,** cast iron w/85% japanning, Stanley No. 5 1/4, corrugated, wooden knob handle, ca. 1950, very good condition...................................... **165**

**Bench plane,** cast iron w/88% japanning, Stanley Bed Rock No. 604, Type 6, wooden knob handle, very good condition .................... **495**

**Bench plane,** cast iron w/90% japanning, marked "Foss's Patent Sept. 3, 1878.," nonadjustable, patent for two piece lever cap, beech handle & knob hand grip, rare, very good condition................. **550**

**Bench plane,** cast iron w/90% japanning, marked "Ohio No. 01," blade marked w/globe of the world trademark, wooden handle & knob, very rare No. 1 model, very good condition w/very small nick in edge of lever cap (ILLUS.) ............................................. **2,970**

**Bench plane,** cast iron w/90% japanning, marked "Standard Rule Co. - Oct. 30, 1883," hardwood handle & hand grip knob, very good condition............................. **495**

*Ohio No. 1 Bench Plane*

*Stanley 1876 Patent Bench Plane*

**Bench plane,** cast iron w/90% japanning, Stanley 1876 Patent Bench Plane, No. 1 size, manufactured under April 18, 1876 patent of Justus Traut & Henry Richards, adjustment mechanism identical to design used on earliest Liberty Bell bench planes, rosewood rear-tote knob design makes for easier grip, it is known that planes of this design were exhibited at Centennial Exposition, so it is believed that this No. 1 was produced to fill out lines of planes on display, unique, fine condition (ILLUS. above).......................... **8,800**

**Bench plane,** cast iron w/90% japanning, Stanley Bed Rock No. 602, Type 6 w/second Sweet Hart logo blade, corrugated, wooden handle & knob hand grip, very good condition.............. **1,815**

**Bench plane,** cast iron w/90% japanning, Stanley Bed Rock No. 604 1/2, Type 6, wooden knob handle, very good condition........... **578**

**Bench plane,** cast iron w/90% japanning, Stanley Bed Rock No. 605 1/2, Type 6, wooden knob handle, very good condition........... **523**

**Bench plane,** cast iron w/90% japanning, Stanley Bed Rock No. 606, Type 4, corrugated, wooden handle, good condition (chip on tote)...................................................... **248**

**Bench plane,** cast iron w/90% japanning, Stanley Bed Rock No. 607, Type 4, corrugated, wooden handle, good condition................ **138**

**Bench plane,** cast iron w/90% japanning, Stanley Bed Rock No. 608, Type 4, wooden handle, good condition....................................... **187**

*Stanley No. 1 Bench Plane*

**Bench plane,** cast iron w/90% japanning, Stanley No. 1, notch logo blade, wooden handle & hand grip knob near perfect, ca. 1925, very good condition (ILLUS.).............................................. **1,200**

**Bench plane,** cast iron w/90% japanning, Stanley No. 5 1/2

Heavy, extra heavy casting, wooden handle & knob hand grip, rare, good condition (small piece missing from edge of tote) **1,486**

**Bench plane,** cast iron w/92% japanning, marked "Sargent No. 708 Auto Set Plane.," blade marked "No. 708," hardwood handle & knob hand grip, very good condition ...................................... **125**

**Bench plane,** cast iron w/92% japanning, Stanley Bed Rock No. 602, Type 5, wooden handle & knob hand grip, very good condition (sides polished) ...................... **523**

*Stanley No. 1 Bench Plane*

**Bench plane,** cast iron w/93% japanning, Stanley No. 1, wooden knob handle, ca. 1915, fine condition (ILLUS.) ................................... **1,485**

**Bench plane,** cast iron w/95% japanning, marked "K 2 Keen Kutter.," No. 2 size, manufactured by Stanley for Keen Kutter Company, "K 2" cast in bed ahead of knob, blade stamped w/Keen Kutter logo, hardwood handle & knob hand grip perfect, rare, excellent condition ..... **1,400**

**Bench plane,** cast iron w/95% japanning, marked "Sargent No. 714 Auto-Set," wooden handle & knob hand grip w/85% original finish, apparently unused, very good condition ............................. **55**

**Bench plane,** cast iron w/95% japanning, marked "Siegley No. 4 Smooth Plane.," hardwood handle & knob hand grip, very good condition (plating bit dull) ................. **425**

*Union No. X0 Bench Plane*

**Bench plane,** cast iron w/95% japanning, marked "Union No. X0 Bench," vertical post No. 1 size, hardwood handle & knob hand grip, rare, near perfect, w/very tight hairline crack at edge of mouth (ILLUS.).............................. **3,850**

**Bench plane,** cast iron w/95% japanning, Stanley Bed Rock No. 603, Type 6, wooden knob handle, very good condition .................... **336**

**Bench plane,** cast iron w/95% japanning, Stanley Bed Rock No. 604 1/2, Type 4, wooden handle.... **264**

**Bench plane,** cast iron w/95% japanning , Stanley Bed Rock No. 604 1/2, Type 4, corrugated, wooden handle, very good condition ......................................................... **303**

**Bench plane,** cast iron w/95% japanning, Stanley Bed Rock No. 605 1/4, wooden knob handle, hardest Bed Rock to locate, very good condition.............................. **413**

**Bench plane,** cast iron w/95% japanning, Stanley Bed Rock No. 605, Type 6, wooden knob handle, very good condition .................... **248**

**Bench plane,** cast iron w/95% japanning, Stanley Bed Rock No. 606, Type 4, wooden handle............. **83**

**Bench plane,** cast iron w/95% japanning, Stanley Bed Rock No. 606, Type 6, wooden knob handle, very good condition .................... **347**

**Bench plane,** cast iron w/95% japanning, Stanley Bed Rock No. 608, Type 4, wooden handle.......... **193**

**Bench plane,** cast iron w/97% japanning, Stanley Bed Rock No. 608, Type 6, corrugated base, wooden handle & hand grip knob fine, very good condition ...... **330**

*Stanley No. 1 Plane in Original Box*

**Bench plane,** cast iron w/97% japanning, Stanley No. 1, Sweet Hart logo, hardwood handle & knob hand grip, in original early script logo box, fine condition w/small chip off top edge of tote, box dirty w/55% label, rare plane in rarer box, fine condition (ILLUS.) .............................................. **1,540**

**Bench plane,** cast iron w/97% japanning, Stanley No. 2, first Sweet Hart logo mark, wooden knob handle, ca. 1920s.................... **253**

**Bench plane,** cast iron w/98% japanning, marked "L. Bailey No. 5 Vertical Post Bench Plane.," banjo level cap, marked "Moulsen Brothers" iron, hardwood handle & knob hand grip fine, great condition w/little use, small chip back of mouth from thin casting, rare & proper (ILLUS. p. 75 right w/other Bailey plane)..... **4,600**

**Bench plane,** cast iron w/98% japanning, Stanley Bed Rock No. 607, Type 6, wood knob handle, very good condition ............................. **402**

**Bench plane,** cast iron w/99% japanning, marked "Union No. 502" #2 size, no vertical post, adjustment via lever, wooden knob hand grip, very rare, very good condition (ILLUS. bottom of page.) ................................................... **330**

*Stanley No. S5 Bench Plane*

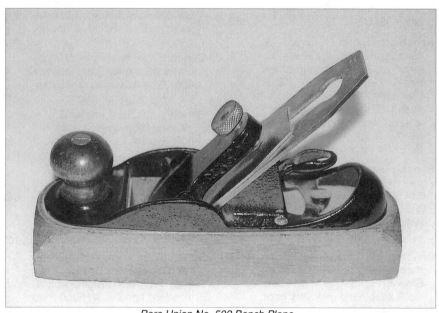

*Rare Union No. 502 Bench Plane*

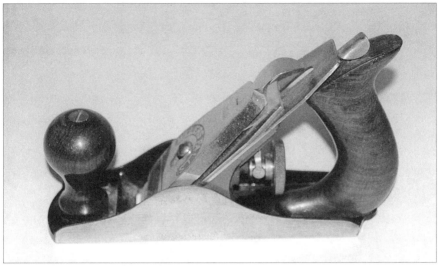

*Millers Falls No. 10 Bench Plane*

**Bench plane,** cast iron w/99% japanning, Stanley No. S 5, Sweet Hart logo, complete handle decal, fine condition (ILLUS. center previous page)............................ **220**

**Bench plane,** cast iron w/cast-brass cap, marked "H.B. Price Patent June 17, 1879," frog seat w/stair-stepped incline that changes the frog pitch as frog moves up ramp, frog adjustable by sliding the seat, four cutter pitches possible, laminated wood handles, very good condition (ILLUS.).................................. **3,960**

*H.B. Price Bench Plane*

**Bench plane,** cast iron w/japanning, Stanley Bed Rock No. 605 1/2, Type 5, w/corrugated bottom, hardwood handle & knob hand grip, good condition (tote w/chips along side, japanning & wood enhanced)..................... **130**

**Bench plane,** cast iron w/near 100% japanning, marked "Millers Falls No. 10," Stanley 4 1/2 size, wood grip & knob, two-piece cap, hard to find, fine condition, tote w/very tight hairline (ILLUS. above)........................................ **88**

*Union X No. 2 Patented Plane*

**Bench plane,** cast iron w/perfect japanning, marked "Union X No. 2 Pat. 12.8.03," vertical post adjustment, mahogany handles w/100% finish, rare in this No. 2 size, fine condition (ILLUS.)....... **3,300**

**Bench plane,** hardwood, marked "Silcock & Co. Patent., "long block-form w/patented screw lock iron attachment, round

*Stanley No. 32 Wooden
Bottom Plane*

style tote probably original, good condition, 2 1/2" w. iron, 22" l. (retipped) ................................. **375**

**Bench plane,** repainted cast iron, Stanley No. 2, Sweet Hart logo vintage, good condition (base of tote broken) ........................................... **154**

**Bench plane,** salesman's demonstration model, cast iron w/75% japanning, Stanley Bed Rock No. 604, Type 5, cut-out sides allows inspection of frog attachment system, rare model demonstrating 1911 patent innovation, very good condition .............. **4,620**

**Bench plane,** steel w/95% japanning, Stanley No. 1, 1892 blade logo, tip of rosewood tote handle w/bit of blonde sapwood, rosewood knob hand grip, complete & perfect, fine condition ..... **1,100**

**Bench plane,** wood-bottomed, Stanley No. 32, Sweet Hart logo, first type, bottom w/finger-jointed rosewood sole, cast iron top w/98% japanning, dated March 1922, wooden handle & knob hand grip, fine condition (ILLUS. above) ............................ **1,650**

**Bench rabbet plane,** carriage maker's, cast iron w/50% japanning, Stanley No. 10 1/2, Type 1 w/adjustable mouth, lever cap nib-type, good condition (tight base crack on tote)............................. **198**

**Bench rabbet plane,** carriage maker's, cast iron w/80% japanning, Stanley No. 10, 5/8" cutter, wooden handle & knob grip, ca. 1910, good condition ....... **143**

**Bench rabbet plane,** carriage maker's type, cast iron w/100% japanning, marked "Union No. 10 1/2 Carriage Maker's Rabbet.," when Stanley purchased Union Tool Co, No. 10 & 10 1/2 rabbet planes were added to line of Union tools sold by Stanley who added hardwood handles stained mahogany, Sweet Hart logo blade w/lever cap marked "Union," overall plane like new, fine condition ...................... **300**

**Bench rabbet plane,** carriage maker's-type, cast iron w/50% finishes, Stanley No. 10, pre-lateral-type, unusual plated cap, frog, blade & cap iron, bed japanned inside & plated outside, wooden handles, good condition... **358**

**Bench rabbet plane,** carriage maker's-type, cast iron w/75% japanning, Stanley No. 10 1/2 Carriage Maker's Rabbet, early type w/adjustable mouth & first pre-lateral level, cutter w/special design for easier removal, extremely rare, hardwood tote handle & knob hand grip fine, ca. 1885-88, good condition (knob base chip) .......................... **350**

*Rare Stanley No. 14 1/4 C Plane*

**Bench rabbet plane,** carriage maker's-type, cast iron w/95% japanning, Stanley No. 14 1/4 C, corrugated bottom, wooden handle & hand grip knob in good condition, very rare Stanley, ca. 1912, very good condition (ILLUS.)................................................. **2,640**

*Victor Bench Rabbet Plane*

**Bench rabbet plane,** cast iron w/90% finishes, marked "Victor No. 11 1/2," patented, w/lever lock cap, hardwood handle & knob hand grip, very rare Victor, very good condition, retains bracket for fence, but fence & stop missing (ILLUS.)..................... **2,420**

**Bench smoothing plane,** cast iron coffin shaped-style, w/overhead cutter locking & adjust-

ment, brass eye section secures to blade & interlocks w/nose section, front knob turns & nose section rotates to lock iron in place while brass knob above iron adjusts blade, complex levers & interlocking pieces, hardwood handle & knob hand grip, very likely patented but research unable to locate, good condition (rear tote poor replacement)....................................... **450**

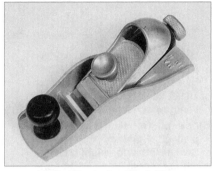

*Limited Production Block Plane*

**Block plane,** aluminum body & cap, Stanley No. 9 1/2 (13-029A), adjustable, hardwood grip, extremely rare, limited production done as test run in 1970s, but never made it to full production, fine condition (ILLUS.) ....................................................... **358**

*Stanley Prototype Block Plane*

**Block plane,** aluminum & cast iron, Stanley No. H1247, prototype, aluminum body & cast-iron cap, standard red cap w/blue body, new produced, new & mint (ILLUS.)............................. **525**

**Block plane,** aluminum, Stanley No. A18, Sweet Hart logo, ca. 1920s, good condition (plating worn off cap)............................... **210**

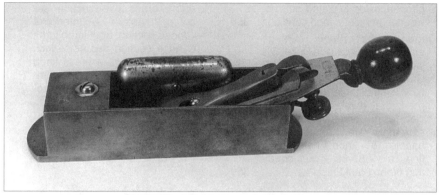

*Stanley No. 9 Cabinetmaker's Block Plane*

**Block plane,** aluminum w/92% cap plating, Stanley No. A 18, Sweet Hart logo, much original lustre, ca. 1920s, good condition (few scratches) ............................ **138**

**Block plane,** aluminum w/98% plating, Stanley No. A 18, Sweet Hart logo, bright & clean, name on both sides, good condition ................................................... **83**

**Block plane,** cabinetmaker's, cast iron & hardwood, Stanley No. 9 prototype plane w/special handle attachment, most likely intended for shooting work, well-made handle, casting supporting it well designed, rare & interesting plane, good condition (cracks at each side of nose) ................................................ **900**

**Block plane,** cabinetmaker's, cast iron, Stanley No. 9, finishes fine, ca. 1910, hardwood end knob handle, very good condition, (few nicks & bangs on wood, otherwise nice example) .... **825**

**Block plane,** cabinetmaker's, cast iron w/90% japanning, Stanley No. 9, w/hot dog side handle, finishes fine, ca. 1900, very good condition (ILLUS. above) .................................................. **1,430**

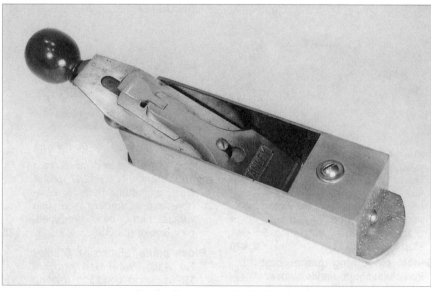

*Stanley Cabinetmaker's Block Plane*

*Cabinetmaker's Block Plane*

**Block plane,** cabinetmaker's, cast iron w/93% japanning, Stanley No. 9, all proper parts, fine condition, ca. 1915 (ILLUS. above)............................................ **1,045**

**Block plane,** cabinetmaker's, cast iron w/98% japanning, Stanley No. 9, blade marked w/earlier "V" logo, 80% cap plating, hardwood grip, ca. 1925, fine condition (ILLUS. bottom of previous page)............................................... **1,760**

*Late Gage Plane*

**Block plane,** cast iron, marked "Gage Tool Co. - Vineland, N.J.," patent dated "Apr. 15, 1913," cutter marked, top of blade only 1/2" above bottom of plane at end of 5" cutter, late Gage manufacture, extremely rare, fine condition (ILLUS.).................... **3,300**

**Block plane,** cast iron, marked "Rodier's Patent Bullnose Block," adjustable, cutter marked "Laflin Manufacturing Company - Patented Mar. 4, 1879 - Westfield, Mass.," one of only two known, good condition (edge of cap very thin & w/large chip)........................................................ **3,520**

**Block plane,** cast iron, marked "Victor No. 0 1/2 Block.," adjustable, 1 3/4" blade, rejapanned otherwise okay w/proper parts, good condition..................................... **220**

*Stanley Prototype Block Plane*

**Block plane,** cast iron, prototype of Stanley #H102, special production tag reads "1962 Block Plane Stanley #H102 Sample-Made Spec to Show Sears Roebuck," one of a kind, fine condition (ILLUS.)............................................. **385**

**Block plane,** cast iron, Stanley No. 131, double-ended type, near new, in original box w/full label, rare............................................. **1,485**

**Block plane,** cast iron, Stanley No. 18 1/4, in original box w/label, fine condition, 18 1/4" l. (light tool use, box taped)................. **220**

**Block plane,** cast iron, Stanley No. 583, wedge dolly-type, an auto body tool, tool new in factory wrapping, original rare purple box w/green & white label, fine condition................................................... **550**

**Block plane,** cast iron, Stanley No. 60 1/2," new in original box, fine condition (box w/torn-out corner)................................................. **88**

**Block plane,** cast iron, Stanley No. 65 1/2, low-angle style, in original box, fine condition (tool w/moderate use).................................. **143**

**Block plane,** cast iron, Stanley No. 9 1/2, Type 1, proper cutter without extended date, very rare type, good condition (two small mouth chips) ............................. **800**

*Stanley No. 9 3/4 Block
Plane in Box*

**Block plane,** cast iron, Stanley No. 9 3/4, w/wooden grip knob end handle, in original box w/full label includes 1926 pocket catalog w/stains on back but fully readable, tool never used, rare in box, fine condition, box top w/45% of its paper peeled off (ILLUS. above) .................................. **2,700**

**Block plane,** cast iron, Stanley No. 95, unused in original box, fine condition.......................................... **226**

**Block plane,** cast iron, unmarked but clearly Boston Metallic Plane Company, adjustable w/cutter adjustment by screw & folded cutter used on Boston Metallic bench planes & some early Bailey planes, cap decorated w/six-petal flower design, tool unused, extremely rare, fine condition...................................... **1,000**

**Block plane,** cast iron w/100% japanning, Stanley prototype No. 120, cutter marked "Stanley Rule & Level" w/patent date "1876," body cast as bullnose w/all the design features of the 120, large hole star cap, ca. 1883, appears company dropped plans to manufacture the 120 bullnose, so prototype is extremely rare, polished surfaces, no rust (ILLUS. right) ....... **4,600**

**Block plane,** cast iron w/20% japanning, marked "Defiance.

Bailey Tool Co. Model B," nonadjustable, cutter marked & proper, fine cap, good condition (ILLUS. top of next page, left w/other block planes)......................... **468**

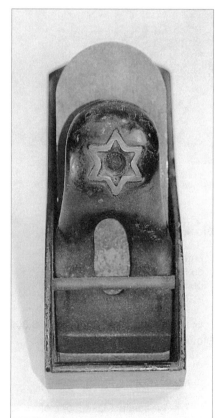

*Rare Stanley Block Plane Prototype*

*Three Block Planes*

**Block plane,** cast iron w/40% japanning, marked "Defiance Block Plane, Model D.," adjustable, cutter marked w/battle-ax & "Defiance," no breaks, rare type, good condition (replacement knob) ............................................. **475**

**Block plane,** cast iron w/45% japanning, marked "Defiance Model B Block," adjustable, all proper parts, front wood knob original but chipped, good condition, 7 1/2" l. ...................................... **495**

**Block plane,** cast iron w/45% japanning, marked "L. Bailey Victor No. 12," good Victor knob, good condition ...................................... **385**

**Block plane,** cast iron w/45% japanning, marked "Standard Rule Block," nonadjustable, marked on both sides, good condition, 7" l. (small mouth chip)................................................. **88**

**Block plane,** cast iron w/45% japanning, marked "Victor No. 1," adjustable, good condition .............. **358**

**Block plane,** cast iron w/45% japanning, Stanley No. 103, wooden front knob, first type, proper blade, good condition......... **110**

*Stanley No. 90J Block Plane*

**Block plane,** cast iron w/45% japanning, Stanley No. 90 J, plated handle, blade marked w/about 3/4" remaining, good condition (ILLUS.) ............................... **385**

**Block plane,** cast iron w/50% japanning, marked "Bailey Victor No. 50 Block," adjustable, original cutter, good condition (some light pitting) .............................................. **165**

**Block plane,** cast iron w/50% japanning, marked "Victor No. 0," button & knob fine, good condition, cutter worn down (ILLUS. top of page, center w/other block planes) ...................................... **193**

**Block plane,** cast iron w/50% japanning, Stanley No. 120, star cap-type, proper front wood knob ................................................................. **39**

*Victor No. 50 1/2 Block Plane*

**Block plane,** cast iron w/55% japanning, Stanley No. 110, first type w/boat-shaped body, original front knob, cutter marked only w/patent in oval border, nick off bump at rear of plane, very good condition (hairline at one edge of mouth) ............................ **550**

**Block plane,** cast iron w/55% plating, marked "Victor No. 50 1/2," adjustable, traces of original orangish red paint, rare, good condition (ILLUS. above) ..... **900**

**Block plane,** cast iron w/60% japanning, Stanley No. 9 1/2, Type 3, first type w/vertical post adjuster, ca. 1876-1879, good condition .................................................. **110**

**Block plane,** cast iron w/65% japanning, marked "Bailey Tool Co.," B model, w/"Bailey Tool Comp." on sole, rare, good condition (ILLUS. at right).................... **1,870**

*Bailey Tool Co. Embossed Block Plane*

**Block plane,** cast iron w/70% japanning, marked "Defiance. Bailey Tool Co. Model F," adjustable w/adjustable mouth, cutter marked & proper, cap find, good condition (ILLUS. top of page 89, right w/other block planes) ...................................................... **880**

**Block plane,** cast iron w/70% japanning, marked "L. Bailey No. 0 1/2 Block," adjustable, no breaks, good Victor cap, good condition ...................................................... **330**

**Block plane,** cast iron w/75% japanning & plating 85%, Stanley No. 63, very hard to find, good condition (cap slight nick in edge) ... **375**

**Block plane,** cast iron w/75% japanning, Stanley No. 101 1/2, bullnose w/proper finger rest on nose, clean, very good condition ...................................................... **385**

**Block plane,** cast iron w/80% japanning, Stanley No. 15 1/2 w/tail, wooden knob handle, ca. 1900, good condition ........................ **330**

*Rare Stanley No. 90A Block Plane*

**Block plane,** cast iron w/80% plating, Stanley No. 90 A, marked blade w/7/8" remaining, rare Stanley plane, very good condition (ILLUS.) ............................. **1,870**

**Block plane,** cast iron w/85% japanning & enhanced, Stanley No. 9 3/4, Type 5, wooden handle, name on side ............................... **220**

**Block plane,** cast iron w/85% japanning, marked "Victor Bailey. No. 12.", pocket-style, very nice example, very good condition (well worn on sides) ........................... **700**

**Block plane,** cast iron w/85% japanning, Stanley No. 9 3/4, Type 2, w/pebbled cap, wooden knob handle, very rare plane only manufactured in the years 1874 & 1875, very good condition (very small mouth chip) ............ **500**

**Block plane,** cast iron w/90% japanning, marked "Sargent No. 507 Rabbet," open sides for rabbeting work, proper blade, wooden knob hand grip, very good condition ....................................... **165**

**Block plane,** cast iron w/90% japanning, marked "Victor No. 0 1/2.," nonadjustable mouth, adjustable cutter, cutter marked "L. Bailey's Patent Dec. 12, 1876," worn on outside, bright inside, no mouth chips, rare, very good condition, (cutter dinged over a bit) ................................. **400**

*Victor No. 51 Plane*

**Block plane,** cast iron w/90% japanning, marked "Victor No. 51," patented, complete & proper, ca. 1880, very good condition (ILLUS.) ............................... **440**

*Rare Bullnose Stanley Block Plane*

*Winchester W102
Block Plane*

**Block plane,** cast iron w/90% japanning, Stanley No. 101 1/2, bullnose type w/finger rest on nose, rare version, very good condition (ILLUS. bottom of previous page) .............................................. **495**

**Block plane,** cast iron w/90% japanning, Stanley No. 131, no damage, good condition ...................... **94**

**Block plane,** cast iron w/90% japanning, Stanley No. 131, Sweet Hart logo, wooden handle & hand grip knob fine, very good condition ......................................... **94**

**Block plane,** cast iron w/90% japanning, Stanley No. 9 3/4, w/tail handle, Type 1, wooden knob handle, very good condition............................................................... **605**

**Block plane,** cast iron w/92% finishes, Stanley No. 140, Type 1, lever adjuster, wooden hand knob grip, early & hard to find, very good condition ............................. **220**

**Block plane,** cast iron w/92% japanning, Stanley No. 110 Shoe Buckle, Type 2, wooden knob handle, apparently unused, fine condition (ILLUS.) ................................ **990**

**Block plane,** cast iron w/98% japanning, marked "Winchester W102," very good condition w/light storage stain on polished surfaces, in original box, box dirty & faded but label complete & full (ILLUS. above) ......................... **605**

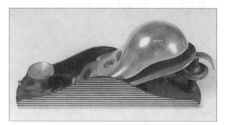

*Experimental Stanley Block Plane*

**Block plane,** cast iron w/99% paint, Stanley No. S18, experimental model w/grooved sides for improved grip, fine condition (ILLUS.) ................................................... **506**

**Block plane,** cast iron w/about 99% finishes, Stanley No. 18 1/4, rare version w/nonadjustable mouth, ca. 1950 ...................... **83**

*Stanley No. 110 Block Plane*

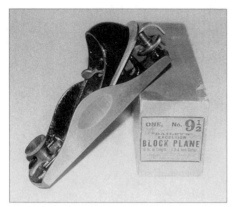

*Bailey's Excelsior Block Plane*

**Block plane,** cast iron w/nearly 100% japanning, Stanley No. 9 1/2 Bailey's Excelsior model, in original green box, little sign of use, box w/full bright label, some corner wear (ILLUS.)............ **660**

**Block plane,** cast iron w/worn japanning, marked "L. Bailey Victor No. 1," proper parts, cap w/Bailey logo, good condition ....... **220**

**Block plane,** hardwood, marked "Wm. Hopper Patent Jan. 16, 1855," early patent w/wedge behind cutter & steel mouth plate, from Pittsburgh, also stamped w/name of hardware dealer "Victor Keller, Alleghany," very good condition ................... **297**

**Block plane,** hardwood, probably fruitwood, turned front knob & carved mouth, Holland, 18th c., very good condition (19th c. iron)............................................................ **88**

**Block plane,** iron, ebony & gunmetal, marked "Moseley & Simpson, Covent Garden, London," bullnose-type, gunmetal w/adjustable mouth, near full Ward iron & ebony wedge, rare maker, English, very good condition, 1 9/16" w., 3 3/8" l.............................. **375**

**Bossingschaaf plane,** hardwood, marked "Bossingschaaf. 1731," highly decorated w/scroll-carved mouth & pinwheel on wedge, iron very early & could be original, worm holes add character, good condition, 7 1/2" l. (ILLUS. below).................... **660**

**Box scraper,** cast iron w/90% japanning, marked "Bailey Pat'd. July 26, 1870," lever-action cutter holder, 1 5/8" cutter near full, wood handle & brass ferrule w/traces of original finish, seldom found in this fine condition, overall 11 1/2" l.................................... **130**

*Bossingschaaf 1731 Plane*

**Box scrapers,** cast iron, Stanley No. 70, six new scrapers in original Stanley wrapping, original box w/inside & outside labels, wrapped in Stanley orange paper, very rare box, fine condition (top of box torn)................................. **248**

**Bullnose plane attachment,** cast iron w/80% finish, front bullnose section for the Stanley No. 72 chamfer plane, as supplied w/cutter screw only, very good condition................................................. **240**

*Rare Stanley No. 64 Bench Plane*

**Butcher block plane,** cast iron w/90% japanning, Stanley No. 64, heavy duty low-angle bench-type, fine wood handle & knob hand grip, rare, very good condition, ca. 1915 (ILLUS.)....... **1,155**

**Cabinet maker's block plane,** cast iron w/75% japanning, Stanley No. 9, wooden handle, short-neck lever cap, ca. 1900...... **770**

*Carriage Maker's Planes in Fitted Box*

**Carriage maker's planes,** cast brass w/bone infill, rosewood wedges, four rabbets, vee & matched inverted vee, pair of hollow & rounds, in fitted dovetailed box decorated w/inlaid eight-pointed star & banding on top, fine condition, the set (ILLUS.)................................. **2,090**

**Carriage maker's planes,** cast iron w/90% plating, Art Deco design, intended for use on auto bodies, matched pair of hollow & rounds, a single hollow, a rabbet & a vee groove, 1930s, the set (ILLUS. below)............................... **550**

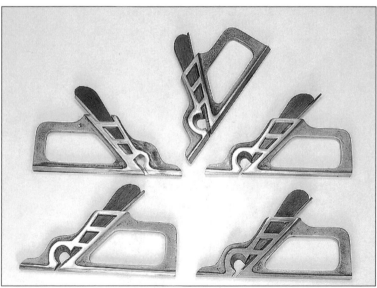

*Carriage Maker's Planes*

*Stanley No. 72 1/2 Chamfer Plane*

*Stanley No. 72 Chamfer Plane*

**Chamfer plane,** cast iron, Stanley No. 72 1/2, w/beading & molding attachments, beading attachment in separate orange box w/earlier green box label, also includes bullnose attachment, tools near new, main box w/picture label, fine condition, the set (ILLUS.) ................................. **3,850**

**Chamfer plane,** cast iron, Stanley No. 72, w/bullnose attachment, hardwood handle & knob, in original picture box, ca. 1905, like new, some storage stains, box fine w/dime-size scuff on bottom edge of label (ILLUS.) .. **1,320**

**Chamfer plane,** cast iron w/60% japanning, Stanley No. 72, rare bullnose attachment, ca. 1915 (tote w/edge chip,wooden knob cracked)...................................................... **330**

**Chamfer plane,** cast iron w/90% japanning, marked "Lee's Stop Chamfer," Gothic arch design

*"Lee's Stop Chamfer" Plane*

adjustable nose plate, hardwood handle, rare in very good
condition (ILLUS. bottom of pre-
vious page) .......................................... **7,480**

**Chariot plane,** gun metal w/beech
wedge, cupid's bow retainer,
very good condition, 3 1/4" l. ......... **165**

**Chisel plane,** cast iron w/92% japanning, Stanley No. 97, Sweet
Hart logo, good corners on nose
of body, wooden knob
handle, ca. 1920s, very good
condition ............................................... **358**

**Circula plane,** cast iron w/92%
plating, Stanley No. 20, ca.
1908, very good condition .............. **165**

**Circular plane,** cast iron, marked
"George Evans Patent March
22, 1864," brass screw cap
marked w/patent date, Type 1
w/shield cut-out & rabbet blade,
one of only two known, good
condition (ILLUS. below) .............. **9,900**

**Circular plane,** cast iron, Stanley
No. 113, mint & unused, in
original box w/label about 80%,
box good, tool mint
condition, ca. 1929 (label
w/some insect damage) .................. **670**

**Circular plane,** cast iron, Stanley
No. 113, unused, in original box
w/picture label, fine condition ........ **275**

**Circular plane,** cast iron, Stanley
No. 20, adjustable, unused, in
original box, fine condition .............. **413**

**Circular plane,** cast iron w/60%
japanning, marked "Victor
Plane. L. Bailey. No. 10.," adjuster works fine, plating on
Bailey logo cap bright & shiny,
very rare, good condition .................. **950**

**Circular plane,** cast iron w/75%
japanning, marked "Bailey Tool
Co. Woonsocket, RI. Defiance.
No. 9.," David Williams patented
adjuster, battle-ax emblem on
cutter, rare, very good condition..... **525**

*Bailey Victor No. 10 Circular Plane*

**Circular plane,** cast iron w/80%
japanning & 95% plating,
marked "L. Bailey Victor No.
10.," w/early-style cutter adjuster used in very earliest Victors,
very hard to find, fine condition
(ILLUS.) ............................................... **1,430**

**Circular plane,** cast iron w/80%
japanning, marked "Sargent No.

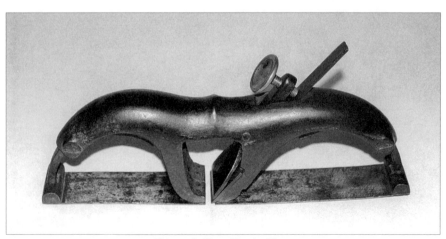

*Extremely Rare Circular Plane*

76," a Stanley No. 113-style, wooden grip knob, good condition ................................................ **154**

**Circular plane,** cast iron w/80% japanning, Stanley No. 13, Type 2, first production run w/cutter stamped w/L. Bailey's Patent logo, very fine example (japanning worn) .................................... **140**

**Circular plane,** cast iron w/80% plating, marked "Victor No. 20," L. Bailey buttons on both ends, key-type adjuster on top, polished surfaces, rare, good condition (ILLUS. below) .......................... **825**

**Circular plane,** cast iron w/90% japanning, Stanley No. 113, later type w/lever cap & Bailey adjuster ................................................ **121**

**Circular plane,** cast iron w/90% japanning, Stanley No. 113, Type 2, wooden handle & hand grip knob, clean, good condition ... **132**

**Circular plane,** cast iron w/95% japanning, marked "L. Bailey Circular No. 13," solid adjuster wheel marked "Patented Aug. 31, 1858. Aug. 6, 1867," important Bailey/Stanley plane, very good condition ................................ **2,420**

*Bailey Victor Circular Plane*

**Circular plane,** cast iron w/clean, bright finishes, marked "Bailey Victor No. 20 Circular," original buttons & button-type cap, early type, very good condition (ILLUS.) .................................... **550**

**Circular plane,** hardwood & brass, marked "Evans Patent Circular Plane," complete & proper down to brass tag on side of body, few made, cap screw marked "Patented Jan. 28 1862," good condition ................. **325**

**Combination croze & howel plane,** birch & beech, marked "A. Heald & Son, Milford.," hol-

*Victor No. 20 Circular Plane*

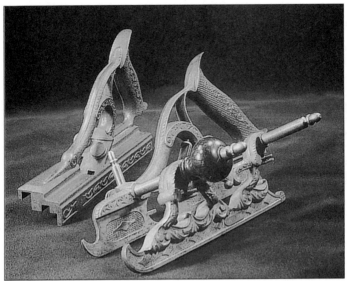

*Rare Miller's
Patent Planes*

low wedge w/wooden screw at top end as invented by the maker's son, David Milton Heald, used, clean & fine, very good condition ................................................. **200**

**Combination match plane,** cast iron w/copper wash, marked "12" & "Patented August 19, 1873," Miller's patent plane, designed to cut both tongue & groove when doing match work, no cutter, one of only two known examples, 1873 patent was replaced by Charles Miller's

patent for the swing fence in 1875, so 1873 patent model unlikely to have ever made it to full production (ILLUS. above left w/Miller's light plow plane) ...... **19,250**

**Combination match plane,** hardwood, marked "Ohio Tool Co. 1/2 inch. No. 70," combination match plane cuts groove in one direction, tongue in other, reshaped wedges, wedges done long ago & perhaps done at factory, bit of extra beauty, very good condition ............................. **200**

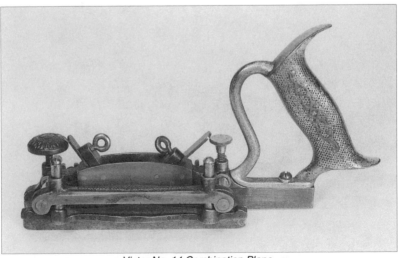

*Victor No. 14 Combination Plane*

*Stanley No. 141 Planes*

**Combination molding plane,** cast iron w/90% plating, Stanley No. 45 Plow, Rabbet, Slitter & Beading Plane, Type 7B, 19 cutters, S casting marks, wooden handles, includes two catalogs, one w/unusual cover - Stanley name & address was left off the bottom half, in original chestnut box w/rare original lid & 75% label, very good condition (very small sliver off side of handle, catalogs w/considerable silverfish damage) ............................................ **260**

**Combination plane,** cast iron, marked "Victor No. 14 Light Combination, L. Bailey. Patent July 6, 1875.," seldom found complete, totally original, good condition (ILLUS. bottom of previous page) ........................................ **2,750**

**Combination plane,** cast iron, Stanley No. 141 Bullnose Plow, Rabbet & Match Plane, complete w/filletster bed & nine cutters in original wooden holder, in original repaired box w/full label, cutters w/minor storage rust, otherwise near mint condition (ILLUS. above) ................................ **3,300**

**Combination plane,** cast iron w/45% plating, marked "Miller's

*Stanley No. 141
Combination Plane*

Patent Plane." Stanley No. 141, wooden handle, hard to find, good condition (ILLUS. bottom of previous page)............................................ **633**

**Combination plane,** cast iron w/80% japanning, Stanley No. 45 Type 1, 18 cutters, two depth stops, short & long rods, early design box w/some carved decoration, in custom case, good condition.................................................. **250**

**Combination plane,** cast iron w/95% japanning, Stanley No. 54, World War II-type w/proper plated fence, eight cutters, in original wooden box, very good condition, the set................................. **303**

**Combination plane,** cast iron w/99% plating, Stanley No. 45 E, Type 17 Late, marked for the English market, 2/23 cutters, original box w/90% label, fine condition...... **385**

**Combination plane,** cast iron w/99% plating, Stanley No. 45, in original lift-top metal box w/paper label & good color, includes instructions, fine condition.................... **660**

**Combination plane,** cast iron w/99% plating, Stanley No. 45, Type 15, made in Canada, in original worn box, no instructions, 75% box labels........................ **275**

**Combination plane,** cast iron w/rosewood handle, marked "Fales Patent Combination,"

consists of main plane & five boxed bottoms for center beads, side beads, rounds, plow & dado cuts, in five small boxes fitting into original larger walnut box, four original slide-top boxes w/sizes listed on paper labels, fifth box modern replacement, some 40 sets of bottoms plus seldom-seen flat skates for a plow plane, unique & near complete, very good condition, the set (ILLUS. bottom of page)...................................... **3,410**

*Miller's Patent Plane Stanley No. 44*

**Combination plane,** gunmetal, marked "Miller's Patent Plane." Stanley No. 44, slitter-type, eight cutters, tip off tote, polished years ago, very good condition (ILLUS.).................................... **2,805**

**Combination plane,** rosewood, marked "Gladwin's Patent," absolutely mint, w/six tools including the rule, in original worn box

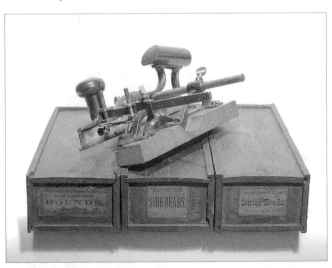

*Combination Plane*

*Fales Patent Combination Plane with Bottoms*

w/partial picture label, fine condition................................................................ **1,540**

**Combination plane set,** cast iron w/95% finish, marked "Sargent No. 1080," 16 cutters in rolls & all the parts, in custom box, the set...... **138**

**Combination plane w/bottoms,** cast iron & rosewood, marked "Fales Patent Combination Plane," w/eight hollow & round sets w/10 cutters, two single rounds w/cutters, single hollow w/cutter, three plows w/cutters, two coves w/cutters, one ogee w/cutter, nosing w/cutter, three center beads w/cutters, six side beads w/cutters, additional parts & about 10 extra cutters, good condition (ILLUS. above)................ **1,100**

**Combination plow plane,** cast iron, marked "Siegley," many combo variations, adjustable fence in two pieces, rear section stops at cutter & held by cutter edge, front section runs back to cutter hole, extra short rod holds in place, depth stops all hand-set, cutter adjustment w/toothed block dates from time of wheel adjust stops, original thumb screws w/oval head eye bolts, "Siegley" cast in side & cast-iron wear plate along bottom surface, appears early production yet

w/many later patents, complete & original, very good condition............. **900**

**Combination plow plane,** cast iron w/50% japanning, marked "Phillips Plough Plane," patentee Russell Phillips designed plane in Gardiner, Maine, square frame design, rosewood tote handle, one cutter, good condition (both sides off tote) ............................................. **575**

**Combination plow plane,** cast iron w/75% plating, marked "Victor No. 14. Charles G Miller and Leonard Bailey's patent of July 6, 1875.," complete w/both cutters & depth stop, complete plane very hard to find, good condition (repainted & an old repair)................... **1,250**

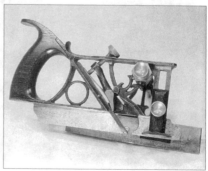

*Rare Phillips Combination Plane*

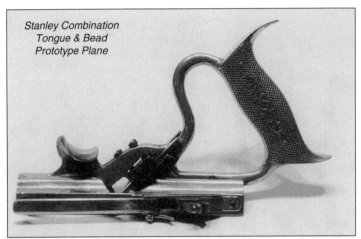

*Stanley Combination Tongue & Bead Prototype Plane*

**Combination plow plane,** cast iron w/80% finish, marked "Phillips," first type w/box frame, six cutters, wooden tote, sliver off one side of tote, very good condition (ILLUS. bottom of previous page) **1,050**

**Combination plow plane,** cast iron w/black japanning, marked "Phillips' Improved Plough Plane. Babson & Repplier. 7 Doane St." on skate & "M. C. Mayo's Improved-Jan 1, 1872" on fence, gold, red & blue accents on black japanning, rosewood tote & fence handle near perfect w/most original finish, two cutters, paint 85% & bright, very fine condition (ILLUS. below)................................... **4,000**

**Combination tongue & bead plane,** cast iron w/90% plating, Stanley Combination Tongue and Bead prototype, plane

*Phillips' Combination Plane*

would first cut the tongue, then the beading plane would be engaged to cut edge bead, appears to be Traut's design, but no patent for the spring-loaded edge beader has been located, clearly from Plane Plant of Stanley Rule & Level Co., fine condition, 6 3/8" bed, overall 9" l. (ILLUS. top of previous page) ............................ **5,500**

**Complex molder plane,** hardwood, marked "Bensen & Crannell," unusual profile, good condition, 3" w. ........................ **220**

**Complex molder plane,** hardwood, marked "Speight - Leeds," handled, double irons & wedges, triple boxing, very complex, very good condition, 3 5/8" w. ................... **468**

*Wooden Planes*

**Complex molding plane,** beech, marked "I. Walton In Reading.," flat chamfers, Pennsylvania, ca.

1775, good condition, 10 1/8" l. (ILLUS. far right with other wooden planes) ............................... **990**

**Complex molding plane,** beech, marked "Tho. Grant. New:York.," A mark w/crown, initials "IT," astragal & bead complex molder, wide flat chamfers, good condition, 1 5/8" w., 10 1/4" l. .............................. **260**

**Complex molding plane,** hardwood, marked "Alford, New York.," double boxing w/deep cut, New York's earliest plane maker & very hard mark to find, rare & choice, very good condition, 5/8 size mark ................... **180**

**Complex molding plane,** hardwood, marked "H. Hazlet.," double boxing, unlisted Philadelphia maker, good condition (missing 1/1/2" of tail boxing) ......... **358**

**Complex molding plane,** hardwood, marked "Isaac Field - Providence," double boxing, mark w/overstamped initials, very good condition, 1 3/16" w. ..... **154**

**Complex molding plane,** yellow birch, marked "I. Nicholson In Cumberland (w/double crown & initials "PP")," A wedge, flat chamfers, fine profile, very good condition, 1 1/8" w., 9 7/8" l. (ILLUS. far left w/other wooden planes) ............................................. **2,640**

*Cooper's Long Jointer*

**Cooper's long jointer plane,** twin stocks make separate planes that are pegged together, w/stand, good condition, 59" l. ..... **165**

**Cooper's croze plane,** hardwood w/bone inlaid wear strips & double boxing, boxing follows arc of plane head & is carved to match radius, good condition........................ **275**

**Cooper's jointer plane,** maple, marked "John Veit - Corner New Market & Green Streets - Phila.," 3" single iron, large, 56" l. (top of wedge dinged)........................ **165**

*Circular Connected Plane*

**Cooper's plane,** applewood, circular design, topping or leveling-type used to even ends of staves after barrel assembled, composed of four sun planes connected together to work set size barrel, four irons & four wedges in full circle, sections appear to be mortised & pinned together, works 17" barrel, extremely rare & beautiful, very good condition (ILLUS.)............... **1,300**

**Cooper's sun plane,** lignum vitae, marked "L. & I.J. White - 1837," very good condition............. **446**

**Corebox plane,** cast iron & brass, marked "W. H. Groat. 1886.," unique w/very complex mechanism that rotates cutter around the cut, handle carved in tee & deer foot combination that matches handgrip, highest quality & finest castings, main fence adjustable via brass knob when rotated, moves fence to match work, main body cast-iron w/brass parts, name & date cast into brass cross bar that helps hold wings, only known example, fine condition (ILLUS. below)..................................................... **4,200**

**Corebox plane,** cast iron, marked "Collins & Co. Pat. Corebox

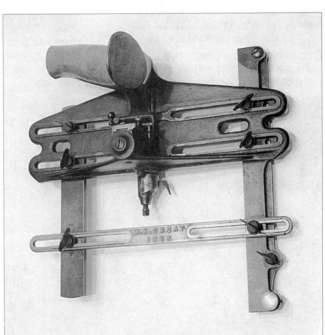

*Corebox Plane*

Plane. Newark, N.J.," early type, perhaps original idea for Stanley No. 57, fewer than half dozen known, plane w/100% finish, perfect in all respects, fine condition ........................................................ **750**

**Corebox plane,** cast iron w/92% plating, Stanley No. 57, complete w/three extensions, w/all the rods & turnbuckles, wooden handle & hand grip knob clean & fine, hard to find, very good condition ........................................................ **935**

**Corebox plane,** cast iron w/98% finishes, marked "G-I-C Co. Springfield, O.," made by Gray Iron Casting Co., cutter set up on ratchet that rotates cutter as pressure applied to handle, fine condition ........................................................ **375**

**Corebox plane,** cherry, smaller size w/excellent eye appeal, wings, very good condition, 5 x 5 1/2", 9 1/2" l. ........................................... **160**

**Corebox plane,** cast brass, patented Bayley model, cast from new owner-made patterns, working w/one cutter, well made, good condition ........................... **176**

**Corebox plane,** cast iron, Stanley No. 57, near new, in original box w/picture label, fine condition ..... **1,870**

**Corebox plane,** cast iron w/85% japanning, Stanley No. 56, wooden handle, small size, good condition ...................................... **963**

**Corebox plane,** cast iron w/95% japanning, marked "G-I-C-CO - Springfield, O.," ratchet mechanism rotates cutter w/each forward stroke, w/two cutters, very good condition ...................................... **220**

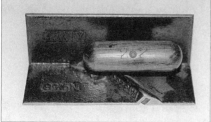

*Stanley No. 56 Corebox Plane*

**Corebox plane,** cast iron w/95% japanning, Stanley No. 56, rosewood handle stamped "22," fine condition (ILLUS. bottom of page) ........................................................ **1,100**

*E.W. Lewis Patented Plane*

**Corebox plane,** cast iron w/nearly 100% japanning & brass, marked "E.W. Lewis - Pat. Dec. 4, 1866," geared mechanism advances the cutter around a half circle as knurled wheel to right of handle is turned, rosewood tote, rare, fine condition (ILLUS. above) ............................... **3,400**

**Corebox plane,** cast iron w/wood handle, marked "Elisha W. Lewis - Patented Dec. 4, 1866," mechanism rotates bit through 180-degree arc, notch for larger core on each side, good condition ........................................................ **605**

**Corner rounding plane,** cast iron, Stanley No. 144 1/4, early type w/first Sweet Hart logo on cutter, "Pat. Apl'd For" cast into plane, lightly used, original box w/label, very good condition (box w/light wear & two torn out corners, label dark) ............................ **413**

**Corner rounding plane,** cast iron, Stanley No. 144 3/8, early type w/first Sweet Hart logo on cutter, "Pat. Apl'd For" cast into plane, appears unused, original box w/95% label, very good condition (box worn & stained, label dark) ............................................ **440**

**Corner rounding plane,** cast iron w/98% japanning, Stanley No. 144 3/8, first Sweet Hart logo on cutter, "Pat Apl'd For" on body, ca. 1920s, bright, pol-

*Mark on J.C. Jewett Crown Molding Plane*

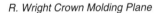

*R. Wright Crown Molding Plane*

ished surfaces clean & fine, fine condition ................................................ **475**

**Cornering plane,** cast iron w/90% japanning, Stanley No. 144 1/2, ca. 1940, nice clean example, very good condition ....... **325**

**Crown molding plane,** beech, end marked "R. Wright - Philad.," w/wide flat chamfers, applied fence, Newbould round-top iron, 1793-97, very good condition w/some roughness on edge of tote, 2 3/4" w., 13" l. (ILLUS. above right) ......................... **853**

**Crown molding plane,** beech, marked "Isaac Field, Providence," A1 mark, offset tote, flat chamfers, fine condition, 5 1/8" w. ................................................. **1,430**

**Crown molding plane,** beech, marked "J. Bracelin - Dayton," handled, fine condition, 3 1/4" w. ............................................... **198**

**Crown molding plane,** beech w/yellow birch wedge, marked "P.H. Wehrley," zig-zag boarder mark, offset tote, flat chamfers, good condition, 6 1/2" w.

w/5 1/8" w. iron (crack on nose, top off tote, slightly dark finish) . **1,045**

**Crown molding plane,** boxwood boxing, marked "James Mfg. Co. - Wmsburg. MS," handle ogee, applied fence, large size, uncommon maker, 5 1/2" w., 18" l. (some wormholes in nose) .... **413**

**Crown molding plane,** cast iron & hardwood, marked "J.C. Jewett. Waterville" (Maine), large ogee crown w/4 5/16" iron, applied fence, rare, very good condition (ILLUS. of mark above left) ............ **770**

**Crown molding plane,** hardwood, marked "B. Sheneman," A1 mark, massive double wedge style, very good condition, two 2 5/8" w. iron, 6 5/8" w. ................. **6,270**

**Crown molding plane,** hardwood, marked "C. Warren - Nashua," owner's name stamp "H. Hall Jr.," massive ogee w/4" cut, wooden tote, good condition, overall 5" l. (body w/some checking from age) ............................ **375**

**Crown molding plane,** hardwood, marked "H. Hills. Springfield, Mass.," original applied fence & pull stick, very clean, excellent condition, 3 1/2" iron, overall 4 5/8" l. ........................ **850**

**Crown molding plane,** hardwood, marked "Hachenberg - Union Co. PA," offset tote, flat chamfers, round top James Cam iron, one of a set of two planes used to make an extra wide crown, good condition, 3 5/8" w. (top off tote) ........................ **281**

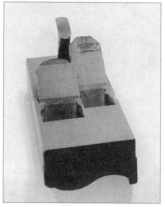

*I. C. Titcomb Handled Molding Plane*

**Crown molding plane,** hardwood, marked "I. C. Titcomb. N.P.," B mark, double iron & wedge, cuts 5" crown, w/no hole for pull rod, cabinetmaker & master plane maker of Newburyport, Massachusetts, ca.

1840, very clean, fine condition, 6 1/4" w. (ILLUS.) ........................ **2,400**

**Crown molding plane,** hardwood, marked "J. Bear," handled, offset tote, round top iron, possibly early 18th c., fine condition, 4" w. ........................ **550**

**Crown molding plane,** hardwood, marked "P. Sargent - Concord, N.H.," ogee & bevel, good wooden tote handle, very clean, very good condition, 3 3/16" w, iron, overall 15" l. ........................ **375**

**Crown molding plane,** hardwood, marked "P. Sargent. Concord, N. H.," ogee, good wooden tote, very clean, very good condition, 3 1/4" w. iron (one worm hole & couple shrinkage checks) ........................ **330**

**Crown molding plane,** hardwood, marked "Tho. Napier.," B mark, handled, cuts pilaster-style molding, wide flat chamfers, round top iron & offset tote, steel strike button, perfect wooden tote handle, one of Philadelphia's earliest makers, good condition (old rivet at pull stick early repair to shrinkage check) ........................ **1,200**

**Crown molding plane,** hardwood, marked "Wm. Martin Philad.," w/wide, flat chamfers, full stick, applied fence, offset tote, round

*Giant Crown Molding Plane*

*Cooper's Croze Planes*

top iron marked w/what appears to be "C. Lawrence," widest known example of this maker, good condition, 5 1/16" iron, 13 3/4" l. (ILLUS. bottom of previous page) .......................... **3,200**

**Crown molding plane,** yellow birch, marked "F*Nicholson. Wrentham," B1 mark, round top wedge & iron, wide flat chamfers, 3 3/4" iron, rare, first American plane maker, good condition, 4 3/4" w. (old shrinkage check repaired w/rosehead nail) ................. **4,600**

**Crown molding plane,** yellow birch, marked "I. Walton In Reading," round top wedge & iron & offset tote, Reading, Massachusetts, third quarter 18th c., good condition, 3 1/4" w. & 11 3/4" l. (tip off tote, several worm holes, otherwise in remarkable state of preservation) ................................ **1,800**

**Crown molding starter plane,** hardwood, marked "D. Lose," w/a James Cam iron, made in Center County, Pennsylvania, ca. 1800, very good condition, 3 3/4" w. ......................................... **660**

**Croze plane,** cooper's tool, hardwood & cast iron, decorated & chip carved, Dutch, 1828, good condition w/a few worn holes (ILLUS. above, left w/other croze planes) ............................. **90**

**Croze plane,** cooper's tool, hardwood & cast iron, small sized model, Dutch, 1846, good condition (ILLUS. above, center w/other croze planes) ......................... **235**

**Croze plane,** cooper's tool, hardwood & cast iron, w/three-arm adjustment, wedge cutter & two spurs, Dutch, fine condition (ILLUS. above, right w/other croze planes) ................................................ **95**

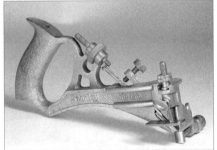

*Rare Stanley Curved Rabbet Plane*

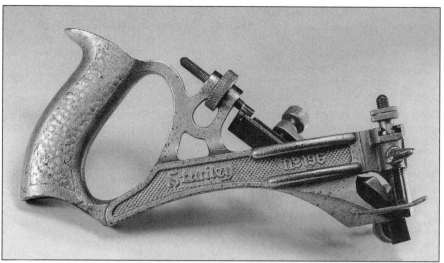

*Stanley No. 196 Curved Rabbet Plane*

**Curved rabbet plane,** cast iron w/94% plating, Stanley No. 196, Sweet Hart logo, cuts rabbets round curved edges, rare, very good condition (ILLUS. bottom of previous page) ............................ **1,540**

**Curved rabbet plane,** cast iron w/99% plating, Stanley No. 196, Sweet Hart logo, complete & original w/few signs of use, fine condition ............................................. **2,640**

**Curved rabbet plane,** cast iron w/near 100% plating, Stanley No. 196, ca. 1910, complete, very good condition (ILLUS. top of page) ................................................. **1,595**

*Rare Traut - Millers Dado Plane*

**Dado plane,** cast iron & gunmetal, marked "Traut - Miller," earliest type, open hand cast w/gunmetal cutter hold down & screw, rare & important, metal cracked,

*Stanley No. 39 13/16 Dado Plane*

good condition (ILLUS. previous page)...................................................... **5,060**

**Dado plane,** cast iron, Stanley No. 39 1/2, light use, original box w/picture label, fine condition (box w/some edge wear, label taped on corners)................................ **220**

**Dado plane,** cast iron, Stanley No. 39 3/4, lightly used, in original box w/picture label, fine condition (edge wear on box)................ **275**

**Dado plane,** cast iron, Stanley No. 39 3/8, new tool, in original box w/picture label & only light wear, fine condition............................. **248**

**Dado plane,** cast iron, Stanley No. 39 7/8, improved-type, Sweet Hart logo vintage, in original box w/picture label, unused tool, fine condition ............................... **248**

**Dado plane,** cast iron w/100% japanning, Stanley No. 39 13/16, Sweet Hart logo, in original box, like new, box w/minor edge scuffs & printed label, mint (ILLUS. bottom of previous page) . **6,490**

**Dado plane,** cast iron w/60% japanning, Stanley No. 39 13/16" IN., Sweet Hart vintage, manufactured from 7/8" dados, the body milled to 13/16" wide, original & proper w/all markings removed, very rare, good condition (ILLUS. below) ......................... **1,320**

**Dado plane,** cast iron w/70% japanning, Stanley No. 46, Type 5, wooden handle & grip knob, w/11 cutters in original wooden case, plane in custom wooden display case, good condition .......... **259**

**Dado plane,** cast iron w/80% japanning, Stanley No. 39, early 1-inch type, complete........................ **127**

**Dado plane,** cast iron w/85% japanning, Stanley No. 39 5/8 Inch, complete w/proper parts, very good condition............................. **105**

**Dado plane,** cast iron w/85% plating, Stanley No. 46, Type 8, rare nickel crossover depth stop, w/nine cutters, hard to find, good condition ...................................... **220**

**Dado plane,** cast iron w/90% japanning, marked "Sargent No. 34," proper working parts, 1/2" size, ornate scroll decoration, hard to find, very good condition.... **220**

**Dado plane,** cast iron w/90% plating, Stanley No. 46, original box w/picture label, very good condition (some tool & box wear)........ **440**

**Dado plane,** cast iron w/92% japanning, Stanley No. 39 7/8 Inch, complete w/proper parts, very good condition............................. **105**

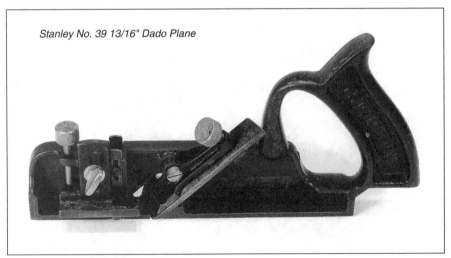

*Stanley No. 39 13/16" Dado Plane*

*Rare Stanley No. 39 13/16 Dado Plane*

**Dado plane,** cast iron w/95% japanning, Stanley No. 39 13/16, Sweet Hart logo, rarest of the 39s, ca. 1920s, mint condition (ILLUS.)...................... **1,430**

**Dado plane,** cast iron w/98% japanning, Stanley Improved Dado Plane No. 239 5/32-Inch, in original box w/label (box dark & dirty)............................ **468**

**Dado plane,** hardwood, marked "M. C. Vaile.," wedge nicker, possibly unlisted maker, very clean & near new, fine condition 5/16" size ............................ **65**

**Dado plane,** hardwood, marked "Tyler, P." in tee shape stamp, one mark vertical, another horizontal, early Marlow, New Hampshire maker, large oval wedge finial, good condition, 1 9/16" w., 9" l. ......................... **70**

**Dado, plow & filletster plane,** cast iron w/98% finish, Stanley No. 46, in original box w/picture label, very good condition (light use, box well worn)..................... **798**

**Door coping plane,** hardwood, cuts cope in cross rails to match into side rails, door rail planes extremely rare, ones making coping cuts very rare, fine condition............................ **300**

**Door plane,** hardwood, marked "M. Crannell. Albany," screw adjusts for width, cuts the edges & sides of rails to receive door panels in one operation, very good condition ......................... **99**

**Door router plane,** cast iron w/90% japanning, Stanley No. 171, double wood handles, complete w/fence, good condition (minor roughness on tote edges)......................... **253**

**Door router plane,** cast iron w/90% japanning, Stanley No. 171, wooden handles, w/all four cutters, ca. 1900, very good condition ......................... **413**

**Dovetail plane,** cast iron, Stanley No. 444, tool new & mint, w/four cutters in wooden box, includes two spur blocks & instructions, all in original cardboard box w/layout blueprint inside top of lid, fine condition ................. **1,760**

**Dovetail plane,** cast iron w/80% plating, Stanley No. 444, four cutters & both spur blocks, w/owner-made box.......................... **660**

**Dovetail plane,** cast iron w/90% plating, Stanley No. 444, includes two spur blocks, screwdriver, four cutters & cutter box, sample dovetail, original instructions & 1927 Stanley pocket catalog, in original cardboard box w/full label, box good, tools very good condition (plating w/some rust spots) ....................... **1,400**

**Dovetail plane,** cast iron w/95% plating, Stanley No. 444, complete w/four cutters in the original wooden case, w/color instruction sheets & screwdriver, like-new tool, all in original box, fine condition (some box edge wear, no dovetail sample)............... **990**

**Duplex rabbet plane,** aluminum w/frosted original finish, Stanley No. 78 A, Sweet Hart logo, proper original parts, light use, very good condition............................ **275**

**Edge trimming block plane,** cast iron, Stanley No. 95, mint tool in original mint box................ **209**

**Edge trimming plane,** cast iron w/80% japanning, Stanley No. 95, Type 1 w/New Britain trademark on blade............................ **116**

**Farrier's scraper,** hand-hammered iron blade w/turned boxwood handle, unclean stamped mark, ca. 1830............................ **61**

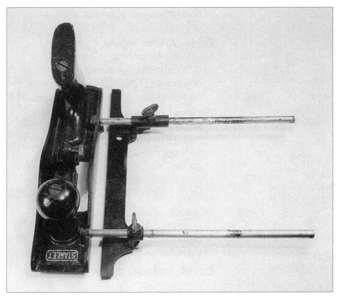

*Prototype*
*Fiberboard Plane*

**Fenced dado plane,** yellow birch, marked "Jo. Fuller. Providence.," double nickers, unusual, good condition .............................. **193**

**Fenced rabbet plane,** yellow birch, marked "C.E. Chelor. Wrenthem.," flat chamfers, nice wedge, even light color, very good condition, 1 3/16" w., 9 15/16" l. (ILLUS. p. 103 second from right w/other wooden planes) ................................................. **1,760**

**Fiberboard plane,** cast iron w/100% japanning & hardwood, Stanley prototype, "Stanley" in notched logo cast into nose & painted orange, probably used in the development of the No. 193 plane w/added complex wraparound cutter clamp, rare & unique (ILLUS. above) ................. **2,400**

*Metallic Plane Co. Filletster Plane*

**Filletster plane,** cast iron w/80% japanning, marked "Metallic Plane Co. Auburn, NY.," patented by William Loughborough, May 10, 1859, cutter marked "Excelsior Cutter," adjustable fence, wooden handle & knob grip, chip in bottom edge of tote, good condition (ILLUS.) ......... **700**

**Filletster & rabbet plane,** cast iron w/98% japanning, Stanley No. 289, wooden handle w/60% decal, original box w/picture label, complete & proper, fine condition (edge wear & scuffing on box) ...................................... **303**

**Filletsters & rabbet plane,** cast iron, Stanley No. 289, in original box, good condition (tool w/fair amount of use, box worn w/90% paper label) ............................ **385**

**Floor plane,** cast iron, Stanley No. 74, long tapering cylindrical wood handle, good condition (repainted) ................................ **193**

**Floor plane,** cast iron, Stanley No. 74, rare all-original long wooden push handle in fine condition, new blade, good condition (plane pitted) ....................... **1,125**

**Floor plane,** cast iron w/70% japanning, Stanley No. 74, original handle w/the proper parts, rare w/handle, ca. 1900, good condition ................................................. **880**

**Floor plane,** cast iron w/long turned beech handle, Stanley No. 11 1/2, rare, good condition (repainted) ........................................... **440**

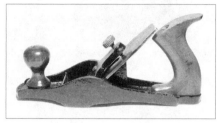

*Stanley No. 340 Furring Plane*

**Furring plane,** cast iron w/92% japanning, Stanley No. 340, wooden handle & knob grip, cutter marked "Pat'd 3-3-03 - SR&L" in arch trademark, ca. 1910, very good condition (ILLUS.) ............................................. **1,045**

*Stanley No. 340 Furring Plane*

**Furring plane,** cast iron w/99% japanning, Stanley No. 340, Type 1, cutter marked "Pat. Apld. For," wood handle & knob grip, mint condition except for slight edge chip to tote (ILLUS.) **1,450**

**Gage plane,** cast iron w/100% japanning, marked "No. 4 Gage Self-Setting Plane. H.IS.B. & Co. OVB. Our Very Best," corrugated, wooden handle & knob hand grip, made by Stanley for HSB & Co., uncommon, mint condition .............................................. **165**

**Gage plane,** hardwood, marked "O.V.B. H.S. B. & Co. No. 26," transitional-type, self-setting plane by Stanley, wood near perfect w/80% original finish, nice color, fine condition (only one edge ding) ..................................... **220**

**Framing plane,** carpenter's, hardwood, marked "John Weiss," giant size w/tee handle on front & closed tote on rear, marked on only the iron but shown in catalogs, good condition, 3 1/2" w. iron, overall 49" l. (ILLUS. at left) ..... **385**

*Large Weiss Carpenter's Plane*

*Stewart Spiers
Infill Panel Plane*

**Groove plane,** hardwood, marked "L. Cook," name stamped in maker's slot, possibly unlisted maker, good condition ................................................. **250**

**Groove plane,** hardwood, marked "T. Tilefton," D mark, odd groove plane, early mark, few w/'f' instead of 's' in name stamp, fine condition ........................... **160**

**Gutter plane,** fruitwood, marked "N. Schauer.," round top James Cam iron, weak stamped mark, worn but rare plane, early Pennsylvania maker, good condition, iron 2", 16" l. ............................. **120**

**Halving or shiplap plane,** beech, marked "Cristerini.," flat chamfers, nice wedge, early Lancaster, Pennsylvania area maker, good condition, 1 7/16" w., 10 1/8" l. ................................... **275**

**Hand beading plane,** cast iron w/100% plating, Stanley No. 66 Universal, very light use, box w/90% paper label, very good condition ................................................ **176**

**Hard board beveler,** cast iron w/98% japanning, Stanley No. 195, wood handle w/good finish, fine condition .............................. **160**

**Hollow & round-bottom planes,** wooden, marked "John Mosley & Son," sizes 2, 4, 6, 8, 10, 12, 14, 16 & 18, good cutters & wedges, the set ................................... **523**

**Ice plane,** cast iron w/well used finishes on wooden base, table model, used to make shaved ice for drinks, rare, good condition ................................................ **225**

**Infill bullnose plane,** gunmetal body & lever cap w/mahogany infill, very good condition ................. **187**

**Infill jointer plane,** cast iron, tiger stripe maple & walnut, bird's-eye rear infill & tote, front infilled w/dark tiger stripe wood, possibly maple in back & walnut on front, attractive combination using different woods, heavy iron body, good condition, 3" w., 19" l. (tip of toe broken at bottom edge & reglued) ....................... **550**

**Infill mitre plane,** cast iron w/rosewood overstuffing, gunmetal transitional style cap w/crossbar, well-made, very good condition, blade 2 11/16" w., overall 10" l. ...................... **303**

**Infill mitre plane,** cast-iron body w/beech infill, low angle, round ends, very good condition ............... **138**

**Infill panel plane,** cast iron & rosewood, marked "Stewart Spiers," dovetailed construction w/rosewood stuffing, gunmetal cap, 2 1/2" iron, very good condition, 13 3/8" l. (ILLUS. above) .... **605**

*Baker Infill
Plane*

**Infill panel plane,** cast iron w/rosewood infill, marked "Spiers Ayr Panel," dovetailed construction, Mathieson cap iron, very good condition, 13 3/4" l. ...... **358**

**Infill parallel side jointer,** cast iron, marked "Spiers, Ayr," dovetailed, rosewood infill, rare, good condition, cutter 2 3/8" w., 20 1/2" l. (tip off tote) ......................... **750**

**Infill plane,** beech, rhino horn-shaped shoulder, unmarked, good condition, 1 3/8" w., 7 1/2" l. (small nick on rear edge) ... **160**

**Infill plane,** brass w/ebony infill, marked "Rob't. Baker 1980," mitre-type w/steel sole, dovetailed body, fine condition (ILLUS. above) ....................................... **935**

**Infill plane,** cast iron, marked "Mathieson & Son," coffin-shaped smoother-type, dovetailed, rosewood infill, gunmetal lever cap, small size, very good condition, iron 2 1/8" w., 7 1/4" l. ........................................ **385**

**Infill plane,** cast iron, marked "Norris - London - A 5 Smoother," adjustable, gunmetal lever cap, stained wood infill, good iron length, very good condition ... **440**

**Infill plane,** cast iron, marked "Norris - London," No. 4 coffin-shaped smoother, dovetailed, rosewood infill, gunmetal cap, early Norris stamp, very good condition, iron 2 1/8" w., 7 3/8" l. ............................................ **385**

**Infill plane,** cast iron, marked "Spiers - Ayr," jointer-type, rosewood infill, gunmetal lever cap, round nose & tail, very good condition, iron 2 3/4" w., 20 3/4" l. .............................................. **1,100**

**Infill plane,** cast iron, marked "Spiers - Ayr," panel-type, dovetailed, rosewood infill, gunmetal lever cap, very good condition, iron 2 1/2" w., 14" l. .............................. **605**

**Infill plane,** cast iron, marked "Spiers - Ayr," smoother-type, dovetailed, rosewood infill, clean, very good condition (tight base craft in wooden handle) ......... **358**

**Infill plane,** cast iron, rosewood stuffing, gunmetal cap, round ends, straight sides, carved wood knob w/ivory infill, panel on tote handle w/checkered carving, very good condition, iron 2 3/8" w., 10" l. ........................... **248**

**Infill plane,** cast iron, rosewood stuffing, gunmetal cap w/special seat for applying even pressure from the locking screw, iron 2 3/8" w., 14" l. .............................. **314**

**Infill plane,** cast iron w/gunmetal shoulder & rosewood infill, much original lacquer, finger grip in nose fits the hand, awkward to use, fine condition .............. **248**

**Infill plane,** cast steel w/mahogany infill, stepped front w/over stuffing, gunmetal cap, good condition, 2 3/8" w. iron, 8 1/2" l. (cutter does not seat well & plane may have been designed for cutter backing strip) ...... **140**

**Infill plane,** gunmetal & maple, gunmetal chariot, maple wedge, steel filler plate closes mouth opening & adjustable, 1 3/8" w., 3 7/8" l. ................................. **120**

**Infill plane,** gunmetal shoulder & mahogany infill, craftsman-made, good condition, 1 3/8" w., 6 3/4" l. ............................. **130**

*Modern Wayne Anderson Infill Plane*

**Infill plane,** gunmetal & steel, marked "Wayne A. Anderson," No. 1 size, gunmetal body & dovetailed steel sole, rosewood infill w/ivory strike button, modern maker, new w/wooden box, fine condition (ILLUS.)....................... **880**

*Spiers Infill Plane*

**Infill plane,** gunmetal, steel & rosewood, marked "Spiers Ayr" on nose, blade & on 2 1/4" cap iron, w/gunmetal round side smoother w/dovetailed steel sole, overstuffed rosewood, gunmetal cap, very good condition, 7 1/2" l. (ILLUS.) ................ **1,980**

**Infill plane,** gunmetal w/steel sole, rosewood infill, shoulder w/stylized screw lock wedge, full cutter, unusual form, very good condition (ILLUS. below)...... **633**

**Infill plane,** hardwood, marked "Spiers, Ayr," dovetailed shoulder, rosewood infill, about 3/8" of Ward iron remains, very good condition, 1 1/2" w. ................. **325**

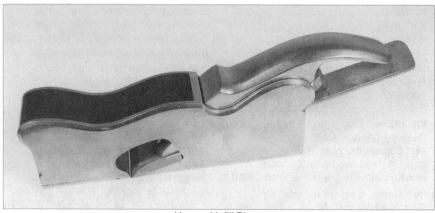

*Unusual Infill Plane*

*Norris London No. A5 Infill Plane*

**Infill plane,** steel & hardwood, marked "Norris London No. A5," w/round sides, adjustable, in original box, like new except for very light flaking of finish on wood, box fine w/full label (ILLUS.)................................ **1,540**

**Infill shoulder plane,** cast iron w/mahogany infill, long wedge tail, blade 1 1/2" w., 8" l. .................. **110**

**Infill smoother plane,** cast iron & rosewood, marked "Spiers Ayr Smoother," dovetailed con-struction, rosewood overstuff-ing, gunmetal cap, Mathieson cap iron, very good condition, overall 7 1/2" l. ..................................... **330**

**Infill smoother plane,** cast iron & rosewood, marked "Spiers Ayr Smoother," dovetailed con-struction, rosewood overstuff-ing, gunmetal cap, round sides, good condition, 9" l. (hairline crack in nose infill) .............................. **330**

**Infill smoother plane,** cast iron & rosewood, square side w/round tail, overstuffed w/rosewood, gunmetal lever cap, unmarked, good condition, iron 2 3/16" w., overall 9" l. ............................................. **275**

**Infill smoothing plane,** cast iron, dovetailed & filled w/walnut, scroll-carved front knob, gun-metal cap, craftsman-made quality, good condition, 2" w. iron, 8 3/4" l............................................. **325**

**Infill smoothing plane,** gunmetal, marked "Spiers, Ayr," gunmetal round side-style w/dovetailed steel sole, overstuffed w/rose-wood, gunmetal cap, very good condition, cutter 2 1/8" w., 7 1/2" l. (ILLUS. top of next page) ...................................................... **1025**

*Various Planes*

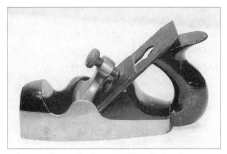

*Smooth plane by "Ayr Spiers"*

**Infill smoothing plane,** hardwood, marked "Spiers, Ayr," handled round side-style, dovetailed, overstuffed w/rosewood, good condition, iron 2 1/8" w., 7 1/2"l. (tote w/old crack repaired from bottom) ............................ **300**

**Instrument maker's plane,** brass, tailed-type w/wooden knob palm rest, fine condition, 1 3/8" l. ............. **127**

**Jack plane,** aluminum, Stanley A5, Sweet Hart vintage, plane mint, includes store tag for aluminum planes, box w/original full label, like-new condition, ca. 1920s (couple scuffs on corners of box) ............................................. **1,700**

**Jack plane,** cast iron, marked "E.H. Morris No. 8, 1870," diamond sole, hardwood tote handle, Ohio Tool Company cutter, very good condition, 16" l. (tip of tote round, wedge w/some hammer marks) ................................ **2,090**

**Jack plane,** cast iron, marked "Keen Kutter KK 5," in original box, good condition, box worn but w/strong label (ILLUS. previous page center w/router plane & tonguing & grooving plane) ....................................... **275**

**Jack plane,** cast iron, marked "Rodier Patent Jack - Patented Mar. 4, 1879," walnut handle, hard to find, very good condition (ILLUS. below) ................................ **1,265**

**Jack plane,** cast iron, Stanley Bed Rock No. 605, tool new & mint, in original box w/label, fine condition (box w/some masking tape at corners of label) .................... **908**

**Jack plane,** cast iron, Stanley Four Square, Sweet Hart logo on blade, Four Square marketed before age of home handyman & never became popular, middle quality tools aimed at homeowner market of day, Four Square handle decal & polished sides finishes near perfect, appears unused, three color printing bright & shiny, w/original box, ca. 1925, new condition (slight edge wear on box) ............ **1,150**

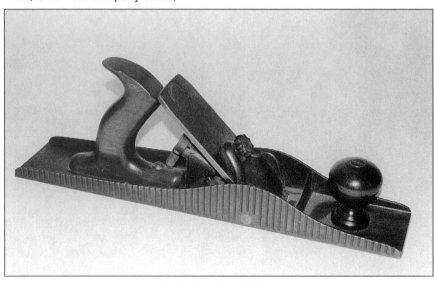

*Rodier Patent Jack Plane*

**Jack plane,** cast iron, Stanley No. 5 1/2 Heavy Jack Plane, tool mint & probably unused, original box w/full label w/factory stick-on "Heavy" sticker, fine condition (box worn w/one bad corner)...................................................... **2,860**

**Jack plane,** cast iron, Stanley No. 5 1/4 Junior Jack, ca. 1930s, in original box w/Sweet Hart label, fine condition........................................ **275**

**Jack plane,** cast iron, Stanley No. 62, low-angle style, in original box, rare boxed item, fine condition (minor storage stain on plane)...................................................... **1,073**

**Jack plane,** cast iron w/60% japanning, marked "Birmingham Plane Mfg. Co. - Mosher Patent Dec. 16, 1884," adjustable, very good condition, 14" l. w/2" iron...... **385**

*Rare Long Patented Jack Plane*

**Jack plane,** cast iron w/95% finishes, marked "Foster's Turn-Table - Patented Jan. 29, 1908," bed & lever cap marked "102," iron by Stanley & correct, wooden handles similar to Ohio Tool Co., only one known in this size, very good condition, 15" l. (ILLUS.)................................................ **3,850**

**Jack plane,** cast iron w/95% japanning, marked "Louis C. Rodier. Patent March 4, 1879.," w/waved corrugated sole & original extra thick Buck Bros. iron, sides w/vertical cast grooves typical of Rodier planes, polished surfaces bright & shiny, portion of original paper label on tail of plane, extremely rare plane, very fine

condition (tote chip on one edge otherwise wood fine w/original finish) .................................................. **950**

**Jack plane,** cast iron w/97% japanning, marked "Steer's Patent. C.E. Jennings & Co. No. 307," rosewood sole strips near perfect, early type 2/lever cap, fine condition (some edge rusting on cutter & cap)............................ **385**

*Stanley No. 62 Jack Plane*

**Jack plane,** cast iron w/nearly 100% japanning, Stanley No. 62, Sweet Hart logo, low-angle type, wooden handle & knob, original polished surfaces, ca. 1920s, fine condition (ILLUS.)........ **825**

**Jack plane,** cast iron w/wooden handle & knob handle, marked "Knowles Patent Jack," patented by Hazzard Knowles of Connecticut in 1827, clean, little used, very good condition, 16 1/2" l. ............................................. **715**

**Jack plane,** tiger stripe maple, marked "W. Mead" w/three sunbursts, razee-type w/burl tote, pronounced wood grain, fine condition.................................................. **446**

**Jenny plane,** cast iron w/80% japanning, Stanley No. 37, Type 9, wooden handle, good blade....... **215**

**Jointer fence,** cast iron w/95% plating, Stanley No. 386, good hardwood knob hand grip, very good condition (polished surface stained)............................................ **121**

**Jointer fence,** cast iron w/99% plating, Stanley No. 386, hardwood knob hand grip w/most original finish, fine condition ........... **132**

**Jointer fence,** steel w/nearly 100% plating, Stanley No. 386, like-new.............................................. **171**

*Jointer Plane*

**Jointer plane,** annealed steel w/gunmetal cap, 97% original finish, marked "Norris" blade, post-war model w/adjustment, appears to be an A-1 but isn't dovetailed, fine condition, 22 1/2" l. (ILLUS.) ............................ **2,970**

**Jointer plane,** beech, marked "M.B. Tidey, Dundee, NY" on nose & wedge, ebony wedge & strike button, decorative ebony crossbar into nose of plane, closed tote of dark rosewood, held by two copper rivets, mouth equipped w/boxwood wear surface, iron by Ohio, rare very fancy jointer, interesting & unusual plane by American maker, good condition, 3 1/2" w., 26" l., ..................................... **450**

**Jointer plane,** beech, marked "S. Sleeper," iron strike button, mouth closed in w/wooden infill, good condition, iron 2" w., 21 1/2" l. .................................................. **110**

**Jointer plane,** cast iron, marked "E.H. Morris Nov. 8, 1870," diamond sole, wooden tote handle & knob hand grip, very good condition, 21" l. (edge chip on tip of tote) ........................................... **2,530**

*Long Cooper's Jointer Plane*

**Jointer plane,** cooper's, hardwood, carved mouth & decorated body w/"1832 - T S I+K," wedge & iron highly decorated, good condition, many worm holes, some distress on lower end, body 5 x 7", overall 52" l (ILLUS. at right).... ................................. **154**

*Cord winder mounted in brass frame that clamps on tabletop, possibly early 19th c., $330.*

All pictures on these pages courtesy Brown Auction Services

*Cast iron corn sheller, ca. 1870, $275.*

*Mining compass, iron and brass, with dovetailed wooden case, $3,740.*

*Light mountain transit, cast iron, with original wooden case with leather covering and tripod, $770.*

*Tool chest, walnut burl with crotch burl on top both inside and out, dovetailed construction, $330.*

*Combination bench and tool chest of mixed soft and hard woods, $330.*

*Oak wall-mounted tool chest with tools, includes about 20 tools, saws, shaves, rules, and chisels, $358.*

*Cast iron and wood boring machine, patented 1843, $2,200.*

*Wrought iron blacksmith leg-type vise, $110.*

*Treadle lathe, grinder and jigsaw, cast iron, $220.*

*Iron treadle model lathe, 19th c., $743.*

*Cast iron boring machine, extremely rare American Industrial Age tool, $3,300.*

*Cast iron foot-powered mortiser, 19th c., $165.*

*Cast iron brace, ca. 1862, brass ring, $171.*

*Brace, beech with ebony pad with ivory ring, $468.*

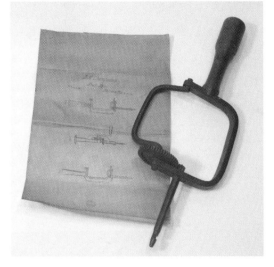

*Cast iron, brass and wood brace, ca. 1854, $1,375.*

*Brace, brass-framed with beech infill, ebony pad with full ivory ring, $660.*

*Brace, rosewood with metal fittings, $880.*

*Rare patented brace, brass, ebony and beech, $743.*

*Cast-iron hand drill with black japanning and red and gold trim, in original box with 15 drills and a chuck wrench, $1,650.*

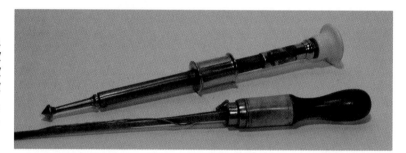

*Brass, iron and rosewood bow drill with box, $605.*

*Above: Wrought-iron hand drill with cast brass gears, wooden tee handle, 18th c. or earlier, $715.*

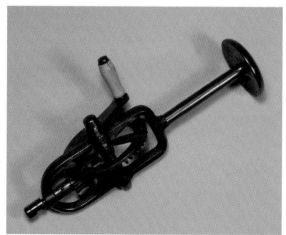

*Brass and ivory frame drill with open 6-spoke wheel and mushroom pad, $193.*

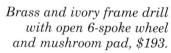

*Handforged
iron chisel,
$275.*

*Tap box,
about 2" wide edge,
$165.*

*Vise, cast iron, huge 70 lb. size, $303.*

*Wrought-iron
goosewing-type ax,
Lancaster,
Pennsylvania, $413.*

*Cast iron and
hardwood double
face hammer, hits
on both forward
and backward
stoke, $600.*

*Layout device, cast iron with hinged brass handle, ca. 1868, one of only three known, $6,380.*

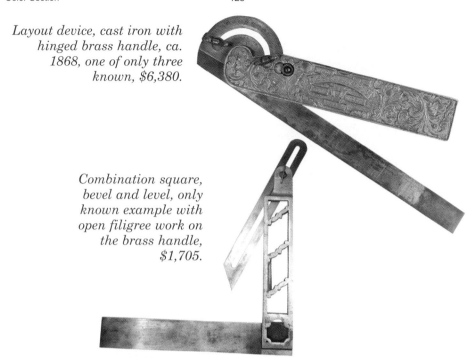

*Combination square, bevel and level, only known example with open filigree work on the brass handle, $1,705.*

*Try square, steel with whalebone handle, dated 1937, $330.*

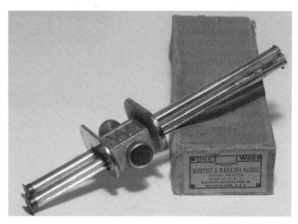

*Mortise and marking gauge with original box, $825.*

*Four-fold ivory rule with brass fittings and joints, ca. 1858, $3,300.*

*Saw, wrought iron and hardwood, possibly for stair work, crude saw blade inserted along the bottom, dated 1808, $193.*

*Turning saw, rosewood and steel, $275.*

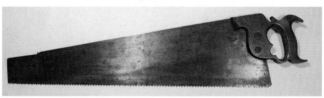

*Hand saw, steel, with triple medallion label screws with split nuts, $1,210.*

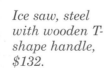

*Ice saw, steel with wooden T-shape handle, $132.*

*Combination mitre saw and vise for picture-frame work, mounted on oak base, $275.*

*Basketmaker's shave, cast iron, initialed and dated on side "1842," hand-cut bolts hold blade, $440.*

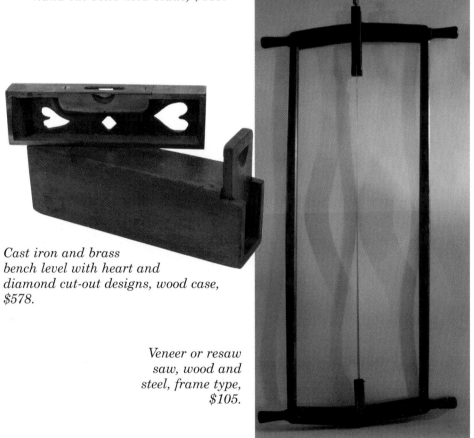

*Cast iron and brass bench level with heart and diamond cut-out designs, wood case, $578.*

*Veneer or resaw saw, wood and steel, frame type, $105.*

*Crooked knife, wrought iron, canted handle with chip-carved dog, ax, and Masonic emblem, $715.*

*Cast-iron level with open framework, rarest of Davis skeleton types, $4,730.*

*Inclinometer, cast iron with japanning and gold leaf, $275.*

*Cast-iron level, sometimes called pretzel level because of open pinwheel filigree design, $1,045.*

*Rare cast aluminum corner level, ca. 1886, $1,980.*

*Plumb and level pendulum-type inclinometer, walnut picture frame design, $8,800.*

*Openwork mantel clock-style inclinometer, ca. 1889, $2,860.*

*Cast-iron plumb bob with built-in reel, $2,310.*

*Wooden dividers with handwrought iron tips, 1879, $330.*

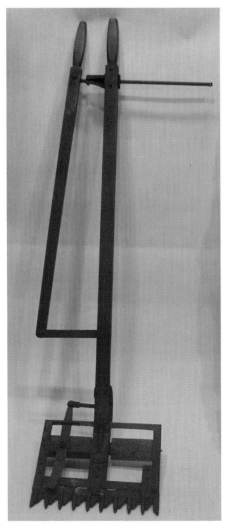

*Patent model marked "G.W. and T. Parker — Saw Gummer — Dec. 14th, 1875," with original tags, $440.*

*Cast-iron hand-powered sickle bar lawn mower, ca. 1900, $248.*

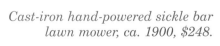

*Cast-iron jack plane, patented 1908, $3,850.*

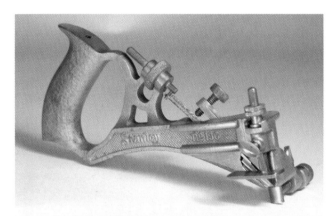

*Cast-iron curved rabbet plane, rare, $1,540.*

*Cast-iron and gunmetal dado plane, $5,060.*

*Chamfer-type molding plane, patented 1883, $5,500.*

*Cooper's jointer plane, $154.*

*Beech plow plane, handled three-arm style, $21,450.*

*Molding plane with several interchangeable parts, $11,550.*

*Carriage maker's plow plane
with adjustable fence,
$10,450.*

*Scraper with wooden bottom
and turned wood side
handles, with original store
tag, $275.*

*Plow plane, three-arm style, Philadelphia,
1830s, $31,900.*

*Coachmaker's plow plane, unusual
router style, $605.*

*Bossingschaaf plane, hardwood, with scroll-carved mouth and pinwheel on wedge, $660.*

*Rare Stanley cast-iron block plane, $1,870.*

*Plow plane, cast iron, marked "Loughborough Patent Iron Plow— Patented May 3, 1864," very rare, $16,500.*

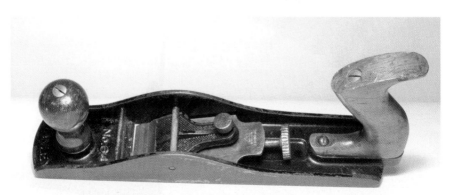

*Butcher block plane, low-angle bench-type, rare, ca. 1915, $1,155.*

*Mannebach Bros. Cooper's Jointer Plane*

*Jointer Plane*

**Jointer plane,** cast iron, marked "Knowles Patent Jointer," original wedge, perfect wood handle & knob, light corrugations on sole, earliest patented plane, fine condition, 23 1/2" l. (ILLUS.) ............................ **1,430**

**Jointer plane,** cast iron w/85% finish, marked "Metallic Plane Co. Palmer & Storkes Patent," nonadjustable cutter marked w/patent dates, adjustable mouth & corrugated sole, hardwood handle & knob hand grip, very good condition, 20" l. ............... **385**

**Jointer plane,** cast iron w/97% japanning, marked "O.R. Chapin. Tower & Lyon. Patented July 4, 1876.," No. 8 size, corrugated bottom, fine condition (handles w/few storage dings otherwise near perfect) ............................... **275**

**Jointer plane,** cooper's, hardwood, marked "Mannebach Bros. 112 Straton St., New York.," very long body, iron w/4 1/2" cutting edge, weighs 4 lbs., marked on the iron & throat, partly cleaned, good condition, 5 1/2" w., 5" deep, 5' 10" l. (ILLUS. above) ........................... **250**

**Jointer plane,** hardwood, long block carved on the top w/"C - 1831 - I," carved mouth, good condition, 30" l. (replaced wedge) ...................................................... **248**

**Jointer plane,** hardwood, marked "E.W. Carpenter. Patent March 27, 1849.," double wedges, very clean, very good condition, 22" l. ........................................................ **116**

**Jointer plane,** hardwood, marked "LGL 1818," long w/carved handle & horn knob, early & proper, some wormholes, good condition (ILLUS. below) .............................. **220**

**Jointer plane,** hardwood w/gold pinstriping, razee-type plane w/good tote, metal fence w/100% japanning & striping, very good condition ............................ **259**

**Jointer plane,** rosewood, marked "Gage Tool Co.," #21 size, special order-type, very good condition (one rear corner chip) ........... **880**

*Early Long Jointer Plane*

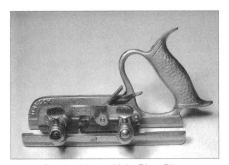

*Stanley No. 54 Light Plow Plane*

**Light plow plane,** cast iron w/100% plating, Stanley No. 54, Canadian military issue marked w/broad arrow & "C" mark, probably made for overseas shipment during World War II, never exported, fine condition (ILLUS.) ........................................... **330**

**Light plow plane,** cast iron w/copper wash, Miller's Patent plane, marked "Patented September 17, 1872" in ovla on fence, rare in copper wash, very good condition (ILLUS. p. 91, right w/Miller's combination match plane ...................................... **20,350**

**Low-angle smoothing plane,** cast iron w/90% japanning, Stanley No. 164, Sweet Hart logo, wood tote w/sapwood on edge, trace of hand decal remains, documented to have once been owned by Edmund A. Schade (Mechanical Superintendent at Stanley Rule & Level Co. 1900-1932 & patentee of overhead adjustment used on No. 164), fine condition (ILLUS. below) .................................................. **6,050**

**Match plane,** cast iron w/70% japanning, Stanley No. 48 Match, Type 1, patent date stamped in skates, early version, very good condition ........... **193**

**Match plane,** cast iron w/80% plating, marked "Sargent No. 1066," flip- over type w/one side cutting groove while other cuts tongue, good condition ...................... **300**

**Match plane,** cast iron w/80% plating, Stanley No. 146, complete ................................................ **121**

**Match plane,** cast iron w/95% plating, marked "Union 41,"

*Low-angle Smoother Plane*

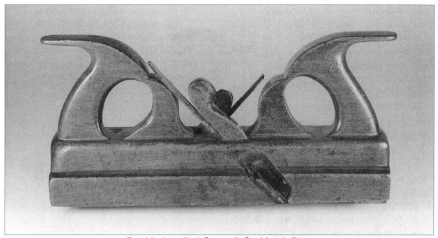

*Double-handled Come & Go Match Plane*

wooden knob grip w/much original finish, fine condition .............. **60**

**Match plane,** cast iron w/95% plating, Stanley No. 147, proper cutters ...................................................... **143**

**Match plane,** cast iron/plating near 100%, Stanley No. 48, hardwood handle w/original finish, very fine condition ...................... **160**

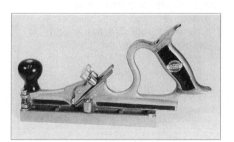

*Stanley No. 48 Match Plane*

**Match plane,** cast iron w/99% plating & 100% japanning, Stanley No. 48 Swing Fence, Sweet Hart logo, handle decal 97%, name on handle & number on fence were ground out & japanned so these planes could be sold as Stanleys, mint condition (ILLUS.) ...................................... **528**

**Match plane,** hardwood, cast iron & steel, double-handled come-and-go type, w/closed totes in both directions, wedged irons for cutting tongue in one direc-

tion & groove in the other, steel skates, very rare & unusual, fine condition (ILLUS. above) ................. **880**

*Come And Go Match Wooden Plane*

**Match plane,** hardwood, come-and-go double-ender type, early & well made, hard to find, good condition, 13 1/4" l. (ILLUS.) .......... **495**

*Match Plane*

**Match plane,** hardwood, marked "Auburn Tool Co.," double-handled style cuts both tongue & groove w/a closed tote on each end, very rare (ILLUS.) ...................... **990**

**Match planes,** hardwood, marked "I. Sleeper," matched pair, good condition, the set (top edge of one notch cut under wedge) ........... **220**

**Matching plane,** cast iron, Stanley No. 48, nearly unused in original box w/picture label, fine condition ............................................... **143**

**Matching plane,** cast iron, Stanley No. 49, in original box w/picture label, fine condition (light use, box w/some wear & taping) ... **198**

**Matching plane,** hardwood, marked "Spear & Wood" A mark & "Gladwin Patent June 9, 1857," near mint ................................. **330**

**Miller's Patent plane,** cast iron w/80% japanning, Stanley No. 41, Type 6A, filletster bed, both fences, 10 cutters, good condition ...... **1,155**

**Miller's Patent plane,** cast iron w/85% japanning, Stanley No. 43, Type 6A, w/nine cutters, good condition ..................................... **385**

**Miller's Patent plane,** gunmetal, Stanley No. 42, much original finish, tip of tote tapers to a fine point, w/nine cutters, ca. 1876, fine condition.................................. **2,970**

**Miller's Patent plane,** gunmetal, Stanley No. 44, Type 6A, rare model w/no filletster, original gunmetal fence & cutter box w/10 cutters, very good condition.......... **5,720**

**Mitre box plane,** cast iron, marked "Langdon Mitre Box Co. Millers Falls, Mass. Pat. Sept. 19, 1883.," two skew cutters set to cut in both directions, guides set at any angle from 45 to 90 degrees, adjustable slides used for fine adjustment, painted red & green, paint bit dull but 85%, brass replacement plane handle, very good condition (ILLUS. at bottom of page)....................................... **400**

*R. Baker Tools Mitre Infill Plane*

**Mitre infill plane,** gunmetal, steel & rosewood, marked "Infill Plane. R. Baker Tools." gunmetal w/dovetailed steel sole, rosewood infill, engraved as presented to William Rigler MWTCA president, Mr. Baker one of top modern planemakers, this early work clearly shows why, fine condition, iron 1", 5 1/4" l., (ILLUS.)...................... **1,155**

**Mitre molding plane,** cocobolo wood, marked "J.P. Storer - Brunswick, ME.," A mark, double-type, very good condition, iron 1 3/4" w., 10" l. (three minor chips on wood) ............................. **110**

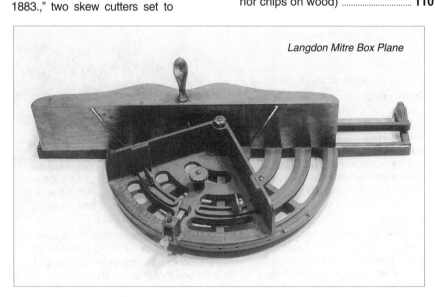

*Langdon Mitre Box Plane*

**Mitre molding plane,** hardwood, marked "Gus. Walker. Concord, NH.," coffin-shaped, Walker was a hardware dealer from 1855-1883, much original finish remains, rare mark, very good condition, blade 1 3/4" w., 9" l..... **150**

**Mitre plane,** gunmetal, pattern-maker-made, very low angle, good condition, 1 7/8" w., 9" l. ......... **83**

**Mitre plane,** gunmetal w/beech wedge cut out to straddle the crossbar, good condition, 8" l. ......... **61**

**Mitre plane,** pattern maker's, cast brass w/rosewood wedge, very good condition, 9" l. .............................. **50**

**Molding plane,** beech, boxwood & brass, marked "Ohio Tool Co. No. 58.," handled filletster-type, beech w/boxwood arms, nuts, washers & boxing, nickers & brass screw stop, rare to find handle filletsters, very good condition (one nicker missing, chip off edge of tote, & some minor thread chips at very end of rods)... **280**

**Molding plane,** beech, marked "A. Wheaton. Philada.," A mark, narrow molder w/flat chamfers, marked "D. Fenimorron" side, strong stamp from rare maker, very good condition, 9 11/16" l. .... **210**

**Molding plane,** beech, marked "Jacob Heiss," sash-type, early Lancaster County, Pennsylvania maker, good condition (mouth open a bit) .............................. **176**

**Molding plane,** beech, marked "Multiform Moulding Plane Pat. Aug. 29, 1854," brass fittings, eight bodies, tongue w/adjustable fence, five beads in sizes 1/8", 1/4", 5/8", 3/4" & 1", 1 1/4" nosing & 5/8" rounding, very good condition, the set........... **495**

**Molding plane,** beech, marked "O. Vinal," apparently maker's mark, ogee, flat wide chamfers, wedge w/small round finial, owner's stamp on side "N.R. Hill," 18th c., fine condition, 1 1/2" w., 9 5/16" l., .......................... **375**

**Molding plane,** beech, marked "T.E. Burley," bead-type w/rounded chamfers, later wedge w/large round finial & curving neck, very hard-to-find mark, very good condition, 10" l..... **290**

**Molding plane,** beech, marked "T.E. Burley," halving-type, wide flat chamfers, large wedged finial at cabinet pitch, early maker from Epping, New Hampshire, 10" l. (broken out at rear edge) .... **240**

**Molding plane,** beech, marked "Tho. Grant. (w/double crowns & "C" initials)," rounded bottom, flat chamfer, good condition, 1 3/8" w., 10" l. ...................................... **72**

**Molding plane,** beech, miniature, rounder, very good condition, 2 3/5" l. ................................................... **50**

**Molding plane,** birch, marked "F*Nicholson. Wrentham.," B1 mark, rounded bottom, original height, good color, strong mark, very good condition, 1/2" w., 9 7/8" l. (ILLUS. p. 103 second from left w/other wooden planes) .................................... **1,210**

**Molding plane,** birch, marked "Jo. Fuller. Providence.," astragal-type, relieved wedge, fine details, very good condition, 1 1/4" w., 10" l. ...................................... **193**

**Molding plane,** boxwood arms & nuts w/double rosewood boxing, marked "Israel White. Corner Callowhill & Fourth St. Phild. Warranted.," K mark, screw sash-type, 'N.N.' initials on bench, very clean, rare initials, fine condition ................................. **250**

**Molding plane,** boxwood, marked "D.P. Sandborn. Littleton.," B mark, ogee-type, single boxwood boxing, very good condition, 3/8" size (fence re-worked) ................................... **100**

**Molding plane,** boxwood, marked "E. W. Carpenter. Lancaster.," wide bead marked 'INCH 1/4.' single boxwood boxing, like-new condition, fine condition (nick on nose) ................................. **110**

**Molding plane,** boxwood, marked "M. Barr & Co. Nashua.," ogee-type, single boxwood boxing, good condition, 2 5/8" w. (bit dark w/couple shrinkage checks) ...................................................... **120**

*Unique Baines Patent Molding Plane*

**Molding plane,** cast gunmetal, marked "J.S. Baines Patented March 17, 1874," several interchangeable parts, iron marked "P*ML" for Boston Metallic Plane Company, complete except for a couple of screws &

clips, only known Baines extant, fine condition (ILLUS.)................ **11,550**

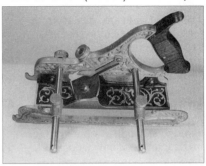

*Stanley Miller's Patent No. 42 Plane*

**Molding plane,** cast iron, copper red gunmetal & hardwood, marked "Stanley Miller's Patent No. 42," early oval trademark, 98% japanning on filletster bed, wooden handle, ca. 1875, crisp & clean condition w/tight hairline in wood (ILLUS.) ................... **3,300**

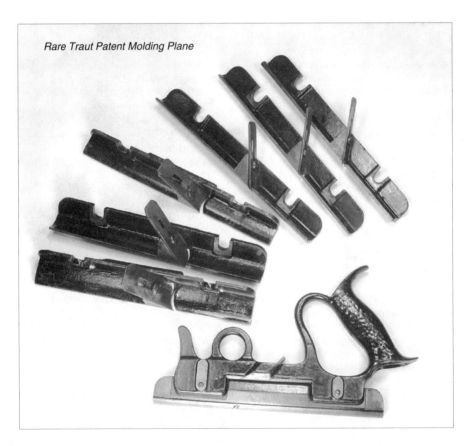

*Rare Traut Patent Molding Plane*

**Molding plane,** cast iron & hardwood, marked "Multiform Moulding Plane Co. Boston," wood bottom w/iron frame, bolt from rear of plane holds cutter in place, wooden tote overhangs tail of plane nearly 2", wooden knob grip, very good condition ..... **310**

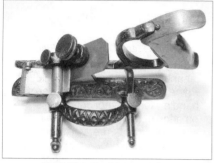

*Rare Chamfer Molding Plane*

**Molding plane,** cast iron, marked "Lee's Patent Feb. 13. 1883," chamfer-type, early model w/brass nose piece, acorn finials on both rods, three cutters, one for bead work, rare, good condition, traces of gilt paint, sliver off side of tote (ILLUS.) ..... **5,500**

**Molding plane,** cast iron, marked "Metallic Plane Co.," filletster

w/floral-decorated fence, most original finish, fine condition ...... **4,180**

*Rare Stanley No. 45 Combination Plane*

**Molding plane,** cast iron, Stanley No. 45 Combination, second Sweet Hart logo, complete w/all parts, cutters & A45 instruction manual, near new, original box w/some wear & missing stick-on aluminum label, glue spot on label, rare, fine condition (ILLUS.) **2,310**

**Molding plane,** cast iron w/100% japanning, marked "Traut Patent Hollow and Rounds - July 30, 1878," cast finger ring & front horn, pebbled handle,

*Stanley No. 41 Plane*

three pairs of bottoms & a single, earliest example using a pebbled handle, fine condition (ILLUS. bottom of page 142) ...... **6,050**

**Molding plane,** cast iron w/65% japanning, Stanley No. 43, Miller's Patent-type, Type 3, one cutter, wooden handle, good condition .................................... **220**

**Molding plane,** cast iron w/85% paint, marked "M.C. Mayo Improved Plane - Patented Sept. 14, 1875 - Boston," four brass screws each w/a letter to spell out "Mayo," w/three original cutters, wooden handle, very good condition ............................................. **6,600**

**Molding plane,** cast iron w/90% japanning, Stanley No. 41, Type 7, Miller's Patent, w/long foot depth stop, filletster bed, slitter & slitter stop, hardwood handle, good condition (ILLUS. bottom of previous page) ................................. **935**

**Molding plane,** cast iron w/85% plating, Stanley No. 141, Miller's Patent-type, slitter type, wooden handle, filletster bed, very good condition (edge chip on handle)................................................. **385**

*Metallic Plane Co. Filletster Plane*

**Molding plane,** cast iron w/90% japanning, marked "Metallic Plane Co. Filletster.," wooden handle, some minor roughness on edge of tote & very tight hairline at one rivet, rare, very good condition (ILLUS.) ........................... **3,850**

**Molding plane,** cast iron w/95% japanning, Stanley No. 41, Miller's Patent-type, Type 8 w/slitter, one cutter, slitter w/stop & filletster bed, very good condition ................................................... **880**

**Molding plane,** cast iron w/98% plating, Stanley No. 141, Miller's Patent-type, filletster bed, wooden handle, w/set of cutters in original box, fine condition, ca. 1915 (ILLUS. below)........................... **880**

**Molding plane,** cast iron w/98% plating, Stanley No. 143, Mill-

*Stanley No. 141 Miller's Patent Plane*

er's Patent-type, Sweet Hart logo, last production run w/number cast into side, wooden handle w/much original finish, fine condition ...................................................... **660**

**Molding plane,** cast iron w/nearly 100% plating, Stanley No. 45 Combination, Type 7B, rods wrapped in paper, possibly never used, in original box w/bright green label, near mint ........................ **440**

**Molding plane,** cherry, marked "H. Pratt," bead & cove, flat chamfers, very good condition, 1 1/2" w. ................................................. **275**

**Molding plane,** fruitwood, marked "C.B. Coomes," quarter-round, relieved wedge, flat chamfers, strong stamped mark, ca. 1800 or earlier, very good condition, 1 1/16" w., 9 7/8" l. ........................................... **248**

**Molding plane,** fruitwood, marked "I.T.," astragal & cove-type, perhaps initials of unlisted plane maker, good condition ........ **100**

**Molding plane,** gunmetal body & fence, Stanley No. 44, Miller's Patent-type, rare slitter type, wooden handle & set of cutters, clean w/good patina, w/custom-made walnut display, very rare, fine condition ..................................... **3,190**

**Molding plane,** gunmetal w/90% japanning, Stanley No. 42 Miller's Patent, Type 3A, filletster-type, patina on body & wraparound fence a pale copper red, ca. 1875, fine condition (ILLUS. below) ...................................... **4,070**

**Molding plane,** hardwood, cove & bead-type, marked "Rowell & Gibson, Albany," clean w/uncommon mark, 2 1/8" w. ................. **33**

**Molding plane,** hardwood, handled hollow & bead-type, very clean, ca. 1810, very good condition, 4 1/4" w. .................................. **154**

**Molding plane,** hardwood, hollow-type, marked "J.J. Angermyer," Western Pennsylvania maker, rare mark, good condition, 1 7/8" w. ...................................... **193**

**Molding plane,** hardwood, marked "Barton & Smith - Rochester" w/reverse "S," ogee & bevel, single boxing, good condition, 2 7/8" w. (a bit dark) ............. **116**

**Molding plane,** hardwood, marked "Bensen & Crannell - Albany," flat ovolo w/fillet, large

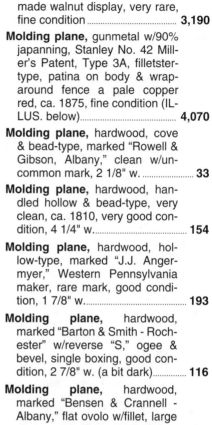

*Stanley No. 42 Molding Plane*

& unusual profile, very good condition, 3 1/16" w. ........................ **110**

**Molding plane,** hardwood, marked "C.S. See - Warranted - 3/4," C3 mark, belection-type, single boxing, very good condition (some minor stain) ...................... **127**

**Molding plane,** hardwood, marked "Columbus - Ohio - 8/8," belection-type, single boxing, tight & mint, fine condition .............. **160**

**Molding plane,** hardwood, marked "D. Heis.," A mark, torus bead & cove-type, flat chamfers, weak mark otherwise great plane, "I.SH" on side, early Lancaster, Pennsylvania maker, very good condition, 1 1/4" w., 9 7/8" l. ........................................... **325**

**Molding plane,** hardwood, marked "D (pine tree) H," fenced rabbet-type, relieved wedge, wrong iron, rare, very good condition (ILLUS. next page, second from left with other molding planes) ...................... **66**

**Molding plane,** hardwood, marked "E. Baldwin - 8/8," bead w/cove & quirk ovolo, single boxing, double wedges & irons, clean, very good condition .............. **281**

**Molding plane,** hardwood, marked "E.F. Saybold - Cini. O. - 6/8," astragal & quirk ovolo, double boxing, very good condition ....... **116**

**Molding plane,** hardwood, marked "E. & J. Evans - Rochester - 8/8," belection-type, single boxing, tight & mint, fine condition ........................................ **138**

**Molding plane,** hardwood, marked "E.W. Carpenter - 1/2," flat w/bead & quirk ovolo, triple boxed, very complex, clean, very good condition ...................... **220**

**Molding plane,** hardwood, marked "F. Nicholson Living In Wrentham.," rounded bottom, painted in old red, good condition, 9/16" w., 9 3/4" l. (opened a bit at the mouth) ...................... **715**

**Molding plane,** hardwood, marked "F. Nicholson - Living In Wrenthem," cove-type, name stamped upside down, owner stamp "IM," good condition, 1" w., 9 7/8" l. (wedge a crude replacement) .................................... **1,045**

**Molding plane,** hardwood, marked "G. Axe - Buffalo," ogee-type, also marked "J.J. Holmes" w/the Masonic emblem, good condition, 1 1/2" w. ..... **110**

**Molding plane,** hardwood, marked "Griffiths - Norwich," complex style w/extra wide profile, pull hole added & needed, very good condition, 4" w. (some stain) .............................. **468**

**Molding plane,** hardwood, marked "I. Sleeper," bead & ogee-type, wide flat chamfers & Sleeper-style wedge, single lignin vitae boxing, overall fine condition, 9 3/4" l., 2 1/8" w. (slightly dark) .............................. **300**

**Molding plane,** hardwood, marked "J. Angemyer," bead-type, rare Zelienople, Pennsylvania, maker, good condition (dark finish w/some dings) .............. **198**

**Molding plane,** hardwood, marked "J. Burt.," hollow cut-type, very rare New England maker, very good condition ............. **242**

**Molding plane,** hardwood, marked "J. & J. Gibson- Albany," astragal & quirk ogee, single boxing, very good condition, 2" w. (cleaned) .............................. **171**

**Molding plane,** hardwood, marked "J. Milton," B mark, ogee & astragal-type, ebony boxing, uncommon Cannon, New Hampshire maker, very good condition .............................. **180**

**Molding plane,** hardwood, marked "J. Morse Jr.," cove & astragal-type, Hopkinton, New Hampshire, maker, first quarter 19th c., very clean w/deep profile, very good condition, 1 5/8" w. .............................. **190**

**Molding plane,** hardwood, marked "J. T. Jones. Eagle Factory. No. 75 St. John St. Phila.,"

*Four Early Molding Planes*

E mark very strong stamp w/full eagle, side bead, rosewood boxing, very good condition, 5/8" size.................................................. **110**

**Molding plane,** hardwood, marked "JJ Angermyer," ogee w/bead & flat, rare Butler County, Pennsylvania, maker, very good condition, 1 7/8" w.................. **358**

**Molding plane,** hardwood, marked "L. Kenney.," A mark, astragal & cove-type, very uncommon maker, fine condition, 1/2 size............................. **240**

**Molding plane,** hardwood, marked "L. Swett," sash-type, relieved wedge, unlisted maker, good condition, 9 5/8" l. (ILLUS. above, second from right with other molding planes) ........................ **303**

**Molding plane,** hardwood, marked "M. Copeland. Warranted. C. Keene. L. Davenport. (all in zig zig border stamps)," special order fluting plane, cuts 3 7/8" flutes at a time, most likely used for door casings or similar work, very unusual & possibly unique, fine condition, 4 3/4" w. w/original applied fence, 14 1/2" l........................... **675**

**Molding plane,** hardwood, marked "Mander & Dillion Manf'r. Phila. Patent March 24, 1885," chamfer-type, adjustable, nickel-plated side plates, screws adjust width of cut, scarce, very good condition............ **209**

**Molding plane,** hardwood, marked "Mockridge & Francis -

Newark, NJ - 1 Inch," belection w/flat & ogee, singled boxing, unique & complex profile, very good condition, 3 1/8" w................... **352**

**Molding plane,** hardwood, marked "N. Little.," astragal & ogee-type, w/great Sleeper-type wedge, rosewood boxing, flat chamfers, early Newbury, Massachusetts maker, trained in style of Sleeper, great plane dating from last quarter of 18th c., fine condition, 9 11/16" l............. **290**

**Molding plane,** hardwood, marked "Ohio Tool Co. - 68 - 7/8," belection-type w/single boxing, tight & mint.............................. **209**

**Molding plane,** hardwood, marked "Ohio Tool Co.," belection-type w/single boxing, very good condition, 2 3/4" w................... **253**

**Molding plane,** hardwood, marked "P. Hayden - Columbus, Ohio," bevel & ogee type, single boxing, very good condition, 2 3/4" w. (slight bump on nose)................................................ **83**

**Molding plane,** hardwood, marked "P. Hayden - Columbus, Ohio," ogee w/single boxing, very good condition........................ **72**

**Molding plane,** hardwood, marked "P. Hills," round w/relieved wedge, early unlisted American maker, good condition (ILLUS. previous page, left with other molding planes).............. **193**

**Molding plane,** hardwood, marked "R. & L. Carter. Troy, N.Y.," cove & astragal 'Inch' size, 1842-46, very good condition (wood fine except for bit of rodent chew on tail edge)................. **110**

**Molding plane,** hardwood, marked "Robert Wooding.," round-type, flat chamfers, one of earliest English plane makers, London, working 1706-28, good condition, 9/16" w., 10 5/16" l. (couple of worm holes)...... **250**

**Molding plane,** hardwood, marked "S. Rowell.," A2 mark, cove & astragal-type, also marked 'INCH.,' very good condition................................................. **75**

**Molding plane,** hardwood, marked "S. Rowell. Albany.," complex molder, double boxing, nice molder w/deep cut, very good condition, 3/4 size.................... **130**

**Molding plane,** hardwood, marked "Sandusky Tool Co.," no number, lazy belection-type, good condition, 2 3/4" w. (darkened finish)................................................ **297**

**Molding plane,** hardwood, marked "T. Fugate. I.D. Conover," flat & quirk ovolo, single boxing, no location stamp, very good condition, 1 5/8" w......... **154**

**Molding plane,** hardwood, marked "Tho. Grant.," side bead-type, single boxing, good mark, very good condition.................... **50**

*Miniature Crown Molding Plane*

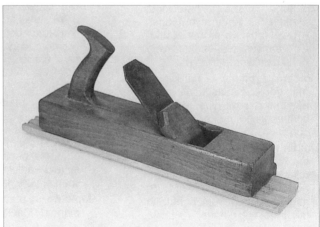

*Wooden Plane 18th Century*

**Molding plane,** hardwood, marked "W. Martin Philada.," B mark, quarter round-type, flat chamfers, classic wedge, early Philadelphia maker, good condition, 1 9/16" w., 10" l. ............................ **94**

**Molding plane,** hardwood, marked "W. Powel.," cove-type, wide flat chamfers, Pre-Revolutionary War maker from Philadelphia, extremely rare, very good condition, 1 7/16" w., 10" l. .... **800**

**Molding plane,** hardwood, marked "W.W. Bottom," ogee-type, single boxing, probably unlisted American maker, good condition ............................................. **187**

**Molding plane,** hardwood, marked "Wm Moss.," ogee & bead-type, single boxing, good condition, 3" w. ............................ **90**

**Molding plane,** hardwood, miniature size, cuts 2" crown molding, w/tote, rare & unique, slight edge chip in tote, 2 3/8" w., 10 1/2" l. (ILLUS. bottom of previous page) ...................................... **1,300**

**Molding plane,** hardwood, round top iron, wrought rivet holds check in nose together, pull handles recent addition, 18th c., good condition 5" iron, 6 3/4" overall width, 12" l. (ILLUS. above) ............................................. **358**

**Molding plane,** hardwood w/intermittent lignum vitae boxing, marked "Iacob (Jacob) Heiss," bead-type w/follower, dark finish, good condition, 1 5/8" w., 9 3/4" l. ...................................... **176**

**Molding plane,** hardwood w/rosewood boxing, marked "J. Milton," B mark, astragal w/quirk ovolo, rare Henniker, New Hampshire, maker, very good condition ............. **116**

**Molding plane,** hardwood w/rosewood boxing, marked "Robert Wooding," wide flat chamfers, applied fence removed, strong mark for very early British maker, good condition (ILLUS. p. 147 far right with other molding planes) ...................... **303**

**Molding plane,** rosewood, miniature, rounder, very good condition, 3" l. ............................................... **105**

**Molding plane,** wooden, marked "Reed - Utica," Gothic bead, double irons & wedges, good condition, 11/16" w. (chip off tail) ................................................... **154**

**Molding plane,** yellow birch, marked "CE. Chelor. Wrentham.," w/wide flat chamfers, mouth open but otherwise great example, very good condition, 9 15/16" l. ............................. **1,650**

**Molding plane,** yellow birch, marked "CE Chelor. Wrenthem.," A2 mark, narrow nosing, flat chamfers, fine example of

Cesar Chelor's work, very fine condition, 9 7/8" l. ............................ **1,950**

**Molding plane,** yellow birch, marked "E. Pierce," Roman quirk ogee, B mark, flat chamfers, early, good condition, 1 5/8" w., 9 1/16" l. (top of wedge broken off).............................. **187**

**Molding plane,** yellow birch, marked "Eli Smith, "round-type, yellow birch wedge, narrow flat chamfers, good condition, 9 1/2" l. (couple of nail holes in side) ........................................................ **110**

**Molding plane,** yellow birch, marked "F. Nicholson, Wrentham.", round-type w/wide flat chamfers, strong mark, good example first American plane maker, fine condition, 9 7/8" l. ... **1,750**

**Molding plane,** yellow birch, marked "I. Iones (Jones).," round-type w/narrow chamfers, African-American plane maker contemporary of Caesar Chelor, extremely rare maker, fine condition 1 5/16" w., 9 7/8" l. ...... **1,550**

**Molding plane,** yellow birch, marked "I. Lindenberger," A1 mark, cove & astragal-type, wide flat chamfers, wide complex molder by early maker, very good condition, 10" l., ............. **230**

**Molding plane,** yellow birch, marked "I. Lindenberger," reverse ogee & bead, early & desirable molder, very good condition, 1 13/16" w., 10" l. (two screws remain where fence removed years ago) ............................. **200**

**Molding plane,** yellow birch, marked "I. Nicholson In Wrentham.," B mark, cove & astragal-type, John Nicholson, son of F. Nicholson, first American plane maker, proper wedge, flat chamfers, dates prior to 1747, very good condition, 1 1/2" w., & 9 15/16" l ................. **1,500**

**Molding plane,** yellow birch, marked "I. Walton In Reading," ogee-type, good condition, 3/4" w., 10 1/8" l ................................. **578**

**Molding plane,** yellow birch, marked "Isaac Field - Providence," very complex w/unusual S-curve forming deep profile, very good condition, 2" w ................. **688**

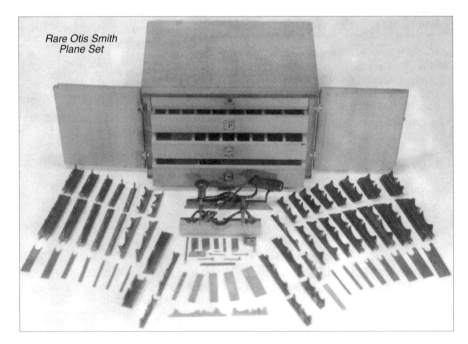

*Rare Otis Smith Plane Set*

**Molding plane,** yellow birch, marked "Jo. Fuller, Providence - 6/8," astragal & round, relieved wedge, very good condition, 1 1/2" w. .......................................... **374**

**Molding plane,** yellow birch, marked "Jo. Fuller. Providence.," D2 mark, ogee-type, flat chamfers, fine example by one of the grand masters, fine condition, 10" l. ............................. **350**

**Molding plane set,** beech handle w/brass fittings, marked "Multiform Moulding Plane Pat. Aug. 29, 1854," five wooden bodies, tongue w/adjustable fence, two beads, a dado & a rabbet, good condition, the set (one replaced wedge) .......................................... **468**

**Molding plane set,** cast iron, marked "Otis Smith - Fales Patent," combination-type w/21 sets of bottoms & many parts including spurs & attachments, in custom-made box w/four drawers probably from the Otis Smith Company, also includes original instruction sheet & bill of sale signed by Otis Smith & dated 1909, fine condition, the set (ILLUS. previous page) ......... **3,850**

**Molding planes,** carriage maker's, cast iron, Art Deco angular openwork designs, new age carriage maker tools required to add wooden detail & trim to new car bodies, classic set includes matched pair of hollow & rounds, single hollow, rabbet, & vee groove, ca. 1930, fine condition, set of five .............................. **1,150**

**Molding planes,** carriage maker's, hardwood, one tailed hollow & four round planes, unmarked, but clearly same maker, the set .......................... **210**

**Molding planes,** hardwood, marked "I.P. Holmes. Berwick, ME.," hollow & round-types, very rare Maine maker, ca. 1850, good condition, 1 3/8" w., the pr. (round w/two holes in side) .............................................. **200**

**Molding planes,** hardwood, marked "J. Milton," B mark, tongue & grooving-types, uncommon maker, good condition, matched pair ................................ **120**

**Multiform molding plane,** hardwood, marked "Multiform Molding Plane Co. Patented Aug. 29, 1854.," adjustable fence groove-type, removable rosewood handle w/brass fittings, fine condition (plane bit stained) .... **425**

**Panel plane,** cast iron, marked "A. Mathieson & Son. Glasgow.," rosewood infill, gunmetal cap, Marples iron, dovetailed body, tight mouth, good condition, iron 2 3/8" w., 13 1/2" l. (knob reglued, sides of tote tip cut square) .......................................... **425**

**Panel raiser plane,** beech, marked "I. Sleeper," produces wide flat chamfers, rosewood diamond strike button & Weldon round top iron, offset tote, very good condition, 2 1/2" w., 13 3/8" l. ...................................... **500**

**Panel raiser plane,** boxwood & iron, marked "E.W. Carpenter - March 27, 1849 - Lancaster," patented double wedges, single boxwood boxing, strong mark, great condition, massive, 6" w. w/skew cutter & wedges .............. **1,485**

**Panel raiser plane,** hardwood, marked "F. Dallicker - Montgomery Co, PA.," applied fence, good condition, 4 7/8" w. (tote cracked at base).............................. **165**

**Panel raiser plane,** hardwood, marked "John Bell," adjustable fence & stop, dark patina, very good condition, 4" w. ......................... **165**

**Panel raiser plane,** hardwood, marked "Ohio Tool Co. 114," skew cutter, wedge nicker, adjustable fence, good condition, 4 7/8" w. ............................................ **149**

**Panel raiser plane,** hardwood w/brass stop, marked "Hall, Case & Co. Columbus, Ohio," C mark, screw-arm adjustable fence, wedged nicker, very good condition, 4" w., 17" l. ............. **303**

**Patent model block plane,** cast iron, marked "Orril R. Chaplin. Patent May 7, 1872.," model for first basic patent of long produced Chapin planes, sole w/33 holes drilled to reduce friction, holes not used on production plane, no other known w/feature, includes tag from O. Rundle Gilbert's Collection of Original Patent Models, very good condition ............................ **3,300**

*Siegley Bench Plane Patent Model*

**Patent model plane,** cast iron & pine, marked "Jacob Siegley, Bench Plane. Patented July 1, 1879.," wooden combination plane model presented to US Patent Office December 6, 1878, as part of patent application for plane that later became well known Siegley plow plane, beautiful example of ingenuity from Industrial Age, pine carved w/vine design, original patent office tag remains (bit tattered), framed copies of patent papers, unique piece of American history, fine condition (ILLUS.) ............ **8,500**

**Patented Plane,** cast iron & hardwood, marked "M. B. Tidey. Ithaca" on nose, & "M.D. Tidey. Dundee" stamped on iron, adjustment mechanism for Tidey March 24, 1857, patent forerunner to Bridges/Gage planes, extremely rare w/only about three examples known, good condition, 2 1/8" iron, 16" l. ...................... **925**

**Pattern maker's plane,** aluminum body w/gunmetal screw lock cap, marked "Simplex," six wooden soles w/matching L. & I.J. White irons, high quality, fine condition ............................ **325**

**Pattern maker's plane,** gunmetal body w/mahogany infill & beech soles, three soles of varying radius, all three matching cutters, quality tool, fine condition ................ **180**

**Pattern maker's plane,** gunmetal body w/mahogany infill w/great squirrel tail design, four interchangeable wooden soles w/cutters, fine condition ..................... **170**

**Pattern maker's plane,** gunmetal, marked "A.F. White.," mahogany infill, three interchangeable soles held in place by tapered dovetails at ends, one cutter, very good condition, 6" l. ........ **100**

**Pattern maker's plane,** gunmetal w/99% japanning, small infill-type w/interchangeable wooden bottoms, mahogany stuffing, plane body, great tail handle, six soles, three cutters, very good condition, 3/4" w., overall 9" l. (front horn knob chipped) ...... **100**

**Pencil sharpening plane,** hardwood, miniature, advertising-type, printed in black "We Smooth the Way - Advertising Results Co.," patent date on end, very good condition ................. **121**

**Pencil sharpening plane,** rosewood, miniature, very good condition, 2 1/4" l. .............................. **138**

**Plane attachments,** cast iron hollows & rounds, Stanley No. 45, 90% plating, full set w/the No. 5 nosing cutter, no cutters, very good condition, the set ..................... **330**

**Plane blade set,** cast iron w/95% plating, Stanley No. 45 attachments, hollow & round blades, full set in sizes 6 to 12 w/the No. 5 nosing attachment, housed in custom-made fitted box, the set.... **825**

**Plane cutters,** cast iron, Miller's Patent Plane Cutters, Stanley Nos. 41, 42, 43 or 44, nine cutters in original box, the set............. **385**

**Plane cutters,** cast iron, Stanley for No. 55 plane, in boxes No. 4 to 8, 41 like-new cutters, cardboard boxes, fine condition, the group .......................................... **1,265**

**Plane cutters,** cast iron, Stanley Special for No. 45 plane, boxes 3, 4 & 5, total of 23 like-new cutters in original boxes, the group ... **495**

**Plane jointer fence,** hardwood, marked "Fairbank's Square Bevel Attachment for Bench Planes. Price $1.25. Patented March 19, 1861. Manufactured by Geo. A. Rollins Co. Nashua, N.H.," all on orange paper tag, clamps to side of wooden jointer, screw adjusts to desired angle, wooden knob & fence, rare, fine condition, large fence at over 10" tall .............................. **275**

**Plane jointer fence gauge,** cast iron, Stanley No. 386, near new tool in original box w/full script label, rare blue & orange store display card included, very good condition (tool dirty w/some storage spots, box worn) ....................................... **176**

**Plane jointer fence gauge,** cast iron w/100% japanning, Stanley No. 386, tool new, in original

box in Kraft color, World War II-type, fine condition ............................. **154**

**Plane & shootboard,** hardwood & cast iron, marked "O.R. Chapin's Patent," clean & mint w/nearly 95% finishes, fine condition .......................................... **3,025**

**Plank match planes,** fruitwood, marked "P. Bossart," slide arm w/edges, tongue plane w/two-piece iron riveted at the top but adjustable at bottom, good condition, pr. ............................... **176**

**Plow & matching plane,** cast iron, Stanley No. 143, bullnose-style, tool mint & unassembled, in original box w/95% picture label, rare version, fine condition (box wear) .......................................... **1,705**

**Plow & matching plane,** cast iron, Stanley No. 143, plane actually a No. 141 w/filletster bed, includes both nose pieces & nine cutters in original wooden box, in an original No. 143 box w/picture label, complete & nice, very fine condition (one box corner torn out) ..................... **2,300**

**Plow matching plane,** cast iron w/97% plating, Stanley No. 143,

*Stanley No. 143 with Original Box*

Miller's Patent type, Sweet Hart logo on skate dates plane to ca. 1925, wooden grip, in original box, fine condition, box fair (IL-LUS. previous page) ...................... **1,155**

**Plow plane,** applewood, box-wood, marked "J. Kellogg - Am-herst MS.," handled screw arm, honey-red patina, w/eight cut-ters, very good condition (cou-ple of chips) .......................................... **853**

*Rare Chapin Solon Rust Patent Plane*

**Plow plane,** applewood, marked "Chapin Solon Rust Patent Mar. 31, 1868," second model w/screw to hold adjuster arm from side of body & brass fence rods, marked w/Union Factory stamp & patent date on nose, one of only three Rust patent types to surface, good condi-tion, fence replaced (ILLUS.) ..... **1,980**

**Plow plane,** applewood, marked "Isaac Field - Providence," A mark, slide arm, wood stop, strong mark, very good condi-tion ....................................................... **138**

**Plow plane,** applewood, un-marked Chapin Solon Rust Patent Mar. 31, 1868, first mod-el w/screw to hold adjuster arm from side of body & cast-iron fence rods, marked on the nose "Pat. Applied For.," earliest Rust design, one of only two pre-patent Rust planes known, good condition (ILLUS. below).. **3,080**

**Plow plane,** beech & cast iron, marked "D. Kimberley Patent," handled, three-arm w/steel cen-ter adjusting screw, original key, good condition ................................ **297**

**Plow plane,** beech & cast iron, marked "D. Kimberley Patent," unhandled, three-arm w/steel center adjusting screw, good condition ................................................ **275**

**Plow plane,** beech, marked "A. Smith. Rehoboth.," B mark, slide arm, hard to find, very good condition ...................................... **248**

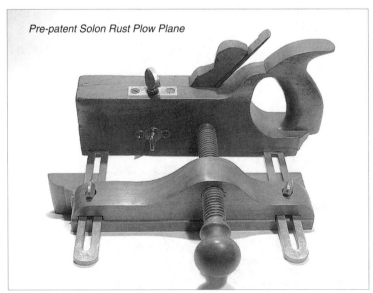

*Pre-patent Solon Rust Plow Plane*

*Early Alender Peeler Plow Plane*

**Plow plane,** beech, marked "Alender Peeler.," wedge w/arm, flat chamfers, distinctive wedge profile, ca. 1790s, very good condition (ILLUS.)...................... **880**

**Plow plane,** beech, marked "C. Keene," slide arm w/wedge locks, unusual depth-stop locking screw, brass depth stop, Maine connection, good condition........................................................ **99**

**Plow plane,** beech, marked "D.P. Sanborn. Littleton.," B1 mark, unhandled, screw lock arm, all

boxwood fence, distinctive thumb screws, wooden depth stop, screws holding skate retain most of original bluing, never oiled or touched, near new, fine condition ...................................... **325**

*Carpenter Patented Plow Plane*

*Early Beech Girffiths Plow Plane*

**Plow plane,** beech, marked "E.W. Carpenter's Improved Arms Patent. Lancaster.," boxwood arms, washers & nuts, w/set of irons, butterfly dovetail let into the tail, very clean, rare patented plow plane, very good condition (ILLUS. right previous page)....... **1,650**

**Plow plane,** beech, marked "Griffins. Norwick.," bridle-style, vee-arms, original rosewood knob, rare, very good condition (ILLUS. bottom of previous page)... **440**

**Plow plane,** beech, marked "H. Libhart.," wedge arm, wide flat chamfers, hand-wrought metal parts, believed to be a Pennsylvania maker, ca. 1800, very good condition ...................................... **330**

**Plow plane,** beech, marked "I. Lindenberger.," slide arm, flat chamfers, uncommon, ca. 1800, good condition ......................... **275**

**Plow plane,** beech, marked "I. Sleeper," slide arm, Sleeper-style wedge, good condition (one replaced thumbscrew)............ **193**

**Plow plane,** beech, marked "I. Teal," A mark, wedge arm, brass depth stop, near mint............... **77**

*Very Rare Israel White Plow Plane*

**Plow plane,** beech, marked "Israel White - No. 106," handled three-arm style w/ivory tips & scales, brass & steel fence rollers, ebony slide arms, one of two known, professionally restored, couple of light burn marks, very good condition (ILLUS.)........................ **21,450**

**Plow plane,** beech, marked "Israel White," unhandled, screw arm, good condition .............................. **99**

*Extremely Rare Israel White Plow Plane*

**Plow plane,** beech, marked "Israel White. Warranted. Philada. - Patent J.E. (over eagle)....," three-arm style, beech body, fence, side arms, & inner lock washer, birch center screw arm, lignum vitae dovetailed fence boxing, boxwood outer lock nut & rosewood wedge, ivory trim w/fine 5" inset scale on front arm, 1" inset depth-stop scale & two ivory finials, original paper label on upper nose, sharp impressed mark, extremely rare, Philadelphia, 1830s, finest example known (ILLUS.)............... **31,900**

**Plow plane,** beech, marked "J.H. Lamb. New Bedford.," handled, screw arm, boxwood arms, nuts & washers, little used, fine condition............................................ **330**

**Plow plane,** beech, marked "Jo. Fuller - Providence," screw lock-arm-type, relieved wedge, wooden depth stop, good condition ...................................................... **154**

**Plow plane,** beech, marked "M.H. Milton Canaan, NH," slide arm, unusual metal depth stop w/wooden thumbscrew, strong mark, rare New Hampshire maker, very good condition............. **110**

**Plow plane,** beech, marked "Palmer.," flat chamfer, carved thumbscrews, New England, ca. 1800, very good condition................................................. **578**

**Plow plane,** beech, marked "R. Harwood.," slide arm, very clean, ca. 1820, very good condition ........................................... **176**

**Plow plane,** beech, marked "S. Chase," slide arm, Sleeper-style wedge, rare New Hampshire maker ................................. **1,045**

**Plow plane,** beech, marked "S. Pomeroy - N+Hampton," slide arm, only example w/location mark known, ca. 1800, very good condition ............................... **660**

**Plow plane,** beech, marked "Sandusky Tool Co. Ohio. No. 119.," beech handle, Elmer Coons' name on side, clean & nice, very good condition (threads clean, w/couple minor chips) ............................................. **290**

**Plow plane,** beech, marked "Solan Rust Patent Mar. 31, 1868 Three Arm Plow. H. Chapin No. 238 1/2," steel screw adjuster, patent information on the side, very rare, good condition (side of wedge dinged) ................. **1,980**

**Plow plane,** beech, marked "Wm. Souder Phidada." w/an eagle, unhandled, screw arm w/brass ferrules on the nuts, rare Philadelphia plane, very good condition ....... **121**

**Plow plane,** beech, marked "Wm. Woodard - Taunton," A mark, slide arm, stamped mark weak, hard-to-find mark, ca. 1820, good condition ............................ **50**

**Plow plane,** beech w/boxwood arms, marked "E. & T. Ring," screw arm, handled, good condition ...................................... **220**

**Plow plane,** beech w/boxwood arms, nuts & washers, marked "A.T. Knapp 1854," moving filletster, screw arm, handled, unusual top escapement, brass depth stop straddles arm, all parts numbered, very good condition ................................................... **286**

**Plow plane,** beech w/boxwood nuts & washers, marked "Israel White," "D.H." bench hand stamp, good condition (few thread chips) ............................. **121**

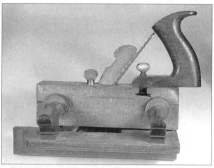

*Multiform Moulding Plane Co. Plow Plane*

**Plow plane,** beech w/detachable rosewood handle, marked "Multiform Moulding Plane Co. Patented Aug. 29, 1854," screw arms, rare, very good condition, few thread chips (ILLUS.) ............. **1,540**

**Plow plane,** beech w/ebony wear strips let into the arms, marked "R. Ionson," double stamp in tee design, fine quality early tool by Johnson, a Connecticut River maker in southern Vermont & New Hampshire, ca. 1800, very good condition .................................. **1,485**

*Unmarked Carpenter Plow Plane*

**Plow plane,** beech w/patented brass handle fittings, unmarked E.W. Carpenter, Lancaster, handled, arms set so far back on body that wood between handle hole & arm holes needs reinforcement, which may account for lack of Carpenter's name, good condition w/minor thread chips (ILLUS.) ................... **1,155**

*Unique Ohio Tool Co. Plow Plane*

*Solon Rust Self-Adjusting Plow Plane*

**Plow plane,** beech w/rosewood arms, marked "Chapin Solon Rust Patented Self-Adjusting No. 236 1/4.," steel bridle w/center screw for adjusting, only a couple of stains, good condition (ILLUS.) ............................ **1,100**

**Plow plane,** beech w/six ivory tips w/ball finials, marked "Ohio Tool Co.," center-wheel self-regulator, believed to be earliest known Ohio-made center-wheel or practice piece because of low grade of wood used (beech most often used for working tools without ivory embellishments), center rod & wheel turned from single piece of wood, fence-locking screw located to side of tote instead of top of plane, bridge between fence rods a special shape w/two delicate points at ends of top arch, single-piece screw wheel/rod & bridge design are known on other center-wheels, but side fence-screw lock believed to be unique to this plane, very good condition (ILLUS. above) ................................ **15,950**

**Plow plane,** birch, Yankee-style, bone wear plates for the arms & depth stop screws, flat chamfers, great wedge, showy, fine condition, 18th c. ............................. **358**

*Sandusky Tool Co. 133 Plow Plane*

**Plow plane,** boxwood & ivory, marked "Sandusky Tool Co. 133," all boxwood w/4 ivory tips, handled screw arm, set of 6 Sandusky blades in a roll, very clean & nice, very good condition (ILLUS.) ..................................... **1,540**

**Plow plane,** boxwood, marked "Auburn Tool Co.," all boxwood w/two ivory tips, handled screw arm, crown-like tips held on with what appear to be original screws, cleaned to great light amber patina, good condition (ILLUS. bottom of page) ............... **1,100**

**Plow plane,** boxwood, marked "C. Warren. Nashua.," unhandled, all boxwood w/great tiger stripe, very good condition (minor thread chips) ............................... **280**

*"DeForest - Birmingham" Plow Plane*

**Plow plane,** boxwood, marked "DeForest - Birmingham," unhandled, screw arm, deep honey-amber patina, fine condition (ILLUS.) ..................................... **523**

*Auburn Tool Co. Plow Plane*

*Rare Patented 1838 Plow Plane*

**Plow plane,** boxwood, marked "E.W. Carpenter's Patent Improved Arms - Lancaster," w/adjustable arms, 1838, rare, good condition w/no chipping on threads (ILLUS.) .................. **3,500**

*Ohio Tool Co. 105 Plow Plane*

**Plow plane,** boxwood, marked "Ohio Tool Co. 105," four ivory tips, great honey-amber patina, very good condition, couple minor chips (ILLUS.) .............................. **935**

**Plow plane,** boxwood, marked "Ohio Tool Co. 105," handled screw arm, fine honey-brown patina, very good condition ............. **572**

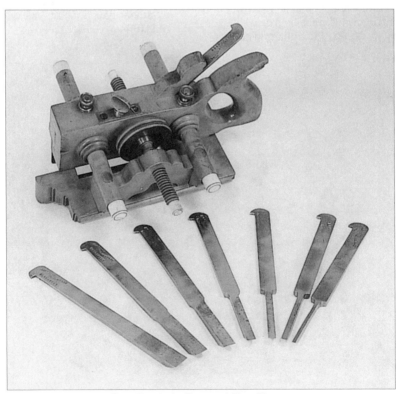

*Rare Sandusky Boxwood Plow Plane*

*"Pond, Malcolm & Welles - New Haven" Plow Plane*

**Plow plane,** boxwood, marked "Pond, Malcolm & Welles - New Haven," screw arm, arms end in turnip finials, light honey-amber patina, uncommon maker, very good condition (ILLUS.) .................... **385**

**Plow plane,** boxwood, marked "Sandusky Tool Co. Ohio 141," center-wheel self-regulating type, six ivory tips, brass center wheel, honey amber patina, includes a set of eight marked Sandusky irons, good condition, minor wear on edge of tote tip & wedge (ILLUS. bottom of previous page) ............................................. **9,350**

**Plow plane,** boxwood, Ohio Tool Co. marked only w/model number "No. 104," handled, screw arm, dark, even, honey-amber patina (some chips) ............................ **220**

*Ohio Tool Co. 110 Plow Plane*

**Plow plane,** boxwood, unmarked Ohio Tool Co. 110, marked only w/number, wooden adjuster wheel on center stem, rare, very good condition, some nicks & bangs (ILLUS.) ................................... **3,190**

*Sandusky Tool Co. Plow Plane*

**Plow plane,** boxwood w/brass wheel, marked "Sandusky Tool Co. Ohio. 140," self-regulating center-wheel type, fine condition, small flake on spindle at wheel (ILLUS.) ................................... **6,380**

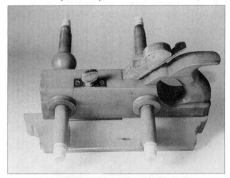

*Extremely Rare L. Hawes Plow Plane*

**Plow plane,** boxwood w/four ivory tips, marked "LH" for L. Hawes, w/handle, extremely rare, mark identical to only other known Hawes plane marked both w/initials & maker's name, very good condition w/very minor thread chips (ILLUS.) ................................... **1,815**

**Plow plane,** boxwood w/four ivory tips, marked "Ohio Tool Co. 105," handled, w/eight Ohio Tool Co. irons, very good condition (a few necks & bangs) .............. **825**

*W.F. Dominich & Co. Plow Plane*

**Plow plane,** boxwood w/four ivory tips, marked "W.F. Dominich & Co. 105," w/handle, uncommon Chicago mark, good color, very good condition w/one small thread chip (ILLUS.) .................. **1,073**

**Plow plane,** boxwood w/four ivory tips, unhandled, screw arm, good condition (couple chips) ....... **523**

**Plow plane,** boxwood w/good tiger stripe, marked "Edward Carter Troy - NY," unhandled, good condition (a few chips) .......... **143**

*Unmarked Hall, Case & Co. Plow Plane*

**Plow plane,** boxwood w/honey amber patina, ivory tips, unmarked, no handle, eight irons all marked "Hall, Case & Co.," fine condition w/one small thread chip & traces of original ink price on nose & tail (ILLUS.) ... **908**

*Sandusky Tool Co. Plow Plane*

**Plow plane,** boxwood w/light tiger stripe, marked "Sandusky Tool Co. 133," handled, w/four ivory tips, very good condition, few minor chips (ILLUS.) ........................ **990**

**Plow plane,** boxwood w/rosewood wedge, nuts, washers & fence, marked "E.W. Carpenter's Patent Improved Arms - Lancaster," unhandled, also marked "Patented Feb. 6, 1838," tail stamped "Wm. McClure, 287 Market St. Phila.," hardware dealer, w/six irons, good condition (couple of chips on adjuster nuts) ............................. **3,300**

*Carriage Maker's Plow Plane.*
*I Sym. 1753-1802*

**Plow plane,** carriage maker's, hardwood, marked "I Sym.," earliest example of carriage maker's plow w/adjustable fence, plane predates Falconer by at least 30 years, only two examples known & both collected in England many years ago, importance of this plow cannot be overstated, ca. 1800, rarest English plow, fine condition (ILLUS. previous page) .................. **10,450**

*Rare Patented Scissors-Arm Plow Plane*

**Plow plane,** cast iron, marked "E.H. Morris Patent Mr. 31, 1871," scissors-arm style, rare design, fence w/80% of original h.p. flower decoration, four original irons, ca. 1887, good condition (ILLUS.) ................ **6,600**

**Plow plane,** cast iron, marked "Howkins Plane Model B," British patent, complete w/seven cutters, part of original catalog & wooden box, good condition, the group .............................................. **550**

**Plow plane,** cast iron, marked "Loughborough Patent Iron Plow. Patented May 3, 1864," earlier attempt at an iron plow, cast-iron fence locked in place w/single screw & wedge device, three loose pieces & the screw, plow unmarked & may pre-date Telford's involvement in production of Loughborough patents, early Rochester, New York designer, very rare, good condition (ILLUS. below) ...................... **16,500**

**Plow plane,** cast iron, marked "Siegley," combination-type, finishes & wood handle good, depth stop made from old bolt, very good condition ............................ **275**

**Plow plane,** cast iron, Stanley No. 248 Weather Strip Plow Plane, apparently never assembled, five cutters & original sheet on weather stripping tools & information on rare No. 78W plane, w/original box & label, mid-1930s, fine condition (box a bit banged, label w/piece out of top edge) ........................................................ **250**

**Plow plane,** cast iron w/55% paint, marked "Phillips Patent Plow," improved model, two cutters, long & short depth stops, oval Boston Tool Co. logo on skate, very good condition .............. **880**

**Plow plane,** cast iron w/80% plating, marked "Rapier," light plow w/two cutters, mahogany fence facing, good condition ............................ **75**

**Plow plane,** cast iron w/80% plating, Stanley No. 50, adjustable cutters, long depth stop, w/17 cutters in original box (chip on deflector) ........................................................ **99**

*Loughborough Patent Iron Plow*

*Miller's Patent Plane*

**Plow plane,** cast iron w/85% japanning, Stanley No. 43, Type 7, Miller's Patent, wooden handle w/sliver off top, one cutter, w/custom-made storage box (no depth stops)...................................... **275**

**Plow plane,** cast iron w/95% copper wash, Miller's Patent light plow-type, marked w/patent date of September 17, 1872 in oval on fence, w/four original cutters, original & proper, very good condition (ILLUS. above) **12,100**

*Jacob Siegley Plow Plane*

**Plow plane,** cast iron w/nearly 100% japanning, marked "Jacob Siegley. Patented Aug. 10,

1881 & Feb. 10, 1891.," wooden handle, w/set of 21 cutters in new wooden box, short & long rods, fine condition (ILLUS.)............ **682**

*Rare Beech Coach Maker's Plane*

**Plow plane,** coach maker's, beech & brass, marked "S. Perrin," unusual router style, brass wear & top plate w/adjustable brass fence, rare, fine condition (ILLUS.) ...................................... **605**

**Plow plane,** coach maker's, ebonized wood body w/inlaid brass plates & adjustable brass fence, marked "CK," adjustable

depth stop, early 19th c., good
condition ................................................ **3,300**

*Boxwood Plow Plane*

**Plow plane,** coach maker's-type,
boxwood, curved skate & fence,
honey-amber patina, very good
condition (ILLUS.)............................ **1,705**

**Plow plane,** coach maker's-type,
cast iron body w/wedge w/wood-
en tail, early & well made, good
condition (ILLUS. below).................. **165**

**Plow plane,** curly boxwood,
marked "C. Morehouse - New
Haven," screw arm, unhandled,
uncommon maker, very good
condition...................................................... **385**

*Plow Plane No. 52*

**Plow plane,** ebony & boxwood,
marked "No. 52," ebony w/box-
wood arms & nuts, showy, jet

*Coach Maker's-type
Plow Plane*

black w/dark brown strips, one cracked washer, very good condition (ILLUS. bottom previous page) ........................................................ **1,540**

*Sandusky Tool Co. Ebony Plow Plane*

**Plow plane,** ebony & ivory, marked "Sandusky Tool Co. Ohio. 137," all ebony w/four ivory tips, handled screw arm, tips bright & ebony jet black, very clean, very good condition (ILLUS.) ................. **5,720**

**Plow plane,** ebony, ivory & rosewood, marked "Ohio Tool Co. 108 (overstamped) 9." ebony w/four ivory tips & rosewood arms, handled screw arm, 7 irons, couple of thread chips, overall fine, good condition (ILLUS. below) .............. **1,540**

*Plow Plane with Shipping Box*

**Plow plane,** ebony w/four ivory tips & boxwood arms, marked "A. Howland - No. 100," w/original wooden shipping box & eight irons, only known example of plow plane shipping box, fine condition (ILLUS.) ........................... **7,480**

**Plow plane,** ebony w/four ivory tips, marked "Sandusky Tool Co. 137," handled, screw arm, rare, good condition (few chips & dings) ............................................. **4,180**

*Ohio Tool Co. 108 Plow Plane*

*Ebony Plow Plane*

**Plow plane,** ebony, wedge arm w/brass tip, ebony plow planes hard to find, very good condition, chip along bottom edge of one arm (ILLUS.) .............................. **578**

**Plow plane,** French coach maker's-type, fruitwood, fenced, cast iron skate & wear plates, traditional wing nuts for fence-locking & depth-stop adjustment, early 19th c., very good condition .......................................... **358**

**Plow plane,** fruitwood, marked "J. Gallup," carved thumbscrews, double-struck mark, early & important, ca. 1790, very good condition ....................................... **880**

**Plow plane,** gunmetal w/100% original copper brown patina, marked "Miller's 1872 Patent Plow Plane.," light combination plow later became Stanley No. 50, "T. Judd." stamped in oval on fence, ca. 1870s, owned by same family for many years, perfect & complete in every detail, rare & in finest condition ... **23,500**

**Plow plane,** gunmetal w/nearly 100% japanning filling recessed detail, marked "Miller's Patent Plane. Plow Plane. Patented June 28, 1870. Stanley Rule & Level Co. No. 42," w/hook above tote, nine cutters w/filletster bed, in original wooden box w/quarter-size portion of original paper label, only three of these hooked gunmetal planes are known, this is the only one

in its previously unknown type of box allowing the plane to be stored fully assembled, fine condition .......................................... **17,600**

**Plow plane,** hardwood, carved mouth carved "M.G. 1854," small size, very good condition, 7" l. (some worm holes) .................... **440**

**Plow plane,** hardwood, fine ram's horn nuts, Dutch Ploeg-type, owner-stamped in several places "F (fleur-de-lis) M," carved date "1747" enclosed by carving, important early tool, very good condition .............................. **440**

**Plow plane,** hardwood, marked "A. Sampson - Portland," screw arm, unhandled, rarest "A" mark w/Portland location, Maine, first half 19th c., dark, good condition ....................................................... **55**

**Plow plane,** hardwood, marked "C. Lindenberger," wedge arm w/wooden depth stop, rare Ohio maker, good condition ......................... **99**

**Plow plane,** hardwood, marked "Collins - Hartford," friction-fit arms w/screw locks, ca. 1800, very good condition ............................. **220**

*Small E.W. Carpenter Plow Plane*

**Plow plane,** hardwood, marked "E.W. Carpenter. Lancaster.," unhandled, wedge arm, small size, probably made for a carriage maker, very good condition, 7" l. (ILLUS.) ................................ **825**

*"Griffiths - Norwich" Plow Plane*

**Plow plane,** hardwood, marked "Griffiths - Norwich," wedge arm, arm wedge & cutter wedge made of bone, England, 19th c., good condition (ILLUS.).................. **231**

**Plow plane,** hardwood, marked "H. Wetherell. Chatham (w/double crowns)," flat chamfers, wooden stop, fancy filigree on riveted skate, early period Yankee-style, ca. 1790, good condition.............................................. **495**

**Plow plane,** hardwood, marked "H. Wetherell. Chatham. (w/double crowns)," rounded chamfers, wooden stop, late period Yankee-style, ca. 1805, good condition ........................................ **77**

**Plow plane,** hardwood, marked "H. Wetherell. Chatham. (w/double crowns)," rounded chamfers, wooden stop, fence extends beyond body, middle-period Yankee-style, ca. 1900, good condition ....................................... **358**

*"I. Clark" Plow Plane*

**Plow plane,** hardwood, marked "I. Clark," w/wedge arm, brass washers for fence bolts run length of arm & are graduated, brass fittings & tips, good condition (ILLUS.)........................................... **165**

**Plow plane,** hardwood, marked "J.R. Tolman - Hanover, Mass.," vee or hawk plane used to strike the paint line around the sides of a ship, steel wear plate on sole, uncommon type, very good condition ..................................... **204**

**Plow plane,** hardwood, marked "Ohio Tool Co. 96 1/2," handled screw arm, marked w/the globe logo, clean, very good condition, together w/eight Ohio Tool irons, the group .................................... **270**

**Plow plane,** hardwood, marked "Spayd & Bell. Philada.," B mark, screw arm, unhandled, rare plane from the short-lived partnership of John Spayd & John Bell, very good condition (chip off tail of fence) ........................ **450**

**Plow plane,** hardwood, screw lock arm type w/riveted skate, hand-cut brass screws hold fence to arms, depth stop locked by thumbscrew, good condition, 18th c. (some minor damage on thumbscrews) ................ **85**

**Plow plane,** heavy lesser grade rosewood, handled, brass center wheel, unmarked but crafts-man-made, probably in New York State, fine condition............. **3,740**

*Unique Plane with Celluloid Tips*

**Plow plane,** Honduras rosewood, brass & celluloid, marked "Sandusky Tool Co. Ohio.," nose stamped "140," then over-stamped "141," brass center-wheel w/four original celluloid tips, believed to be one of the last center-wheels made in Ohio, w/full set of Sandusky

irons, unique in that celluloid is seldom found in tools, fine condition (ILLUS.)..................................... **8,800**

*M. B. Tidey Tiger Stripe Plow Plane*

**Plow plane,** maple, rosewood & copper, marked "M. B. Tidey," tiger stripe maple w/rosewood nuts, washers & wedge, handled screw arm, backer plate for skate copper, not brass, tip of tote rounded, very showy tool, very good condition (ILLUS.) ......... **770**

*Sandusky Center Wheel Plow Plane*

**Plow plane,** rosewood body & wedge w/boxwood arms & fence, marked "Sandusky Center Wheel No. 140.," both A & C marks on nose, brass center adjuster wheel, self regulator-type, brass trim a mellow color, rare, fine condition (ILLUS.).................. **7,000**

**Plow plane,** rosewood handle w/boxwood arms & rosewood wedge, different design, nice color, good condition (threads w/minor chips) .................................... **325**

**Plow plane,** rosewood, ivory & brass, marked "Sandusky Tool

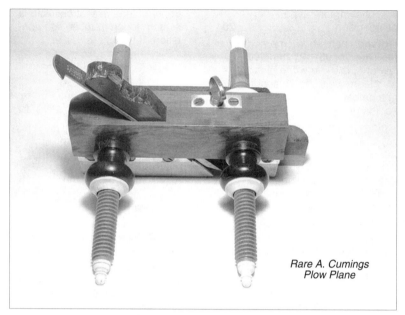

*Rare A. Cumings Plow Plane*

Co. No. 138.," unhandled self-regulating or three-arm plow, six ivory tips, four on arms, two on center screw spindle, brass depth stop & center adjusting wheel, rarest of rare Sandusky Center Wheels, full set of eight Sandusky irons w/fitted box, very good condition (some shrinkage checks, few nicks & bangs)................................ **9,500**

*Ohio Tool Co. 105 Plow Plane*

**Plow plane,** rosewood & ivory, marked "Ohio Tool Co. 105.," rosewood w/four ivory tips, marked w/uncommon plane logo stamp, handled screw arm, one washer reinforced w/copper rings, good condition (ILLUS.)................................ **825**

**Plow plane,** rosewood, marked "Auburn Tool Co. Auburn, N.Y. 96.," body w/about half lighter colored sap wood for very striking contrast, boxwood arms, nuts & washers, handled, very good condition (very minor thread chips), ........................ **775**

**Plow plane,** rosewood, marked "G.W. Denison & Co. Winthop, Conn.," handle w/boxwood arms, nuts & washers, showy, very good condition............................. **715**

**Plow plane,** rosewood, marked "J. Kellogg - Amherst, MS," boxwood wedge arms, nuts & washers, unhandled, boxed fence, good condition......................... **242**

**Plow plane,** rosewood, marked "Ohio Tool Co. No. 110.," self-adjusting center wheel, w/full set of irons, very good condition ...... **4,620**

**Plow plane,** rosewood, marked "Ohio Tool Co.," screw arm, not numbered but appears to be No. 104, good condition ................... **303**

**Plow plane,** rosewood, marked "Union Factory - H. Chapin No. 240 1/2," boxwood nuts, arms & wedge, handled, screw arm, good condition (a few chips).......... **330**

**Plow plane,** rosewood w/boxwood arms & fence boxing, marked "A. Cumings. Boston.," two-piece nuts & washers of rosewood & ivory, arm tips finished w/ivory, outbound set of ivory tips turned w/acorn finials, silver plated metal parts, near-new, rare, chip on wedge but fine condition (ILLUS. top of previous page) ................... **6,600**

**Plow plane,** rosewood w/boxwood arms, marked "Winsted Plane Co. Warranted," handled, very clean, very good condition (minor chips) ............................. **495**

**Plow plane,** rosewood w/boxwood arms, Masonic presentation plane, handled, decorated w/inlays of ivory & silver, dividers w/square on one side of body & "FM" w/shield on other, both in ivory, top of tote decorated w/silver sunburst & square, good condition (ILLUS. below) ..... **798**

**Plow plane,** rosewood w/boxwood arms, nuts, washers & fence boxing, marked "J.E. Boker & Co. Boston.," handled, very striking, arm threads near perfect, fine condition .............................. **600**

**Plow plane,** rosewood w/boxwood arms, nuts & washers & four ivory tips, marked "D.R. Barton. Rochester.," unhandled, fine condition (chip off one tip & a couple thread chips) ........ **1,200**

*Greenfield Tool Co. No. 535 Plane*

**Plow plane,** rosewood w/boxwood arms, nuts & washers, marked "Greenfield Tool Co. No. 535," screw arm, very good condition, couple of chips (ILLUS.) ..................... **264**

*G.W. Denison & Co. Plow Plane*

**Plow plane,** rosewood w/boxwood arms, nuts & washers, nickel-

*Masonic Presentation Plow Plane*

*Lamb & Brownell Plow Plane*

plated fittings, marked "G.W. Denison & Co. Winthrop, Conn.," handled, very good condition w/a couple thread chips (ILLUS. bottom previous page) ..... **825**

**Plow plane,** rosewood w/boxwood arms, nuts, washers, wedge & fence, marked "C. Warren. Nashua.," unhandled, fine condition (minor nick on leading edge of body & on fence nose) ...................................................... **625**

**Plow plane,** rosewood w/boxwood arms, nuts, washers, wedge & fence, marked "J. Bracelin. Hynson. St. Louis.," A mark w/very weak Hynson Hardware Company mark, handled, fence extra long extending 1 1/2" beyond body, possibly a special order, hang hole drilled in fence, very good condition (minor thread chips) ......................... **400**

**Plow plane,** rosewood w/boxwood arms, wedges & fence, marked "Lamb & Brownell - New Bedford," three-piece nuts w/ivory inside & out, ivory washers w/boxwood centers, silver

plated metal fittings, screws retain much original bluing, top-of-the-line plane, Massachusetts, fine condition (ILLUS. above) .... **7,260**

*Rare Plow Plane by Taber Plane Co.*

**Plow plane,** rosewood w/boxwood arms, silver fittings, two fine ivory acorn finials & split rosewood & ivory nuts & washers, marked "Taber Plane Co. New Bedford, Mass.," rare model offered in Taber Company catalog but this is only example to surface, threads & body near perfect , very slightest dings on fence (ILLUS.) ............................... **6,500**

*Greenfield Tool Co. No. 549 Plane*

**Plow plane,** rosewood w/boxwood nuts, arms & washers, marked "Greenfield Tool Co. No. 549," handled, very good condition, few chips (ILLUS.) ........ **468**

*Highly Figured Lamb & Brownell Plow Plane*

**Plow plane,** rosewood w/boxwood nuts, arms, washers & wedge, marked "Lamb & Brownell - New

Bedford," highly figured rosewood, retains most of the original finish, fence screw w/nearly 100% bluing, Massachusetts, fine condition (ILLUS.) .................. **1,925**

**Plow plane,** rosewood w/boxwood nuts, marked "Gladwin & Appleton, Boston," handled, good condition (replaced wedge) ........................................ **440**

**Plow plane,** rosewood w/four ivory tips, marked "J. Bracelin - Dayton - No. 105," handled, rare Ohio maker, very good condition (a few dings) ................. **1,815**

**Plow plane,** rosewood w/ivory nuts & washers, handled, screw arm, unmarked but may have had presentation plate, wood fine, no ivory cracks (ILLUS. bottom of page) ...................................... **5,720**

*Fine Early Rosewood Plow Plane*

**Plow plane,** rosewood w/ivory tips, handled, screw arm, un-

*Rosewood & Ivory
Plow Plane*

signed but fine quality, few thread chips, edges of nuts very thin w/minor dings, good condition (ILLUS. previous page) .......... **468**

**Plow plane,** rosewood w/two ivory tips, marked "Auburn Tool Co. No. 97," unhandled, boxwood arms, nuts & washers, very good condition (a few nicks & bangs) ..................................... **963**

**Plow plane,** solid rosewood body, wedge & tote, Badger-style, very good condition, 3 x 3 1/4" in section, 18" l. ................................... **250**

*Tiger Stripe Boxwood Plow Plane*

**Plow plane,** tiger stripe boxwood w/ivory tips, unmarked except for ink code on nose, handled, very good condition (ILLUS.) ......... **990**

**Plow plane,** wood & handwrought iron, Dutch Ploeg-type, fine wrought wing nuts, friction arms on body, screw locks on fence, 18th c., good condition ....... **132**

*Rare 'D' Mark Plow Plane*

**Plow plane,** wood & ivory, marked "H. Wetherell. Glastonbury. Chatham. 1811.," date underlined w/bar of ivory, thumbscrews, extremely rare 'D' mark, very clean w/even patina, very good condition (ILLUS.) ......... **770**

*C. E. Chelor Plow Plane*

**Plow plane,** yellow birch, marked "C. E. Chelor, Living In Wrentham. A*M." thumbscrew style, strong mark, fence & body both marked w/a '2,' early use of assembly numbers, nice plow, very good condition (ILLUS.) ..... **5,940**

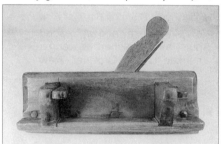

*Very Early Nicholson Plow Plane*

**Plow plane,** yellow birch, marked "F. Nicholson," earliest Nicholson mark, old wedge of coarse-grained wood possibly original, ends w/steps & bold chisel cuts similar to English planes of early 18th c. & unlike Nicholson's other planes, which have lamb's-tongue chamfer ends, does not bear Wrentham location mark, so believed to have been made before Nicholson moved to Wren-

them in 1728, very good condition
(ILLUS. previous page)................. **5,060**

*Rare John Nicholson Plow Plane*

**Plow plane,** yellow birch, marked
"I. (J.) Nicholson In Cumberland.," wedge arm, extremely
rare Cumberland mark, very
good condition (ILLUS.)............... **3,740**

*Rare Early I. Jones Plow Plane*

**Plow plane,** yellow birch, marked
"I. Jones.," slide arms w/fancy
thumbscrews, wooden depth
stop w/finger grips, early & important tool by early African-
American plane maker from
Massachusetts, ca.   1764-67,
very good condition (ILLUS.)...... **2,750**

**Plow plane,** yellow birch, marked
"Jo. Fuller," A mark, flat chamfers, relieved wedge, very good
condition ..................................................... **385**

*Early L. Sampson Plow Plane*

**Plow plane,** yellow birch, marked
"L. Sampson.," B mark, Yankee-style, pre-1800, very good
condition (ILLUS.) ............................... **330**

**Plow plane blades,** cast iron,
Stanley No. 50 Light Plow Plane-
type, early no-notch-type, 15
irons in wooden case, the set.......... **83**

**Plow plane irons,** cast steel,
marked "Sandusky Tool Co. Extra Cast Steel Plow Bits," seven
of eight original cutters all
marked "Sandusky," cutters
bright & shiny, original box retains full top & end labels, fine
condition, the set (missing 1/4"
cutter, box well worn).......................... **725**

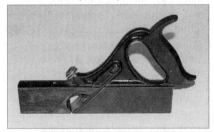

*Stanley No. 42 Type 4 Plane*

**Plow/filletster plane,** gunmetal
w/90% japanning on plow fence
& filletster bed, Stanley No. 42,
Type 4, Miller's Patent type,
cast iron wrap-around fence, six
cutters, patina on body a pale
copper red to gold, ca. 1876,
very good condition, sliver off
side of tote (ILLUS.)........................ **1,100**

*Stanley No. 39 Prototype Plane*

**Prototype plane,** cast iron w/90%
japanning, walnut handle & infill,
Stanley No. 39 prototype used in
development of No. 39 dado
planes, this plane known in two

different styles, this model being the second type w/reinforced-handle design, very rare, very good condition (ILLUS. previous page) ...................... **7,260**

*Early Tiger Stripe Maple Pump Plane*

**Pump plane,** tiger stripe maple, cuts half a circle at a time, very strong striping, pull handle, very good condition (ILLUS.) ................... **165**

**Rabbet block plane,** cast iron, Stanley No. 140, mint & unused, in original unusual grey craft-color box w/perfect Sweet Hart label, mint & boxed, ca. 1920s ................................... **468**

**Rabbet & filletster plane,** cast iron w/92% japanning, Stanley No. 278, Type 1, patent-dated cutter, all parts proper, very good condition ................................ **440**

**Rabbet plane,** aluminum, Stanley No. A78, Sweet Hart logo, duplex-type, all parts appear original, clean w/no pitting, very good condition ................................ **300**

**Rabbet plane,** cabinetmaker's, cast iron, Stanley No. 97, near new, in original box w/full label, fine condition (some storage stain on plane bottom, box w/light edge wear) ..................... **605**

**Rabbet plane,** cabinet maker's, cast iron w/100% plating, Stanley No. 92, new & unused .............. **132**

**Rabbet plane,** cabinet maker's, cast iron w/100% plating, Stanley No. 93, like-new .......................... **132**

**Rabbet plane,** cabinet maker's, cast iron w/93% plating, Stanley No. 94, early type w/applied sole & patent-dated cutter, very good condition ...................................... **308**

**Rabbet plane,** cabinet maker's, cast iron w/95% japanning, Stanley No. 10 1/2, wooden handle, 3/8" of blade left, ca. 1900 ........................................................ **116**

**Rabbet plane,** carriage maker's, cast iron w/100% japanning, marked "Keen Kutter No. KK 10 1/2," near mint ........................... **1,155**

**Rabbet plane,** carriage maker's, cast iron w/45% japanning, Stanley No. 10 1/2, type 1 w/adjustable mouth, wood handle fine, 1/4" of iron remains, good condition (front knob washer broken) ........................................... **187**

**Rabbet plane,** carriage maker's, cast iron w/80% japanning, Stanley No. 101/2, B casting, corrugated bottom, wooden knob handle, good condition ........ **660**

**Rabbet plane,** carriage maker's, cast iron w/95% japanning, Stanley No. 10 1/4, Sweet Hart logo, wood knob handle w/original finish, blade full, ca. 1920s, fine condition, 10 1/4" l. ..................... **743**

**Rabbet plane,** carriage maker's, cast iron w/40% japanning, Stanley No. 10 1/2, early type w/adjustable mouth piece, S casting, 5/8" blade left, hardwood handle & knob hand grip fine, good condition ............................ **290**

**Rabbet plane** carriage maker's, cast iron w/80% japanning, Stanley No. 10 1/4, 5/8" of blade remaining, wooden handle & knob hand grip, ca. 1911, very good condition ............ **550**

**Rabbet plane,** carriage maker's, cast iron/w 97% japanning, Stanley No. 10, corrugated bottom, wood handle fine, very clean, rare, ca. 1915, fine condition ............................................. **725**

*Cast Iron Rabbet Plane*

**Rabbet plane,** cast iron, marked "Birmingham. Standard Angle.," patented, bat-wing design cast into both sides, rare style w/rear handle, English, good condition, 1 1/2" w., 6" l. (ILLUS.) ...................... **523**

*Sargent Lady Bug Rabbet Plane*

**Rabbet plane,** cast iron, marked "Sargent," Sargent Lady Bug No. 15061/2, Albert Page's patent of Jan. 23, 1914 (ILLUS.) .................. **2,310**

**Rabbet plane,** cast iron, Stanley No. 90 J, Sweet Hart logo on box & notched logo on cutter, just before World War II, new & mint in original box (slightest storage stain on one side, box w/some edge staining) ................. **1,350**

**Rabbet plane,** cast iron, Stanley No. 93, new & nearly mint plane, original box w/good label, fine condition, ca. 1915 (box w/some edge wear & taped corners).................................. **160**

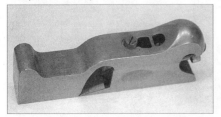

*Stanley No. 94 Rabbet Plane*

**Rabbet plane,** cast iron, Stanley No. 94, "No. 94" cast in top of body & highlighted in orange, unknown type for Stanley cabinet maker rabbets, ca. 1915, new & unused, fine condition (ILLUS.) .............................................. **1,000**

**Rabbet plane,** cast iron w/100% japanning, Stanley No. 90, notched logo, new tool in original box w/some label wear.............. **149**

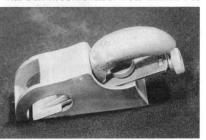

*Rare Stanley No. 90A Rabbet Plane*

**Rabbet plane,** cast iron w/70% plating, Stanley No. 90A, proper cutter nearly full & marked "No. 90A," ca. 1939, only offered from 1937 to 1943, very rare (ILLUS.) .............................................. **2,200**

**Rabbet plane,** cast iron w/80% japanning, marked "Sargent No. 198.," vine pattern on side, complete w/depth stop, 1 1/2" size, good condition................... **55**

**Rabbet plane,** cast iron w/85% japanning, marked "Birmingham Plane Mfg. Co. George D. Mosher - April 1, 1884," 2" cutter, decorative wing design in late 19th c. Egyptian revival style, good condition (ILLUS. p. 193 left w/carriage maker's tee rabbet plane) ........................................ **250**

**Rabbet plane,** cast iron w/95% plating, Stanley No. 94, above average example for uncommon number, fine condition............. **410**

**Rabbet plane,** cast iron w/97% japanning, marked "Sargent No. 196.," 1" size, vine pattern on side, w/all parts, very good condition ............................................... **65**

**Rabbet plane,** cast iron w/97% original finish, Stanley No.

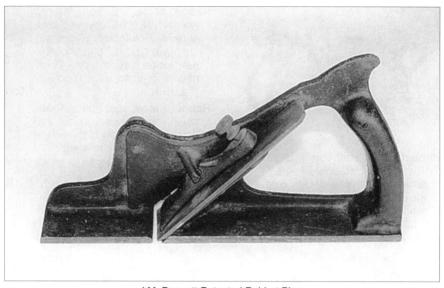

*J.M. Bennett Patented Rabbet Plane*

10 1/2, original picture box w/full label, fine condition (light use, box w/some edge wear & torn corner) .................................... **303**

**Rabbet plane,** cast iron w/98% japanning, Stanley No. 164 with rabbet sides, marked on side "E. Schade 2-4-27," Schade was inventor of this plane & mechanical superintendent of Stanley Rule & Level, probably experimental since rabbet cutout sides never made it into production & Feb. 4 date is seven months before Schade received patent for No. 164 design, fine condition ............................................... **6,380**

**Rabbet plane,** cast iron w/nearly 100% japanning, marked "J.M. Bennett. Patent of Sept. 11, 1883.," manufactured by S.C. Tatum & Co., Cincinnati, Ohio, rare, unused condition w/some light storage stain (ILLUS. above) ...................................................... **1,210**

**Rabbet plane,** cast iron w/rosewood wedges, marked "Spiers Ayr," double irons & wedges, very good condition ............................. **385**

**Rabbet plane,** coach maker's, hardwood, marked "BS" on nose, carved w/integral tail handles, 1 3/8" iron, very good condition, 9 1/2" l. (ILLUS. below) .......... **39**

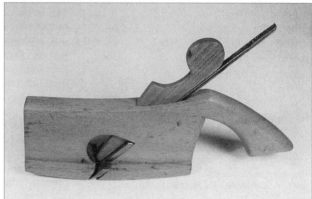

*Coach Maker's Rabbet Plane*

**Rabbet plane,** pattern maker's, cast iron body w/rosewood infill, great form & craftsmanship, good condition, 3/4" w., overall 9" l. ...... **240**

**Rabbet plane,** steel w/complete japanning, Stanley No. 10, only very light use, in original box w/a scuff mark, ca. 1950 ...... **220**

**Rabbet plane,** steel-cased, Stanley No. 80, manufactured without side nicker, No. 80 much rarer than No. 90 w/nicker, nearly unused & mint, fine condition (couple of very minor dings on wood handle) ...... **475**

**Rabbet plane,** steel-cased, Stanley No. 90 Steel Cased Rabbet. Pat. Oct. 5, 1875, stamps visible but faint, some original finish on wood handle, very good condition ...... **225**

**Rabbet-bench plane,** cast iron w/20% japanning, marked "Victor No. 11 Rabbet Bench," knob plating fine, fence & stop good replacements, very rare Victor, good condition ...... **660**

**Reeding plane,** hardwood & boxwood, marked "Thos. Appleton - Boston," w/four beads & six strips of boxwood boxing, very good condition, 5 1/6" size ...... **264**

**Router,** burlwood, old woman's tooth-type, great figure, very showy, fine condition ...... **198**

**Router,** cast iron, marked "E.J. McCulloch.," McCulloch patented the fully adjustable sliding stock Sept. 19, 1893, maple knob handles, rare, only known example w/McCulloch name, very good condition, 10 3/4" l. ...... **500**

**Router plane,** beech, marked "E. Preston & Sons," much original finish, very good condition, 1 x 4" ...... **72**

**Router plane,** cast iron, Stanley No. 71, w/three cutters in original box, fine condition (light wear on tool) ...... **99**

**Router plane,** cast iron w/85% plating, Stanley No. 71 Patent

Router Plane, S casting, in original wooden box w/full green label, tool fine condition ...... **350**

**Router plane,** mahogany, miniature, very good condition, 4" l. ...... **61**

**Router shave,** gunmetal, Stanley No. 71, Sweet Hart logo, complete w/adjustable fence, very good condition, ca. 1920s ...... **220**

**Routers,** beech, brass & steel, marked "C. Nurse & Co. 181 & 183 Walworth Rd. London S.E.," matched pair of routers, right & left, fenced w/brass wear plates for locking screws & steel wear plates for cutter, very clean & nice, fine condition, pr. ...... **175**

**Router plane,** cast iron, marked "Keen Kutter K171," w/original box, good condition w/some staining, box worn but has bright label (ILLUS. p. 117 right w/jack plane & tonguing & grooving plane) ...... **350**

**Router planes,** maple, matched set, identical except for size, one 5 1/2" w., & other 8" w., share cutters & wooden threaded locking bolt that holds cutter, four cutters in sizes 1/8", 1/4", 1/2", & 3/4" inches, very good condition, 2 piece set ...... **100**

**Sash filletster plane,** boxwood edge boxing, marked "P.B. Rider, Bangor," screw lock fence, Maine, very good condition ...... **77**

**Sash molding plane,** beech, marked "A.C. Stevens Maker. No. 82 Race St. Philada. J. Foster, Philada.," screw arm filletster-type, brass depth stop, very rare maker from first half of 19th c., fine condition ...... **750**

**Sash molding plane,** beech, marked "Arad: Simons.," flat chamfers, Sleeper-style wedge, Lebanon, New Hampshire, ca. 1800, very good condition, 9 1/2" l. ...... **230**

**Sash molding plane,** beech, marked "I. Sleeper.," fixed-handle model, split iron, wide flat chamfers, diamond strike button, fine condition, 2 1/2" w., 13 1/2" l. .......... **350**

**Sash molding plane,** boxwood, marked "Wiseman & Ross. Baltimore.," screw arm ovolo-type, boxwood arms okay, strong stamp, short-lived partnership of two makers, rare plane, very good condition ....................... **425**

**Sash molding plane,** hardwood, marked "E.W. Carpenter. Lancaster.," screw adjusts, good condition .............................. **110**

**Sash molding plane,** hardwood, marked "J. H.," ovolo-type, early mark w/zig zag border possibly maker's mark, very good condition .............................. **65**

**Sash molding plane,** hardwood, marked "S. Sayre.," early plane, possibly unlisted maker, good condition, 9 7/8" l. .......... **65**

**Sash plane,** hardwood, marked "J. Kellogg - Amherst, MS," ogee-style, double irons & wedges, like-new ................... **88**

**Sash plane,** hardwood w/rosewood nuts, marked "E.W. Carpenter - Lancaster," ogee screw-arm, double boxing & irons, good condition (edge chips on nuts) ...................... **220**

**Sash plane,** hardwood w/rosewood nuts, marked "E.W. Carpenter - Lancaster," ogee screw-arm, triple boxed, double irons, good condition (few dings) ................................ **231**

**Scraper,** cast brass, marked "Patent March 16, 1897," patent date on side of body, unusual, very good condition .......... **138**

**Scraper,** cast iron, Stanley No. 112, Sweet Hart logo, good wood, original blade, ca. 1920s (repainted) ....................... **165**

**Scraper,** cast iron, Stanley No. 82, new in original box w/instructions (plane w/some light storage rust) ....................... **50**

**Scraper,** cast iron w/100% plating, marked "Bennett Mfg. Co. Buffa-

lo, N.Y. Pat. Apd. For.," one-hand early type, new condition ..... **275**

**Scraper,** cast iron w/100% plating, marked "Keen Kutter No. 79," marked blade, w/original store tag ............................ **193**

**Scraper,** cast iron w/30% japanning & wood, Stanley No. 12, Type 1, marked "L. Bailey Patent Aug. 7, 1855" on rear adjusting screw, w/much smaller inside adjuster nut, very early scraper that may pre-date Stanley production, good condition (replacement blade) .............. **170**

**Scraper,** cast iron w/85% japanning, Stanley No. 12 3/4, extra thick rosewood sole, turned rosewood handles, very good condition ............................ **2,050**

**Scraper,** cast iron w/85% japanning & wood, Stanley No. 112, good condition ....................... **190**

**Scraper,** cast iron w/90% japanning, Stanley No. 283, Sweet Hart logo, proper upright turned wood handle, very good condition ............................... **99**

**Scraper,** cast iron w/93% japanning, Stanley No. 12 1/4, rosewood handles, very good condition ............................... **220**

**Scraper,** cast iron w/95% japanning, Stanley No. 12 1/2, Sweet Hart logo, original marked blade, rosewood handle, very good condition ..................... **83**

**Scraper,** cast iron w/95% japanning, Stanley No. 12 1/4, two-handed type, wood handles fine, very good condition (replacement blade) ..................... **260**

**Scraper,** cast iron w/98% japanning, marked "Boufford Patented May 18, 1899.," ornate delicate cast floral design, like-new, very fine condition ..................... **700**

**Scraper,** cast iron w/wood bottom & turned handles, marked "R.W. Tanner. Pat. Applied For," adjustable pitch cutter, patent dated December 14, 1869, good condition .......................... **578**

*Rare Sargent No. 43 Scraper*

**Scraper,** cast iron w/wooden bottom, marked "Sargent No. 43," turned wood side handles, unused w/much original bluing on blade, original store tag, rare, fine condition (ILLUS.) ....................... **275**

**Scraper,** cast iron w/wooden sole, Stanley No. 81, Sweet Hart blade, good condition (plating very dull) ...................................................... **60**

**Scraper,** cast iron w/worn japanning, marked "Boufford. Patented May 18, 1899," ornate casting in floral design, blade proper w/notch to clear screw head, good condition ..................................... **130**

**Scraper plane,** cast iron, marked "Eclipse Plane Co. Pat. Nov. 24, 74," widely adjustable blade pitch, heavy body, wooden handle & knob hand grip, good condition (sliver off wooden tote, worn plating) ......................................... **495**

**Scraper plane,** cast iron, Stanley No. 12 1/2, tool unused w/blade still wrapped, in original box w/sharpening instructions, fine condition ...................................................... **660**

**Scraper plane,** cast iron, Stanley No. 85 Pat. 04-11-05, tilting handle-type, cutter unmarked, appears to be original, wooden handle & knob hand grip perfect, clean & nice, fine condition.... **750**

*Stanley No. 212 Scraper Plane*

**Scraper plane,** cast iron w/85% japanning, Stanley No. 212, wood knob hand grip, replaced blade, hard to find, good condition (ILLUS.) .......................................... **990**

**Scraper plane,** cast iron w/90% japanning, Stanley No. 85, Pat. Appl'd For type, wood handle & knob grip, very good condition ....... **578**

**Scraper plane,** cast iron w/92% japanning, Stanley No. 212, Sweet Hart vintage, wooden knob grip, marked cutter, fine condition (ILLUS. below)............. **1,760**

*Stanley No. 212 Scraper Plane*

**Scraper plane,** cast iron w/96% japanning, Stanley No. 12 1/4, Sweet Hart era cutter, rosewood handles, very clean example, fine condition........................... **425**

*Stanley No. 212 Scraper Plane*

*Stanley No. 12 3/4 Scraper Plane*

**Scraper plane,** cast iron w/97% japanning & rosewood bottom, Stanley No. 12 3/4, Sweet Hart logo, brass bushing, the use of end grain rosewood for the bottom in this model was discontinued as end grain cracked easily & was subject to humidity changes, rare, fine condition (ILLUS.) .............................................. **1,100**

**Scraper plane,** cast iron w/97% japanning, Stanley No. 212, Sweet Hart logo, marked blade but w/hole drilled where cap screw engages blade, wooden hand grip knob fine, very good condition (ILLUS.) ........................... **1,155**

**Scraper plane,** cast iron w/97% japanning, Stanley No. 85, Sweet Hart blade, hardwood handle & knob hand grip, 50% decal on handle, fine condition, two small nicks on tote (ILLUS. below) ......... **825**

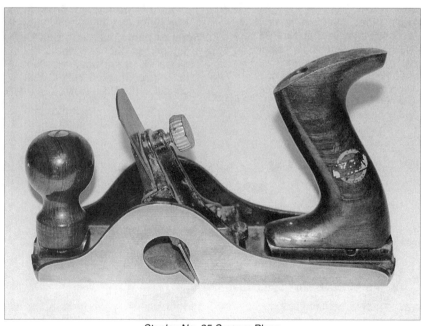

*Stanley No. 85 Scraper Plane*

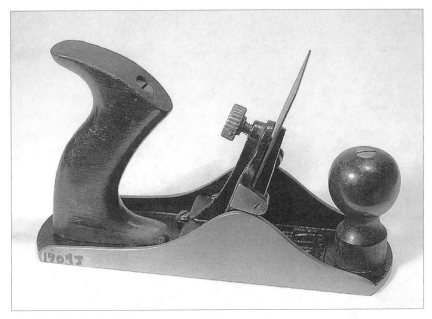

*Stanley No. 87 Scraper Plane*

**Scraper plane,** cast iron w/97% japanning, Stanley No. 87, early type marked "Pat. Apl'd For," wooden handle & hand knob grip, very good condition (ILLUS.) **... 1,540**

*Stanley No. 87 Scraper Plane*

**Scraper plane,** cast iron w/97% japanning, Stanley No. 87, "patent applied for" type, fine hardwood handle & knob hand grip, rarest of Stanley scrapers, very good condition (ILLUS.) ................................................................................................... **2,090**

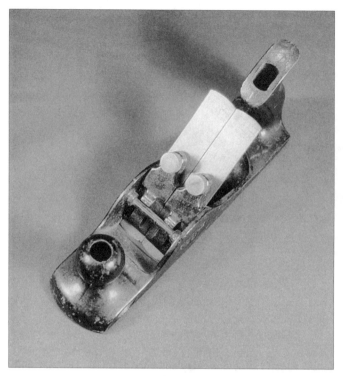

*Sargent No. 162
Scrub Plane*

*Rare Stanley No. 12 3/4 Scraper Plane*

**Scraper plane,** cast iron w/98% japanning, Stanley No. 12 3/4, Sweet Hart logo, wooden side handles fine, all proper parts, ca. 1920s, fine condition (ILLUS.)............................................ **1,155**

**Scrub plane,** cast iron, Stanley No. 40 1/2, nearly unused, handle decal 95%, perfect finish, original sales slip from 1930s, in original rare box, tool fine condition (box worn w/two torn-out corners)............................... **1,045**

**Scrub plane,** cast iron, Stanley No. 40, Sweet Hart logo, tool near new, in original box, fine condition, ca. 1920s............................. **176**

**Scrub plane,** cast iron, Stanley No. 40, unused, mint condition w/complete decal, in original box ................................................. **303**

**Scrub plane,** cast iron w/65% japanning, Stanley No. 40 1/2, Sweet Hart logo on blade, initials "ENM" dotted into side, wooden handle & knob hand grip, ca. 1920s, good condition........ **60**

**Scrub plane,** cast iron w/93% japanning, marked "Sargent No. 162.," double wedges & irons, all cast iron including handles, made for short time before World War I, extremely rare, fine condition (ILLUS. above) .... **3,400**

**Scrub plane,** cast iron w/97% japanning, Sargent No. 161, fine wood handle w/most original finish, lightly used.................................. **127**

**Shoe peg plane,** fruitwood body w/brass fence, cuts single strip

*Stanley No. 51 & 52 Shoot Board & Plane*

of pegs w/each pass, pegs are round w/flat side, sample attached, very good condition............ **625**

**Shoe peg plane,** hardwood, cuts three long peg strips per pass, horn-shaped handle w/a fist carved at top of palm rest behind cutter, rare & unusual, good condition ...................................... **625**

**Shoot board & plane,** cast iron w/95% japanning, Stanley No. 51 & No. 52, Sweet Hart vintage, w/92% handle decal, fine condition (ILLUS. above) ................. **935**

**Shoot board & plane,** cast iron w/95% japanning, unmarked Chaplin patent type, 70% plating on brass cap & handle, plane & board w/cast-in owner's mark "T.W.," oversized mahogany pedestal matching outline of base, stored in fitted dovetailed wooden case, very good condition .......................................... **3,960**

**Shoulder plane,** gunmetal w/steel sole & ebony infill, Ward iron w/plenty of length left, very good condition, 1 1/4" w., 8" l. ....... **220**

*Stanley Shuttle Plane*

**Shuttle plane,** cast iron w/95% japanning, Stanley HFL L2082E, Sweet Hart vintage, hardwood handle & knob hand grip, fine condition, wood w/much original finish (ILLUS.) ........................................ **880**

**Shuttle plane,** cast iron w/95% original japanning, Stanley HFL L2082E, Sweet Hart logo on blade, used to square up shuttles in weaving industry, fine shape, wood perfect w/most of original finish, cap recessed notched logo w/orange background, fine condition .................... **1,100**

**Side rabbet plane,** cast iron, Stanley No. 98, no nickel plating, all recesses painted black, depth stop-type, original box w/full label, ca. 1943 wartime production, rare type, fine condition (box a bit worn) ...................... **170**

**Side rabbet plane,** cast iron, Stanley No. 99, in original early green box w/good label, fine condition .................................................. **358**

**Side rabbet plane,** cast iron w/97% plating, marked "E. Preston & Sons," crossed adjustable blades, appears unused......... **275**

**Side rabbet plane,** rosewood w/steel sole, double wedge & irons for working in both directions, good condition, 2 3/4" w., 4 3/4" l. ...................................................... **130**

**Sill plane,** beech, uncommon cut, used to cut drip stop on underside of sills, fine condition, 5" l....... **130**

**Sill plane,** maple, cuts drip lip in bottom of window sill, rare plane, fine condition, 8 1/2" l. ........... **75**

**Sill plane,** rosewood, unusual router form, rare, very good condition, 5 1/4" l. ................................ **80**

**Skew rabbet plane,** cast iron w/nearly 100% finish, Stanley No. 289, complete proper fence & depth stop, hard to find, ca. 1910, fine condition ............................ **500**

**Smoothing plane,** beech, coffin-shaped w/1" w. iron, good condition, 3 1/2" l. .......................................... **72**

*Beech Plane with Horn Smoother*

**Smoothing plane,** beech, horn-shaped front, carved throat w/bone inlay, 1 1/2" iron marked "Newbould," good condition, wedge a narrow replacement, overall 6 1/2" l. (ILLUS.) ................... **132**

**Smoothing plane,** beech w/rosewood wedge, miniature, marked "Collin Smoother," very good condition, 2 1/4" l. ............................... **121**

*Taber Plane Co. Smoother Plane*

**Smoothing plane,** boxwood coffin-style, marked "Taber Plane Co. Pat. Feb. 26, 65," patented lever cap, wood w/fine honey amber patina (ILLUS.) ...................... **358**

**Smoothing plane,** cast iron, marked "Steers' Patent. June 8, 1880 Canadian and May 11, 1880 US.," Steer's plane allows both cutter adjustment & cutter angle adjustment, production

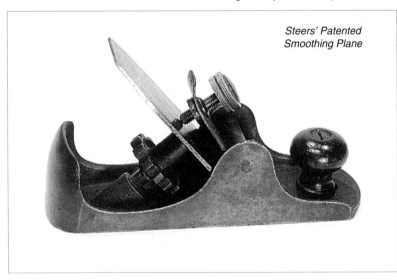

*Steers' Patented Smoothing Plane*

moved to US shortly after patent issued, design completely reworked making these Canadian planes extremely rare, Wm. Steers, pattern maker of Sherbrooke, Quebec at Smith Elkins Mfg. Co., one of only two of this type known, various papers including copies of Canadian patent papers, very good condition (ILLUS. bottom of previous page) ........................................... **2,550**

**Smoothing plane,** cast iron, Stanley Bed Rock No. 603, Type 5, in original box, fine condition (light tool use, box faded) ... **935**

**Smoothing plane,** cast iron, Stanley Bed Rock No. 604, Type 6, tool near new, in original box, fine condition ..................... **1,045**

**Smoothing plane,** cast iron, Stanley No. 4 1/2C, large letter Stanley cutter logo, plane new, ca. 1913, in original box w/full picture label, includes ca. 1909 pocket catalog, very good condition (plane w/some surface staining from storage) ............ **380**

**Smoothing plane,** cast iron, Stanley No. G3C, near new & mint, w/original box w/full label (plane w/very minor storage spots, box w/two paint stains on top) ............ **1,550**

**Smoothing plane,** cast iron, unmarked Knowles type, coffin-shaped, cast body w/wedged iron, wooden tote handle dovetailed into body, first quarter 19th c., good condition (chip on tip of tote) ................................................ **550**

*Ohio Tool Co. Smoothing Plane*

**Smoothing plane,** cast iron w/100% japanning, marked "Ohio Tool Co. No. 9 1/2," ad-

justable w/acorn finial that pivots side to side, new (ILLUS.) ........ **303**

*Patented E.H. Morris Smoothing Plane*

**Smoothing plane,** cast iron w/50% japanning, marked "E.H. Morris Nov. 8, 1870," diamond sole w/1881 mark, wood infill around blade of Butcher iron, rare Sandusky Tool Co. plane, very good condition (ILLUS.) ..... **2,530**

**Smoothing plane,** cast iron w/65% japanning, marked "Buckeye Smoother - Patent Nov. 22, 1904," adjuster on top of blade & part of the level cap, corrugated, wooden knob handle, by John Muehl, very good condition ............................................... **330**

**Smoothing plane,** cast iron w/80% japanning, Stanley No. 164, low angle-type, Sweet Hart blade proper & original, wood fine & tote retains about 70% of original decal, rare & unique overhead adjustment, very good condition (shows some use) ...... **4,100**

*Bailey Tool Co. No. 14 Smoothing Plane*

**Smoothing plane,** cast iron w/90% japanning, marked "Bailey Tool Co. No. 14," lever adjustment, patented split-cap iron w/1867 patent date, wood knob handle w/original finish, very good condition (ILLUS. previous page)............................... **880**

**Smoothing plane,** cast iron w/90% japanning, marked "Birmingham Plane Mfg. Co. - Mosher Patent Dec. 16, 1884," adjustable, very good condition, 9" l. w/2" iron............................................ **440**

*Low-angle Stanley Smoothing Plane*

**Smoothing plane,** cast iron w/90% japanning, Stanley No. 164, Sweet Hart logo, low-angle type, wooden handle & tote w/70% decal, proper blade w/graduated edge, very good condition (ILLUS.)............................. **2,640**

**Smoothing plane,** cast iron w/92% japanning, marked "Metallic Plane Co. Excelsior Cutter. Patented.," corrugated sole, Storke's patents of 1869 &

1875, lever adjustment, adjustable mouth locks in place w/iron mushroom knob, beech tote handle & knob hand grip, little or no use, very fine condition........... **1,600**

**Smoothing plane,** cast iron w/95% japanning, Stanley No. 164, Sweet Hart logo, low angle-type, wooden handle & knob hand grip w/much original finish, fine condition (ILLUS. bottom of page)................................. **3,080**

*Sandusky Tool Co. Smoothing Plane*

**Smoothing plane,** cast iron w/98% japanning, marked "Sandusky Tool Co. No. 3 SC," wooden handle w/original finish (ILLUS.) ..................................................... **385**

*Low Angle Stanley Smoothing Plane*

**Smoothing plane,** cast iron w/98% japanning, Stanley No. 35 Wood Bottom Smoother, transitional-type, Sweet Hart logo, 90% of decal on side of body, beech handles, fine condition (signs of minor use) ............. **160**

**Smoothing plane,** cast iron w/worn japanning, marked "L. Bailey, Woods & Co. No. 35 Smoother," Type 1, banjo lever cap, mushroom wooden knob, rare, good condition (edge of cap iron chipped) ............................. **182**

**Smoothing plane,** ebony, coffin-shaped w/white wood wedge, very good condition, 3" l. ................. **253**

**Smoothing plane,** ebony, miniature, fine condition, 1 1/8" w., 4 5/8" l. ...................................... **440**

**Smoothing plane,** fruitwood, marked "A.M. Rife - Oct. 17, 1879," coffin-shaped, very heavy, very good condition ............... **83**

**Smoothing plane,** fruitwood, miniature, coffin-shaped, good condition, 4" l. ............................. **72**

**Smoothing plane,** hardwood, marked "Adison Heald. Milford, N.H.," A mark, extra wide handled model, closed tote, double iron, strike button, possibly special order, very good condition, 2 3/4" w. iron, 11" l. ............. **220**

**Smoothing plane,** hardwood, marked "Birdsill Holly. Patented July 6, 1852.," round recesses in sole to reduce friction, paint still over 50%, wood tote handle fine, very clean & rare, very fine condition ............................... **2,700**

**Smoothing plane,** hardwood, marked "Defiance No. 3.," patented & produced by the Bailey Tool Co., rare, very good condition (few marks at mouth, tote a proper replacement) ...................... **325**

**Smoothing plane,** hardwood, marked "E.H. Morris - Nov. 1881," diamond sole, wood carved w/an overall wheat sprig design, Sandusky Tool Co. iron, wooden handle & knob hand grip, very good condition (tip of wood tote cracked) ...................... **5,830**

**Smoothing plane,** hardwood, marked "Kieffer & Auxer. Lancaster, PA.," double wedges marked "Patent March 27, 1849.," rare, good condition, 7 1/2" l. ...................................... **88**

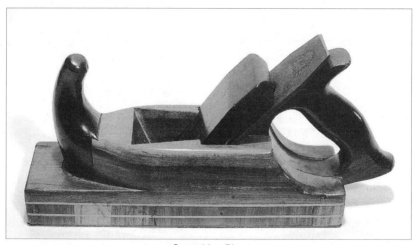

*Smoothing Plane*

**Smoothing plane,** laminated woods w/steel sole, horn, wedge & tote in rosewood, tote in lignum vitae w/inlaid strips of light wood & end grain lignum, very good condition, 9 1/2" l. ............................................................................................................. **220**

*Rare Sanford Patent Smoothing Plane*

**Smoothing plane,** hardwood, marked "Sanford Patent - 1844" on adjuster knob, one of the first adjustable bench planes, early & extremely rare, very good condition (ILLUS.)............................ **440**

**Smoothing plane,** hardwood, marked "Union X No. 3.," patented Union vertical adjustment, unused, very fine condition................................................ **575**

**Smoothing plane,** lignum vitae, marked "J.L. Cluff. Maker.," rare Maine maker, perfect condition, iron 1 7/8" w., 8 3/4" h. ..................... **170**

*Presentation Smoothing Plane*

**Smoothing plane,** presentation-type, mahogany, written in black on one side "Presented By Bro. Wm. G. M'Ardell. - Feb 13 - 1903" & "Chosen Friends Lodge No. 11 - I.O.M." on other, 1" cutter, overall 4 1/2" l. (ILLUS.)................................................. **110**

**Smoothing plane,** rosewood, marked "Sandusky Tool Co.," E mark, coffin-shaped tall type, cutter pitch slightly less than 45 degrees but not low enough for mitre plane, good condition,

2" w. x 2 1/2" h., 9" l. (few nicks & bangs in wood)................................. **725**

**Smoothing plane,** rosewood, miniature coffin-shape, slightly rounded sides, very good condition, 3 1/8" l. ...................................... **110**

**Smoothing plane,** rosewood, miniature, handled coffin-shape, fine detailing, fine condition, 1 3/8" l. ...................................... **303**

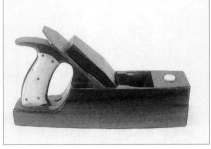

*Rosewood & Ivory Presentation Plane*

**Smoothing plane,** rosewood w/ivory trim, marked "L. & I.J. White.," presentation-type, iron stamped "1837," closed tote w/inlaid ivory grips & ivory strike button, fine condition (ILLUS.)... **1,540**

**Smoothing plane,** steel, Stanley No. S 4 Steel Smooth Plane, new w/complete handle decal & red-backed Stanley logo cap, original cutter sharpening sheets, original box w/95% label, fine condition (one box corner torn out)................................ **578**

**Smoothing plane,** sterling silver w/ebony infill, fine detail, not antique but good quality, 1 1/4" l. ....... **220**

**Smoothing plane,** wood & cast iron, marked "Palmer's Patent Handled Smooths - Palmer's Patent - Pat. Feb. 3, 1857 - No. 18," wooden body carved from single piece of wood including closed tote, rare patented model, good condition ............................. **633**

**Smoothing plane,** wood w/adjustable compass & brass fixture on nose that adjusts sole, captive screw in rear section, well-made, very good condition..... **341**

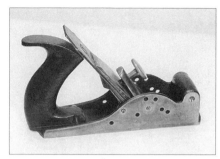

*Bailey's Experimental Smooth Plane*

**Smoothing plane and scraper,** cast iron, rosewood & gunmetal, marked "Leonard Bailey Experimental Smooth Plane and Scraper," principle based on Bailey's 1855 patent, designed w/frog-cap arrangement that allowed blade to be set at several angles, gunmetal cap stamped "L. Bailey's Patent Aug. 7, 1855.," blade "Buck Brothers," replacement rosewood tote but original available, extremely important link to development of Bailey line being only marked example, very good condition (ILLUS.).......................................... **3,600**

*Special Purpose Plane*

**Special purpose plane,** beech & cast iron, marked "T. Tilefton - Front Street," "E. Bordman" stamped on one end in zigzag border, skew iron cuts spiraling U-shaped groove into dowel of approximately 3/8" d., very un-

usual, fine condition, 1 1/2 x 3", 4" l. (ILLUS.)....................................... **1,150**

**Special purpose plane,** hardwood, cuts double tongue on stock over 2 1/2" w., handled, skew cutter 3 1/2" wide, unusual plane made for some special jobs, good condition, 4 5/8" w., 14" l. ........................................................ **200**

**Spill bench plane,** fruitwood, cuts tight spiral spill, fine condition........ **525**

**Spill bench plane,** hardwood, marked "Pat'd. Aug. 26, 73," adjustable fence, rare American spill plane, patent date stamp clear, fine condition ............................ **650**

**Spill plane,** hardwood, V-bottom sides on edge of stock, the ejects spill outside via a half-round escapement, unmarked but clearly a manufactured product ........................................................ **130**

**Split frame plane,** cast iron, marked "Bailey Type Split Frame Plane.," adjusting frame design w/earliest splits w/humped bed, hardwood tote handle & knob hand grip, early style split frame, rarest of frames, good condition................. **7,000**

*Rare Bailey's Split-frame Jointer Plane*

**Split-frame jointer plane,** cast iron, marked "L. Bailey Patent Aug. 7, 55 Aug. 31, 58.," fine example of rare split-frames, wood near perfect & 100% original, polished surfaces w/even brown patina, marked on spring washer cap w/patent dates, very rare, very good condition, 21 5/8" l. (ILLUS.)........................... **19,800**

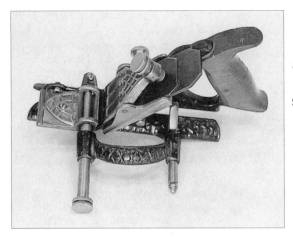

*Rare Lee's Stop Chamfer Plane*

**Stop chamfer plane,** cast iron w/100% japanning, marked "Lee's Patent Feb. 13, 1883," marked on cap screw, side of plane & handle, Gothic arch design & gold pinstriping, hardwood tote w/100% original varnish, rare, perfect (ILLUS.) .......... **8,500**

**Stair maker's plane,** boxwood & beech, marked "G. M. Green Street. Boston.," double bead shave-type, wear surface boxwood dovetailed into beech handle section, 'G.M.' possibly for Gardiner & Murdock, good condition (one cutter improper, dirty) ...................... **170**

**Stair maker's rabbet planes,** beech, three w/tails, one coffin-shaped smoother, from New Jersey stair maker, very good condition, set of 6 ...................... **165**

**Stair maker's rabbet planes & sole plates,** hardwood, all tailed & handcrafted, from New Jersey tool chest, ca. 1900, w/a set of six bone & ivory sole plates, set of 4, very good condition, the group ...................... **743**

**Stair rail plane,** fruitwood, marked "B. Sheneman. No. 735 Market St. Phil'a. Warranted.," B mark, fenced, very good condition, 3" w., 7" l. ...................... **110**

**Sun-style plane,** cooper's-type, yellow birch, curved body w/wide flat chamfers stop at mouth, mitre cut around corners, early tool from master craftsman, fine condition ...................... **150**

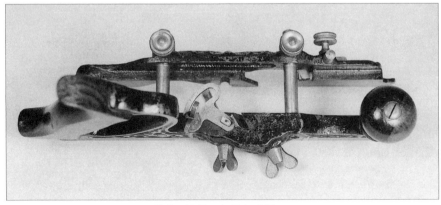

*Rufus H. Dorn's Patent Plane*

**Swing-out cutter plane,** cast iron w/98% japanning, marked "Rufus H. Dorn's Patent of July 16, 1872.," brass screws, complex swing-out cutter design limited to late 1872 production run, manufactured by Stanley Rule & Level Co., very rare, fine condition w/minor scratches to wood (ILLUS.) ...................... **12,650**

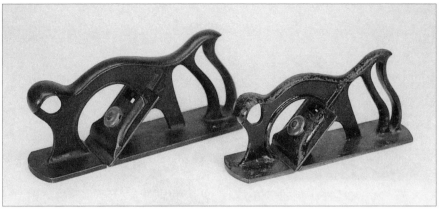

*Mosher Patent Rabbet Planes*

**Tee rabbet plane,** carriage maker's, cast iron, marked "Birmingham Plane Mfg. Co. - George D. Mosher - April 1, 1884," extra wide w/2 1/2" cutter, finish fine, overall 9" l. (ILLUS. right w/Mosher rabbet plane)..................... **450**

**Thumb plane,** hardwood, miniature ogee-style, very good condition, 2" l. .............................................. **165**

**Toboggan plane,** cast iron w/90% japanning, marked "Payson-Brown No. 001.," no patent located but examples known w/"Patent Applied For" markings, early Chicago area plane, fine condition (ILLUS. below) ........ **176**

**Tonguing plane,** applewood, marked "M.B. Tidey," A1 mark, clean & well made, very good condition ....................................... **259**

**Tonguing & grooving plane,** cast iron, Stanley No. 146, tool unused, in original box w/picture label, very good condition (minor storage spots on plane, clear tape on box top)........................ **220**

**Tonguing & grooving plane,** cast iron, Stanley No. 148, tool frosty & unused, in original box w/picture label, very good condition ............................................................ **220**

**Tonguing & grooving plane,** cast iron w/100% plating, marked "Sargent No. 1068 Tonguing and Grooving - Oct. 22, 1912," match plane flips over for matching cut, w/original box, fine condition, box taped but w/full label (ILLUS. p. 117 left w/router plane & jack plane)...................................................... **1,000**

*Toboggan Plane*

*Four Early Stanley Presentation Planes*

**Tonguing & grooving plane,** cast iron w/nearly 100% plating, Stanley No. 147, Sweet Hart logo, tool complete & proper but a bit dull, w/original box w/picture label, very good condition (one side of box missing) .............. **220**

**Toothing plane,** hardwood, marked "H.A. Langhorst - Cini O," weak stamp mark, good condition, 7" l. ........................ **83**

**Transitional bench plane,** cast iron w/96% japanning, rosewood & boxwood, Stanley No. 27, Type 5, presentation-type, possibly produced for the 1876 Centennial Exhibition, dovetailed rosewood & boxwood sole, wood handle & hand grip knob, wood w/most original finish, tight base crack in tote, fine condition (ILLUS. above, second from right) .................................... **2,640**

**Transitional bench plane,** cast iron w/98% japanning, rosewood & boxwood, Stanley No. 25 Block, Type 5, presentation-type, possibly produced for the 1876 Centennial Exhibition, dovetailed rosewood & boxwood sole, wood handle & hand grip knob, wood w/most original finish, fine condition (ILLUS. above, far right with other transitional planes) ...................................... **3,300**

**Transitional bench plane,** cast iron w/98% japanning, rosewood & boxwood, Stanley No. 29, Type 5, presentation-type, possibly produced for the 1876 Centennial Exhibition, dovetailed rosewood & boxwood sole, wood handle & hand grip knob, wood w/most original finish, fine condition (ILLUS. above, third from right) ................. **3,740**

**Transitional bench plane,** cast iron w/98% japanning, rosewood & boxwood, Stanley No. 32, Type 5, presentation-type, possibly produced for the 1876 Centennial Exhibition, dovetailed rosewood & boxwood sole, wood handle & hand grip knob, wood w/most original finish, relief check at sole mouth opening, fine condition (ILLUS. above, far left) .......................... **2,640**

**Transitional block plane,** hardwood & cast iron w/50% japanning, Stanley No. 25 Block, Type 7 w/first lateral adjuster, wooden bottom, iron & cap proper, cap iron stamped w/Bailey patent dates, good condition ............................ **200**

**Transitional block plane,** wood & cast iron w/55% japanning, Stanley No. 21 Block, Type 7, wooden bottom, w/first lateral adjuster, rare No. 2 size, proper cutter & cap iron (wood w/chip at mouth) .................................. **120**

**Transitional smoothing plane,** hardwood & cast iron w/95% japanning, marked "Belknap, H & M. Co. Bluegrass No. 70. Wood Bottom Smoother.," wood fine, clean, very good condition ............. **100**

**Try plane,** hardwood w/decorative carving, Europe, ca. 1800, very good condition, 43" l. ............... **198**

**Universal plane,** cast iron, Stanley No. 55, w/original instructions, in original rare lift-top wooden box painted light yellow w/90% box label, tool new & mint ......................... **715**

**Veneer scraper,** cast iron, Stanley No. 12, in original picture box w/near perfect paper label, only light use, fine condition .......... **633**

**Veneer scraper,** cast iron w/nearly 100% japanning, Stanley No. 212, in original box, ca. 1915, fine condition (very minor surface staining, box dirty) ................ **3,600**

*Wagon-wheel Felloes Plane*

**Wagon-wheel fellows plane,** hardwood, marked "Felloes Plane 4.," designed for finishing wagon-wheel fellows, four

wedges: two for cutters, two for nickers, wedge lock arms allow adjustment to about 5," very clean, like new, fine condition (ILLUS.) ................................................ **1,815**

**Weatherstrip plane,** cast iron, Stanley No. 378, mint plane w/original parts & instructions, in original box w/complete label, fine condition ................................... **160**

**Weatherstrip plane,** cast iron w/100% japanning, Stanley No. 248, w/seven cutters, complete w/instructions, ca. 1930s, like-new in worn & taped box, the set .... **143**

**Weatherstrip plane,** cast iron w/90% japanning, Stanley No. 239, Sweet Hart logo, fenced, 1/8" size, ca. 1920s, good condition ................................. **154**

**Weatherstrip plane,** cast iron w/95% japanning, Stanley No. 78W, Sweet Hart logo, wooden handle, detachable sole plate w/captive screw, complete w/bottom, fence & stop, ca. 1920s ................................................... **286**

**Wooden-bottom plane,** cast iron w/97% japanning, Stanley No. 21, Type 14, wooden handle, never used .................................... **385**

**Wooden-bottom plane,** hardwood & cast iron w/92% japanning, Stanley No. 34, Type 9, wood w/much original finish, very good condition .............................. **94**

*Stanley No. 32 Test Run Plane*

**Wooden-bottom plane,** various hardwoods & cast iron w/98% japanning, Stanley No. 32, Sweet Hart logo, first type, pencil date of March 1922, factory-applied finger-jointed rosewood sole, from test run made in 1922, unique, fine condition w/some nicks & bangs to wood (ILLUS.) ............. **1,375**

**Miniature molding plane,** zebra wood, hollow cut-style, honey brown w/darker strip, very good condition, 1/2" w., 1 9/16" l. .............. **65**

**Miniature molding planes,** carriage maker's, boxwood, hollow & round-types, 5/8" w., 2 1/2" l., the pair (chips on both wedges) ... **175**

**Miniature plane,** beech w/rosewood wedge, marked on nose "D. Farr," good condition, 5/8" iron, 2 1/2" l. (ILLUS. below, middle row, second from right, w/other miniature planes) .............. **220**

**Miniature plane,** chisel plane, brass body w/steel sole, in the style of the Stanley No. 97, good condition, 1 3/16 x 4 1/2" (ILLUS. below, top row, right, with other miniature planes) .......... **220**

**Miniature plane,** instrument maker's, brass body w/wooden tail handle, slightly rounded shape w/screw-type lever cap, good condition, 7/8 x 7/8" (ILLUS. below, top row, left, w/other miniature planes) .............................. **209**

**Miniature plane,** instrument maker's, brass w/wooden tail handle, very slight radius sole, fine condition, 1 1/4 x 2" (ILLUS. middle row, second from left, w/other miniature planes) .............. **160**

**Miniature plane,** whale plane, brass w/rosewood wedge, fine condition (ILLUS. below, middle row, second from left, w/other miniature planes) .................................. **160**

**Miniature planes,** boxwood, compassed hollow & round pair, good condition, 1/2 x 2 1/4", pair (ILLUS. below, bottom row, right, w/other miniature planes) ..... **198**

**Miniature planes,** boxwood, smoother & round pair, 7/8 x 2 1/4", good condition, pair (ILLUS. of both below, bottom row, left, w/other miniature planes) ......................................... **176**

**Miniature planes,** rosewood, w/radius sole, whale-like shape w/horn/tail, good condition, 1 1/8 x 3 1/2" & a rosewood tailed compassed hollow model, 1 3/8 x 3 1/4", lot of 2 (ILLUS. of one below, middle row, left, w/other miniature planes) ................. **226**

**Miniature smoothing plane,** applewood, marked "Sandusky Tool Co. Ohio.," probably I mark, no number, coffin-shaped, fine condition, w/1" iron, 4 1/2" l. ............................................ **500**

**Miniature smoothing plane,** beech, coffin-style, nice form, fine condition, 3 1/2" l., 13/16" w. ................ **50**

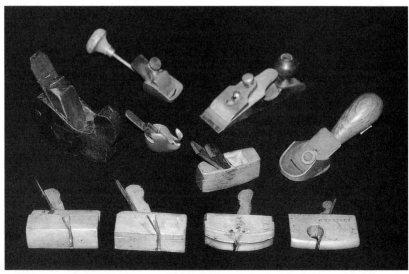

*Miniature Planes*

# Rules & Gages

Although no one knows for certain, it is likely that the first man-made measuring device was a straight stick with notches cut into it. By the time the ancient Egyptians were constructing the Great Pyramids, more refined techniques had evolved, but they still relied on very basic materials such as sticks and cords.

It is known that the Romans were using jointed metal rulers, and more accurate measuring devices continued to evolve in the following centuries. By the Renaissance era more specialized rulers and measuring devices had become the tools of various trades, such as architecture.

It wasn't until the 18th century that commercial production of rules began, and England was the first country to develop this industry. It continued to be a leading

center of production well into the 19th century. American manufacturing arrived during the first quarter of the 19th century, and by the 1860s automated production of folding rules was under way in this country.

The favored material for rules since the 18th century has been boxwood, often with the sections joined by brass or German silver (an alloy) fittings. High quality rules were also made from ivory, and these choice examples are much sought after by collectors. The Stanley Rule and Level Company, as the original name implies, became a leader in the production of this tool by the mid-19th century. In the early 20th century Stanley introduced the multi-hinged "zigzag" type rule, followed some years later by the steel push-pull tape measure that has remained the favorite style ever since.

**Angle bisecter,** cast iron, marked "Angle Bisecter - Patented June 1894," gear mechanism moved both handles while blade centers, very good condition........ **$165**

**Architect's rule,** ivory, Stanley No. 86 1/2, four-fold, good condition, 2' l. (tobacco yellow color, pins missing)............................. **250**

**Architect's rule,** ivory w/German silver fittings, marked "J. Rabone & Sons. Birmingham.," beveled edges, drafting scales, edge markings, arch joint, overall clean & very readable, very good condition (tiny flake & missing one pin, slight yellowing)............................... **525**

**Architect's rule,** ivory w/German silver joints & trim, marked "Halden & Co. Manchester & London," edge markings, four-fold, scales w/beveled edges, arch joint, w/leather case, one-foot architect rules w/beveled edges extremely rare, fine condition, 12" l............................................ **700**

**Barn builder's gauge,** Cuban mahogany, beam graduated to 18" in both Roman & Arabic numerals, wedge lock head, found in Pennsylvania, very good condition..................................... **374**

**Bench gauge,** cast iron w/98% japanning & most of gold highlights, marked "Randel & Stickney. Waltham, Mass.," adjustable table & lever action dial indicator, fine condition, 12" h. (ILLUS. below).......................... **116**

**Bench or school rule,** boxwood, Stanley Special 12" Bench or School Rule, appears to be boxwood, graduated in inches only from 0 to 12 starting at 1/4" in from each end, rule marked in center in block capital letters, special order rule w/unknown purpose, very good condition, 12 1/2" l. (couple of paint spots but overall clean & nice)................... **375**

*Randel & Stickney
Bench Gauge*

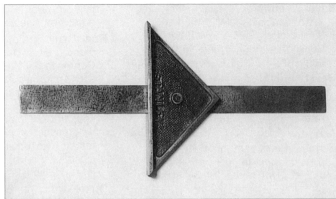

*Extremely Rare Bevel*

**Bench rule,** maple w/brass tips, Stanley No. 35, board tables for boards 6-19" wide & up to 19' long, offered only until 1892, extremely rare, good condition...... **225**

**Bevel,** cast iron, fixed head marked "Stanley," rule stamped "Mar. 4, 89," which appears to be error, since tool clearly manufactured from patent submitted by Justus A. Traut on Mar. 4, 1890, unique, first known example to appear, surface pitting (ILLUS. above)... **1,300**

**Bevel gauge,** cast iron double-blade model, Stanley No. 225 12", Sweet Hart logo, traces of blue on blades, ca. 1920s, very good condition ...................................... **292**

**Bevel gauge,** cast iron, marked "Boss - Pat. Aug. 26, 84," spring & clip mechanism locks blade at various set points, cast iron handle without clips, rare, good condition ......................................... **110**

**Bevel gauge,** cast iron w/rosewood & brass handle in Gothic design, marked "R.J. Robinson - Pat. June 14, 1870," made by the St. Johnsbury Tool & so marked, very good condition, 6" l......................................... **220**

**Bevel gauge,** cast iron w/walnut infill, marked "Traut's Patent," offered only a few years in the 1870s, good condition (blade w/light pitting) ......................................... **209**

**Bevel layout device,** cast iron w/95% plating, marked "The Calhoun Rafter & Polygon Bevel," scales & table to do any layout, also marked "A.O. Calhoun. Victor, MO. Pat. Feb. 5, 07," bright & shiny, fine condition..... **550**

**Bevel square,** brass & rosewood, marked "F.E. Witter. Patent US Feb. 22, 87. Canada Aug. 13, 87," double blades w/much original plating, uncommon, very good condition............................. **440**

**Bevel square,** brass & walnut, marked "Langlais Patent. June 12, 1894," single blade connected to pair of handles geared to maintain same angle to blade, lever locks, good condition..................................................... **237**

**Bevel square,** cast iron blade w/metal-framed wood handle, marked "L. Bailey Patent Mar. 19, 1872," lever lock on handle end, very good condition, blade 10" l.................................................... **127**

**Bevel square,** cast iron w/80% handle decal, Stanley No. 225, Sweet Hart logo, double blades, very good condition, ca. 1920s, 12" l.................................................... **275**

**Bevel square,** cast iron w/two-piece cast-iron handle, marked "Pat. Nov. 5, 1867," uncommon Howard's patent model, very good condition, 8" l............................. **319**

**Bevel square,** cast iron w/wooden handle inlaid w/brass band & star, marked "P.C. Crouch & Co. Middletown, CT" w/full eagle trademark, rare, very good condition............................. **182**

**Bevel square,** cast iron w/wooden handle, marked "Woodrough & McParlin. Cincinnati.," etching legible but faint, 10" l. ............................................ **220**

**Bevel square,** cast iron & wood, Stanley No. 25, Sweet Hart vintage, 70% decal on handle, rare in this size, fine condition, 14" l. ............................................ **132**

**Bevel square,** cast metal w/90% plating, unmarked, protractor dial at pivot reads "S" & "SM" (possibly for "Square" & "Square Mitre"), butt-locking screw as on Stanley 18, good condition, blade 6" l. ...................... **127**

**Bevel square & protractor,** cast iron w/45% japanning, marked "Standard Tool Co. Pat. Mar. 11, 1884," w/original locking pin & fully readable rule, rare in this complete condition, good condition ............................................ **250**

*Stanley Board Caliper*

**Board caliper,** hickory w/brass jaws, Stanley Rule & Level Co., for boards from 1 to 16 feet, German silver spring clip, early & rare, surface stress crack on one side (ILLUS.) ............................ **770**

**Board cane,** hardwood, Stanley No. 48, marked only w/model number, complete & legible, good condition ............................ **100**

**Board rule,** hardwood & brass, marked "C.T. Younglove, Fitchburg, Mass.," calculates board feet in boards to 20 feet long, brass pointer spins and keeps tally as boards are measured, brass tips, fine condition .................. **250**

**Board rule,** hardwood & brass, marked "R.B. Haselton. Maker. Contoocook, N.H.," hand-held stick-type, calculates the board footage in boards from 7 to 16 feet, brass-tipped, tally holes keep track of total as the scaling progresses, stock 1/2 x 1 3/8", retains two original yellow finished tally pins, like-new, very fine condition, 24" l. .......................... **350**

**Board rule,** hardwood, marked "R.B. Haselton. Maker. Contoocook, N.H.," stick-type, scales for boards from 3' to 20' long, stock 1 x 1 1/4", much original orangish yellow finish, fine condition, 24" l. .............................. **110**

**Board rule,** hardwood, marked "Stephens & Co. No. 18," likenew w/original finish, fine condition .............................. **210**

**Board rule,** maple w/brass tips, marked "H. Chapin. Union Factory No. 81," special rule w/board tables for 8- to 19-foot boards up to 19" wide, edge marking in tenths of a foot, rare, very good condition, 24" l. (shrinkage cracks at pin tips) ............ **95**

**Bridge square,** cast iron, marked "Eagle Square Mnf'g Co. 75, Patented Jan. 3, 1870," early double-leg style w/cross beam, offered only for a short time, blades clean, rare, good condition ............................ **605**

**Builder's square,** iron w/60% finishes, marked "Starrett," used, very good condition .............. **185**

**Butt gauge,** cast iron, marked "Sargent No. 11.," adjusted w/screwdriver, w/original instructions, tool near new, in original box w/full label, very good condition (box worn) ............ **475**

**Butt & rabbet gauge,** cast iron, Stanley No. 92, Sweet Hart logo, tool new, in original box, ca. 1920s, fine condition (box w/some edge wear, one taped corner) ............................ **253**

**Button caliper,** boxwood, Stanley No. 23, marked w/SR & L logo, most of the original finish, very rare, fine condition...................... **1,320**

**Calculating rule,** brass half bound hardwood w/tips, marked "Merrifield & Co. New York," log, trig & sector scales, unbound edge is round for ease in reading charts, brass studs for setting dividers, uncommon, very good condition, 24" l. ............ **300**

**Calculating rule,** maple, marked "Thomlinson's Equivalent Paper Slide Scale - J. Thomlinson Ltd. Publishers. Patrick, Glasgow," double slide w/scales to determine information about paper (i.e. weight, number of sheets, etc.), A, B, C, D & E scales, unusual, fine condition, 26" l. ...................... **250**

**Calculator,** cast iron, marked "G.A. Clark. Newburyport, Mass. - Pat. Applied For," traveler-type device, w/wheel that rotates & has seven circular scales, propeller-like double-ended pointer, remnants of paper label, fine condition ................. **60**

**Caliper,** burlwood, good form & grain pattern, very good condition, 16" l. ...................... **176**

**Caliper,** cast iron, lady's leg form, full leg w/extra long toes tapering to form a point for inside or outside measuring, very good condition ............ **165**

**Caliper,** cast iron, miniature, double-type, fine condition, 8 1/2" l. ............................. **165**

**Caliper,** German silver, lady's leg form, long legs & stocking feet, very good condition, 12 1/2" l. ...... **149**

*Gunner's Calipers*

**Caliper,** gunner's type, brass & cast iron, marked "Adams. Fleet Street. London," w/several scales including sector, cannonball, etc., designed for inside & outside measures, steel tips dovetailed onto points, late 18th c., fine condition, 23" h. (ILLUS. of detail) ............... **1,300**

**Caliper,** hand wrought iron, legs worked into round section, opens to 25 1/2", unusual tool, good condition, 21" h. ...................... **80**

**Caliper,** wrought iron, double-style, each half w/wings & locking screws, rare, good condition, 20" h. ...................... **235**

**Caliper,** wrought iron, double-style, large loop handle, good condition, 19" h. ...................... **80**

**Caliper,** wrought iron, lady's leg double proportional-type, brass center joint & locking screw, dancing legs at bottom take outside measure while arms at top repeat same dimension, fine condition ...................... **70**

**Caliper,** wrought iron, marked "G. Scheetz" (owner), lady's leg-type, outside, wing w/locking screw, tight joint, long legs 6 3/4" l., fine condition ...................... **65**

**Caliper,** wrought iron, rare triple-style, double on one end, single on other, good condition (needs cleaning, some pitting) ...................... **135**

**Caliper,** wrought iron w/75% red japanning, full-figure lady's leg form, two adjustable legs flank the center section resembling the silhouette of a mermaid, fine condition, 15 1/2" l. ...................... **523**

**Caliper rule,** boxwood, Stanley No. 32 English, four-fold, English graduations, arch joint, very good condition, 12" l. ............... **100**

**Caliper rule,** boxwood, Stanley No. 36 1/6 E Caliper Rule, Sweet Hart logo, finger notch for caliper highlighted w/Stanley orange paint (first rule to turn up w/that painted detail), English layout, 99% original finish, near mint ...................... **715**

**Caliper rule,** boxwood w/brass slide, Stanley No. 36 1/2 EM,

Sweet Hart trademark, two-fold, slide marked in metric units inside & inches outside, fine condition, 12" l. ............................ **475**

**Caliper rule,** hardwood w/brass fittings, marked "Lufkin No. 172," two-fold, good condition ......... **65**

**Caliper rule,** hardwood w/half-round jaw reinforced w/brass plates, marked "E.H. Taylor. Patent.," bottom section of rule slides to open jaws, unusual, good condition ...................................... **171**

**Caliper rule,** maple w/brass fittings, marked "Kenosha Klosed Krotch. The Lufkin Rule Co.," takes measurements for "The Three Seasons Underwear," tables for "Regular," "Stouts" & "Slims," lettering fully readable, very good condition, jaws 10" w., beam 36" l. ............................ **300**

**Caliper-rule,** boxwood, marked "J. Rabone & Sons," metre on edge, fine condition, 6" l. ..................... **50**

**Caliper-rule,** ivory, marked "Stanley No. 40 Caliper," four-fold, strong lettering, medium yellowing, very good condition, 12" l. ..................................................... **198**

**Calipers,** bronze, screw sets the jaw width, very good condition ......... **46**

**Carpenter's gauge,** brass & maple, marked "Alexander A. Welsh. Patented Feb. 3, 1891," much original finish remains, fine condition ................................. **193**

**Carpenter's rule,** boxwood, marked "Keen Kutter K 180.," two-fold, similar to Stanley No. 18. Square joint, near new, very fine condition, 2' l. ............................ **240**

**Carpenter's rule,** boxwood, marked "Standard Rule Co. Unionville, CT. No. 2.," two-fold, brass arch joint, good condition, 2' l. .......................................................... **65**

**Carpenter's rule,** boxwood, marked "Stephens & Co. Riverton, CT. No. 4. U.S. Standard.," two-fold, square joint, fully bound, good condition, 2' l. (some staining otherwise fine) ............................ **55**

**Carpenter's rule,** boxwood, marked "W. Lambert. Boston.," two-fold w/Gunther's slide, edge marking in tenths of an inch, square bitted joint, early Boston maker, 2' l. (slide slot w/chip & a bit dark) ............................ **325**

**Carpenter's rule,** boxwood, Stanley No. 4, two-fold, extra thin, drafting scales, brass arch joints, rare, very good condition, 2' l. ..................................................... **330**

**Carpenter's rule,** brass-bound boxwood, Stanley No. 78 1/2, four-fold, arch joint, much original finish, fine condition, 24" l. ................................................... **115**

**Carpenter's rule,** brass-bound boxwood, Stanley Rule & Level Co. No. 15, Type 2 trademark, two-fold, w/Gunter's slide, brass arch joint, very clean w/traces of original finish, fine condition, 2' l. ............................ **300**

**Carpenter's rule,** brass-bound boxwood, Stanley Rule & Level Co. No. 78 1/2 English, four-fold, special order rule w/English marking on inside, brass arch joint, fine condition, 2' l. (rule new except some staining at joint) ........................ **240**

**Center finder,** cast iron, marked "Darling, Brown & Sharpe," Ames Patent model, very good condition, 8" l. ............................ **70**

**Chamfer gauge,** cast iron, marked "The Audell Mfg. Co. Orange, Mass.," non-slipping type, w/double-acting screw adjust, in original box, tool & box near new, fine condition ............... **50**

**Chamfer gauges,** brass, marked "Chandler's Chamferer Gauges," new in fine original box w/picture label & directions on back, fine condition, the set .............. **94**

**Clapboard gauge,** mahogany & brass, marked "Nester's Patent. December 31st, 1867,"

*W.T. Fisher Combination Gauge*

all adjustments working, uncommon, good condition.......... **220**

**Cloth chart,** cast iron w/95% plating, marked "Putnam's Improved Cloth Chart - Pat. May, 07," calculating rule, rod-style w/adjustable calipers, from Washington, Iowa, bright & fine condition ...................................................... **65**

**Combination bevel, level & protractor,** brass & walnut, marked "W.T. Fisher. Pat'd. June 23rd, 1868," w/original wing nuts & blade, uncommon layout tool, good condition.............. **400**

**Combination bevel, plumb, level & square,** mahogany w/brass trim, marked "F.W. Ritchie's Pat. Aug. 19, 84," 6" blade graduated in 1/16"

increments, w/vial protectors, proper lock nut for bevel blade, very good condition.............................. **900**

**Combination gauge,** brass & rosewood, marked "W.T. Fisher. Pat'd. June 23rd, 1868.," marked "Fisher" on dial, "Disston" on handle, w/level vial in handle, blade adjusts to angle via two adjustment screws, can read the degree of angle in window of body, manufactured by Disston & Morss of Philadelphia, very good condition (ILLUS. above)........ **578**

**Combination gauge,** cast iron, marked "W.T. Fisher Patent June 23, 1868 - Disston & Morss. Philada.," w/brass-fitted wood handle, much original finish including bluing on blade, fine condition ...................................... **715**

*Combination Gauge & Trammels*

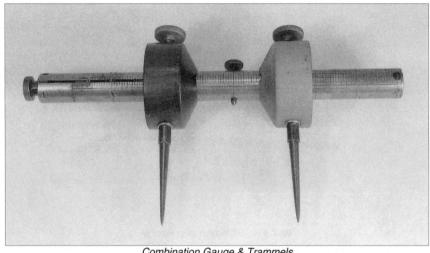

*Combination Gauge & Trammels*

**Combination gauge & trammels,** brass & hardwood, marked "George Kenny Nashua, NH," patent dated "Jan. 4, 1870," for marking & layout work of all kinds, heads of two different color woods for quick identification, trammel points perfect & original, gauge complete down to center scribe point screw, great condition (ILLUS. bottom of previous page) ........................................... **1,210**

**Combination gauge & trammels,** hardwood & brass, marked "George Kenny. Nashua, NH.," patent dated "Jan. 4, 1870," for marking & layout work of all kinds, uncommon especially without broken heads or missing parts, fine condition (ILLUS. above) ................. **715**

**Combination layout device,** brass & rosewood, marked "Man'f'd By C. Farn Co. St. Louis. Pat. Apr. 10, 77. J.F. Klinglesmith Patent," combination square & gauge, blade marked in degrees, inches & other scales, traces of plating on blade, good condition ....................... **605**

**Combination layout device,** cast iron w/90% plating, marked "Crookston Tool Co. Pat. Feb. 16, 1909," a do-it-all device, clean, very good condition ............. **275**

**Combination layout gauge,** brass protractor & walnut handle, marked "Disston & Morss. Tool works Phila. W.T. Fisher Pat'd June 23, 1868," level in handle, rare, good condition ................................................ **688**

**Combination rule,** hardwood & brass, marked "Stephen's Patent Combination Rule No. 036," rule new, in original worn box w/clear top label, very rare, fine condition (box corners taped) .............................. **935**

**Combination rule,** wood & brass, Stanley No. 036, good vial, clean blade, traces of original finish, w/rare oversize page of original instructions & box w/about 90% of the label, ca. 1930, fine condition (ILLUS. next page, left & center top w/various measuring tools) ........ **1,705**

**Combination rule, level, inclinometer, etc.,** boxwood & brass w/steel blades, Stanley No. 036, Stanley acquired patents from Chapin-Stephens & offered the 036 starting in 1929, Stanley-marked 036s very rare, very good condition ....... **450**

**Combination rule, level, protractor, scale, etc.** boxwood, marked "Lufkin No. 863L," clean w/original finish, very good condition ............................. **110**

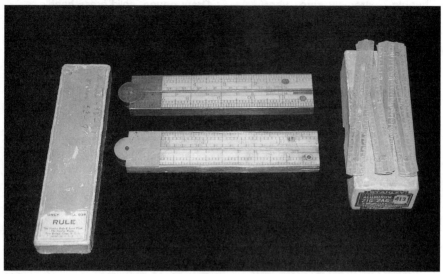

*Various Measuring Tools*

**Combination rule, plumb & level,** boxwood & brass, marked "J. Rabone & Sons. Birmingham.," brass top & bottom wear plates, English, uncommon size, good condition, 10" l. ........................................ **90**

**Combination rule, protractor, scale & level,** boxwood, marked "Rabone No. 1190," four-fold type, fine condition, 12" l. ........................................................ **121**

**Combination square,** cast iron, marked "Nicholls Mfg. Co. Ottumwa, Iowa. Pat. Oct. 18, 04.," square, bevel & angle gauge, very uncommon, very good condition, 8" size ..................... **310**

**Combination square,** cast iron w/nearly 100% japanning, marked "P.L. Fox. Pat. Oct. 2, 88.," try square w/adjustable bevel & mitre, blade bright & shiny, fine condition ........................... **413**

**Combination square, mitre, center finder & level,** cast iron w/80% japanning, marked "S.H. Bellow Pat. Nov. 22, 1881," blades overstamped w/"Chapin's Patent. Reissue May 4, 1889," double bladed, original scribe, good level

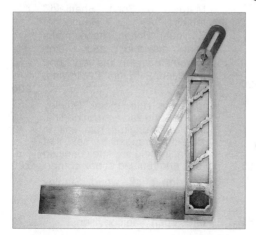

*Combination Square, Level & Bevel*

**Combination square, bevel & level,** cast iron w/75% plating, marked "Ritchie's Patent August 8, 1884," only known example w/open filigree work on the brass handle, Maine inventor, good condition (ILLUS.) .............. **1,705**

bubble, extremely rare, very good condition .................................. **550**

**Combination square, protractor & center finder,** cast iron w/95% japanning, marked "The L.S.S. Co.," fine condition .................. **88**

**Combination try square & bevel,** rosewood & brass, Stanley No. 24 Patent Combination Try Square and Bevel, marked on rosewood handle "Stanley Rule & Level Co. Pat. Apr. 5, 1864," 4" size, early type but w/slotted blade, fine condition w/98% original finishes ........................................ **325**

**Cord wood caliper,** painted wood & brass, marked "F.M. Greenleaf, Littleton, N.H. Maker.," earliest Flossie Greenleaf stamp, yellow paint perfect, brass natural patina, edge & one face calculate units of cord in tree length, trees from 8 to 21 feet, backside stamped in inches, very uncommon caliper, 19th c., very fine condition ........................... **2,100**

**Cotton spinner's rule,** ivory w/German silver fittings, marked "William Slater. Bolton. Designer. Aston & Mander. Makers. London.," two-fold w/Gunter's slide, tables & instructions for cotton spinning, revolution of spindles, counts of yarn, draught of mules, etc., arch & bitted joint, edge markings, rare, fine condition, 2' l. (some yellowing) ........................ **1,450**

**Desk rule,** boxwood, marked "Stephens & Co. Riverton, CT.," straight & unjointed, w/Gunter's slide, beveled edge, rare rule, very good condition, 12" l. (chip one end of slide groove) ........ **120**

**Door-butt gauge,** cast iron, marked "Wright's Door-Butt Gauge," in original box w/detailed picture label & instructions, used, very good condition (some rust) .......................... **95**

**Draw gauge,** brass & rosewood, marked "C.S. Osborne & Co.," clean, very good condition, 5" beam ............................................. **55**

**Draw gauge,** solid brass handle, marked "C.S. Osborne Pat. Aug. 1, 76," handle w/lever to lock the beam in place, very rare, good condition ............................ **310**

**Engineer's rule,** boxwood & brass, marked "Routledge Engineer Improved Rule.," two-fold, calculating rule w/many tables, Gunther's slide, extra wide to allow tables, steel tips, brass arch joint, mint condition, 2' l. ........................................... **475**

**Engineer's rule,** hardwood, Stanley No. 6,. Type 2 mark, two-fold, engineering scales, arch joints, edge marking, very specialized use & very expensive, rare rule very clean & well above average, very good condition, 2' l. ............... **525**

**Engineer's rule,** ivory w/German silver fittings, marked "I. Routledge. Engineer. Bolton.," two-fold w/slide, initials "R.T." engraved on arch joint, w/Routledge calculating table advertised exclusively as made by Jones, an optician located in London, German silver fittings & slide, arch & bitted joints, edge markings, early & extremely rare today, markings fill rule & are clear & fully readable, near fine condition, ca. 1820, 2' l. (chip on one leg & hairline in other) ........... **1,350**

**Engineer's rule,** ivory w/German silver trim & slide, marked "Wm. Marples & Sons. Sheffield," tables by "L. Routledge. Engineer. Bolton," edge marks faint, two-fold, arch joint, extremely rare in this very good condition, 24" l. (light yellowing, wear) .................................................. **900**

**Engineer's rule,** metal, Stanley No. 116, zig zag-type, in original box, one original rule still in slide-on wrapper in box that originally held six, fine condition (one end reglued at box corner) .... **260**

**Extension stick,** wood, Stanley No. 510, in original paper wrapper w/full label, wrapper ends open, fine condition ................. **72**

**Extension stick,** hardwood, Stanley No. 510, new in original paper tube w/full label, fine condition (paper has some tears)...................................................... **80**

**Flooring gauge,** cast iron, hand-wrought clamping device locks sliding beam in place, unusual, good condition ................................. **40**

**Framing square,** cast iron, marked "Pat. July 24, 94. Sep. 2, 99," folding-type, interlocking corner joint slides to lock at 90 degrees, made from Eagle Square Co. squares w/portions of Eagle mark visible, rare & unusual, very good condition ........ **193**

**Frammer,** metal, marked "Sharp's Automatic Frammer," adjust-able blade covered w/tables & is clean & legible, very good condition (most finish worn off metal handle)................................. **60**

**Gauge,** boxwood, marked "Star Tool Co.," light yellow patina, very good condition ............................ **171**

**Gauge,** brass beam, marked "Otis Smith Patent July 5, 1887," combination panel & marking, beam w/point & tee slide on one end for panel work, adjustable steel point on other end for marking, steel w/60% japanning, rare, good condition **1,265**

**Gauge,** brass & mahogany, marked "Chas. A. Miller. Sole Agent. Phila. Made by L.C. Stevens & Co. No. 221, Thompson Patent Oct. 12, 1858.," brass blade w/many scales read direct through window port in handle, scales include sides of polygons, degrees, inches, etc., mahogany handle w/some light tiger stripe that adds character, clean & fine, good condition................................. **1,450**

**Gauge,** cast iron & rosewood, marked "Adjustable Gauge Co. Lexington, Ky. Pat. Aug. 11, 08," gears open blades at equal angles, rosewood handle, very good condition ................................ **160**

**Gauge,** cast iron w/80% japanning, Stanley No. 60, Traut's patent-type, polished surfaces, very good condition........ **110**

**Gauge,** cast iron w/90% plating, marked "Nicholls No. 17. Pat. Apl. Mortise.," double telescoping stem, good condition.................................... **138**

**Gauge,** hardwood w/bronze head, marked "Bates Patent Oct. 20, 1896," head tilts to match bevel edges on one side, other side fits curved edges, uncommon, very good condition.............................. **182**

**Gauge,** iron w/98% plating, marked "W. Brackett. Jordan, NY. Patent Oct. 13, 1885.," rolling across a surface records length of travel, fully working, very good condition.............................. **303**

**Gauge,** metal, marked "Kinney's Patent Rotary Marking," notched rotating head, one of only two examples known, good condition.................................... **1,100**

**Gauge,** rosewood beam & metal w/98% plating, marked "Winslow's Adjustable Face Gauge," face hinged in center & adjusts for both angle & pitch, fine condition ................................. **253**

**Gauge,** rosewood & brass, marked "C. Sholl. Patented March 2, 1864," four-stem mortise-type, very good condition.................................... **242**

**Gauge,** rosewood & brass, marked "Philips Pat. Jan. 15, 1867," nearly unused, fine condition.................................... **105**

**Gauge,** rosewood & brass w/brass mortise slide, marked "A.H. Blaisdell. Pat'd June 23, 1868," lever adjustable cams can be set for concave or convex surfaces, early & important patent, rare, very good condition .................................. **358**

**Gauge,** rosewood head w/steel wear plate, Stanley Rule & Level mark w/eagle trademark & "A. Williams Patented May 26,

*Very Fancy Layout Device*

1857," brass beam w/screw adjust mortise points, strong mark, very good condition .............. **220**

**Gauging rod,** boxwood, marked "Cock. Maker. London.," two-fold rod for beer & wine, brass tip, unusual rule, very good condition, 20" l., ................................. **425**

**Hatter's rule,** boxwood w/slide, inches on one side & tables on other, clean w/some original luster, fine condition .......................... **110**

**Horse measure,** hardwood folding-type, opens to measure a full 18 hands, removable caliper jaw w/level, owner-made, very good condition.............. **138**

**Inclinometer,** ivory w/German silver fittings, marked "L.C. Stephens Co.," folding, earliest patented Stephens inclinometer, very good condition .............. **3,300**

**Inclinometer,** mahogany, marked "Manufactured by L.L. Davis No. 14," good condition w/some wear, 24" l. ........................................... **385**

**Lathe sizing tool,** cast iron w/tiger stripe handle, fine condition ..................................................... **83**

**Layout device,** cast iron w/hinged brass handle, marked "Disston & Morss. Tool Works Phila. W.T. Fisher Pat'd June 23. 1868," handle decorated w/ornately cast leafy scroll design, near perfect, one of only three known, fine condition (ILLUS. above).............................. **6,380**

**Layout square,** cast iron blade swings out from brass handle w/hand-hold grip, marked "Halsted & Ackerman," first patented square, clean, no rust, very good condition, blade 14" l..... **138**

**Ledger rule,** ebony w/jet black finish, six-sided, very good condition, 15" l............................... **29**

**Log caliper,** hardwood, marked "H.M. Co. [diamond logo] Decimal Cord Measure.," all-wood w/tables for lengths 8 to 17 feet, fine condition......................... **140**

**Log caliper,** hardwood, marked "Manufactured by V. Fabian, Milo, ME.," caliper calculates board footage from logs to 24 feet long, tally holes along one jaw w/tally pins, rare to find pins, original yellow finish about 85%, fully readable, Mr. Fabian made calipers & rules of all types for logging industry prior to 1930, very good condition, jaws 19", beam 36" l. ........................................... **110**

**Log caliper,** hardwood w/steel jaws w/much original black finish, brass heads, unmarked, appears to be a Haselton, beam retains trace of finish, fine condition, 36" l. ................................... **200**

**Log caliper,** mahogany beam w/maple jaws, marked "M.E. Hatheway 1881," scales unusual & may not be for logs, fine condition, beam 41" l. ............... **180**

**Log caliper,** maple w/metal fittings at L-bracket ends, marked "G.B. Sanborn, Bristol, N.H.," tall holes to 10,000 board feet, scales to 28-foot logs, 95% finishes, slightly used, fine condition ................................................. **220**

**Log caliper,** wood beam w/brass slide & head, steel jaws, marked "Haselton" w/eagle & "Improved Log Calipers. Cubic Measure," good condition, 48" l. (mark weak but fully readable) ................... **150**

**Log caliper w/wheel,** hardwood & brass, marked "E.S. Lane. Upton, ME. Maker.," wheel & caliper both stamped by Mr. Lane, cast-brass joint, wood fine w/strong markings, wheel near perfect w/tight spokes, very good condition ........................ **2,300**

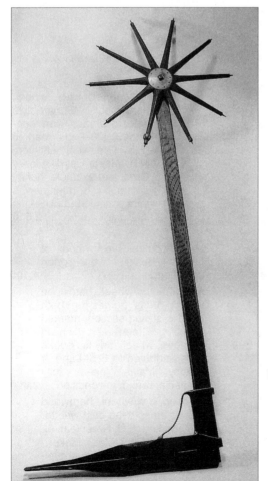

*Log Caliper with Wheel*

**Log caliper w/wheel,** hardwood w/cast-brass joints & wooden steel-tipped jaws, marked "Wm. Greenlief," maker's name stamped on both sides of jaws, wheel is a "Grover" w/unusual round ball weight, early, good condition, dark but still readable (ILLUS.) ......... .**1,650**

*Log Caliper with Wheel*

**Log caliper with wheel,** hardwood w/Grover-style wheel w/brass arm supports & steel tips, marked "F.M. Greenleaf. Littleton, N.H. Maker," early Flossy Greenleaf example, honey amber finish, near new & mint condition (ILLUS.) ............................................. **2,530**

**Log caliper w/wheel,** hardwood & brass, marked "F.M. Greenleaf. 62 Oak Avenue, Belmont, Mass.," w/original unmarked E.S. Lane wheel, Miss Greenleaf learned trade from her father & made calipers while playing in a Boston orchestra, brass jaw supports letter "G" & serial number 1033, F.M. Greenleaf calipers rare, very good condition, (original yellow finish cracked & crazed) **2,550**

**Log caliper w/wheel,** hardwood, marked "Wm. Greenlief," early caliper w/name stamped into edge of brass jaws, scales laid out on both sides of beam, good overall patina, fine wheel of Grover design, very good condition ...................................... **1,100**

**Log caliper w/wheel,** hardwood w/cast brass frames on both head & sliding section, marked "Wm. Greenlief," shield windows, wheel early flat-spoke style attributed to E.S. Lane of Upton, Maine, beam fully readable, rare, fine condition ..... **2,600**

**Log caliper w/wheel,** hardwood w/cast brass head cast w/letter "G," marked "F.H. Greenleaf. 62 Oak St. Belmont, Mass. Maker," wheel is a C.W. Grover-type w/brass hub & plumb bob weight, steel-tipped jaws, wood

*Patented Marking Gauge*

infill, beam retains much original yellow finish & is fully readable, very good condition (one replaced ferrule)................... **1,200**

**Log caliper with wheel,** hardwood, E.S. Lane-style, Grover-style ten-spoke open wood wheel w/metal tips, long flat board handle, unmarked, finish a bit dark, good condition.... **880**

**Log cane,** hickory w/brass cap & tip, Stanley Rule & Level Co. No. 48 1/2, appears to be Scribner's scales, clean, ca. 1879, very good condition.............. **358**

**Log rule,** hardwood, marked "The Maine Log Rule. R.B. Haselton. Maker. Contoocook, N.H.," stick-type, eagle in full flight stamped mark, bright yellow original finish near perfect, fine condition, 4' l.......................... **300**

**Log rule,** hickory w/steel tip, marked "The Chapin Stephens Co. Pine Meadow. Conn. USA," measures logs 12-20' long & up to 35" diameter, fine condition ........ **65**

**Log rule,** wood, 90% paper label reads "V. Fabian Maine Log or Holland Rule," four-foot square w/hook, excellent finishes, used to measure floating logs, uncommon & unused ........................ **110**

**Log scale rule,** white-painted hardwood, marked "Lufkin Doyle Log Scale No. 524," zig-zag folding-type w/hook, like-new, fine condition ................................. **27**

**Marking gauge,** cast bronze w/ash beam, marked "Pat. Oct. 20, 1890" & "Bloomsburg, PA.," Richard Bates patent, faces adjust for curved & mitred edges, rare, fine condition (ILLUS. above)................................. **138**

*Marking Gauges*

**Marking gauge,** cast iron, Stanley Odd Jobs. No. 1, w/original box & instruction sheet, tool like new, box has complete bottom, top & end w/label (ILLUS. bottom left with other gauges)........................................ **660**

**Marking gauge,** cast iron w/95% plating, Stanley No. 198, patternmaker's double stem, rosewood head, very clean &

above average for rare gauge, fine condition.................................. **230**

**Marking gauge,** cast iron w/95% plating, Stanley Odd Jobs. No. 1, includes Stanley No. 62 rule, but early versions did not come with rule, fine condition (ILLUS. previous page top left with other gauges)..................................................... **297**

**Marking gauge,** cast iron w/97% original finish, Stanley No. 165, clearly marked w/"165," Sweet Hart vintage, circular fence plate, fine condition.............................. **100**

*Rare Marking Gauge*

**Marking gauge,** hardwood, marked "John L. Pringle's Patent - Oct. 29, 1906," three interlocking pieces of wood make up stem, w/center section sliding & acting as moving point of mortise gauge, three fixed points allowing for multiple layouts, patent write-up indicates four-in-one tool all set w/single setting, patent submitted by Union Manufacturing Co. in 1905, but patent issued in 1906 after Stanley Rule & Level Co. purchased Union, so gauge most likely made by Stanley, only known example (ILLUS.)................................ **2,200**

**Marking gauge,** cast iron w/98% plating, Stanley Odd Jobs. No. 1, mint but no scribe, 12" l. (ILLUS. previous page right with other gauges) ............................**330**

**Marking gauge,** hardwood, marked "P.B. Rider. Bangor," fixed wooden gauge for laying out lines, weak stamped mark,

only known gauge marked by Rider, good condition............................ **65**

**Marking gauge,** hardwood, Stanley No. 65 3/4 w/pencil, Sweet Hart logo, clean, near mint, ca. 1920s.................................... **171**

**Marking gauge,** metal w/nearly 100% plating, rosewood head, Stanley No. 198, double stem, "Stanley" in script on one beam dates this to ca. 1915, fine condition ................................................ **240**

*1868 Patented Marking Gauge*

**Marking gauge,** rosewood & brass, marked "A.H. Blaisdell. Newton Corners, MS. Patented. June 23, 1868.," used for inside & outside marking on curved surfaces, both screws proper, mechanism fully functional, very good condition (ILLUS.)..................... **495**

**Marking gauge,** rosewood & brass, marked "Star. Tool Co. Pat'd April 21, 1868." W. Broadhead's patent, twist lock, brass trimming, very good condition ......... **65**

**Marking gauge,** rosewood w/full brass plates the length of beam, marked "Phillips Patent Jan. 15, 1867", very good condition.............. **303**

**Marking gauge,** several contrasting woods & inlaid ivory w/brass trim & slide, full brass wear plate on head, ends of beam dovetailed to center section w/standard dovetails & spade-shaped dovetail, fine condition (ILLUS. top of next page) .................................................. **935**

**Measuring pole,** mahogany & brass, four-section, interlocking measuring stick, graduated inches to 120", mahogany w/solid brass joints, quality tool, fine condition, 10' l................................ **250**

*Inlaid Marking Gauge*

**Measuring tape,** steel, Farrand Rapid Rule, open version, marked "Compliments of M.A. Coe Mgr. - S. L. & L. Plant," in original red box, both mint (ILLUS. below) ..................................... **550**

**Measuring tape,** steel w/nearly 100% plating, marked "Stevens by K.&E. Pat. Mar. 23, 86, and June 15, 02," wooden handle, fine condition, 50' ............................... **248**

**Molding gauge,** brass, marked "W.T. Farrell Pat. Mar. 29, 87," heavy body w/scales for setting blade at various angles, wood blocks at base appear to hold a blade, good condition (bolt for blade old replacement) ..................... **140**

**Mortise gauge,** boxwood w/brass trim, marked "S.S. Norton. Colchester, CT," beam stamped to 4", good condition ........................... **110**

**Mortise gauge,** brass & walnut, multi setting-type, four brass slides set & lock, brass head w/four locking screws hold each slide individually, walnut beam, unmarked but at least one other

*Farrand Rapid Rule with Box*

is known, quality indicates manufactured piece may have been patented, fine condition ........ **525**

**Mortise gauge,** ebony & brass, full brass wear plate on head & beam, screw lock, good condition ........................................................ **37**

**Mortise gauge,** rosewood beam w/brass heads, marked "Philips Patent. Jan. 13, 1867," beam-wear plates & mortise slide, good condition (wood shows dings) ...................................................... **90**

**Mortise gauge,** rosewood & brass, marked "M.M. Brainard, Green River, N.Y.," wear plates in head & on beam, screw adjuster, very rare mark from 1870-71 period, near mint .............. **110**

**Mortise gauge,** rosewood head w/steel-wear face & brass beam, marked "A. Williams. Patented May 26, 1857," by Stanley Rule & Level Co., w/early spreadwinged eagle & shield trademark, one movable & four fixed marking points, rare, good condition .......................... **280**

**Mortise gauge,** rosewood, marked "C.G. Siewers. Cincinnati," screw adjust, good condition ...................................................... **83**

**Mortise gauge,** rosewood, marked "Star Tool Co. Pat'd.

Apr'l. 21, 1868.," w/patented twist lock, turn beam locks into position, uncommon gauge, very good condition ............................. **170**

**Mortise gauge,** rosewood w/boxwood slide & screw, marked "E.W. Carpenter. Lancaster.," good condition ............. **209**

**Mortise gauge,** rosewood w/half-bound brass beam, marked "C.G. Siewers. Cincinnati.," screw adjusts from end in the English style, head w/full bone wear plate, good condition .............. **226**

**Mortise gauge,** steel & walnut, walnut stem w/steel head & slide, head appears to be cut from solid block of metal, good condition, 11" l. ...................................... **65**

**Mortise & marking gauge,** cast iron w/99% plating, marked "Winchester Model W 98," in original box w/fine full label, rare boxed item (ILLUS. below) .............. **825**

**Odd-Jobs rule,** cast iron, Stanley No. 1, tool bright & mint complete w/scribe, original green box w/full label, fine condition (box dark w/some wear) ...................................................... **275**

**Odd-Jobs rule,** cast iron w/95% plating, Stanley No. 1, original & w/proper pointer on one end, w/scribe, very good condition ........ **198**

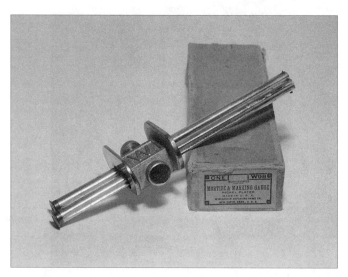

*Mortise & Marking Gauge*

*Stanley Panel Gauge*

**Panel gauge,** beech, marked "Stanley Rule & Level Co. - New Britain, Conn. U.S.A. - No. 84," rare & unusual design, ca. 1900, fine condition (ILLUS. of part) ............................................. **825**

**Panel gauge,** rosewood & brass, Stanley No. 85 1/2, Sweet Hart logo, fine condition ............................. **330**

**Pattern maker's combination rule,** brass-bound hardwood, marked "E. Smith. Rockford, Ill. Pat'd Oct. 24, 1876," slide stick for inside measure scaled for direct read to 44 3/4", trammel points attached to rule & can be located as needed, board scales on one side, inches & shrinkage scales on other sides, hang hole, rare w/trammel points, very good condition ....................................... **300**

**Pitch gauge,** cast iron, Stanley, attaches to end of wooden levels, graduated slide extends from bottom to set desired pitch, very hard Stanley item to find, fine condition ............................ **350**

**Plotter,** German silver-trimmed mahogany, marked "John A.F. Svenson. Scranton, PA.," patent dated "October 27, 1891," adjustable-angle square for draftsmen, can be used to lay out lines at any angle from another line, copy of patent papers attached, fine condition, ... **165**

**Proof rule,** ivory body & slide, German silver tips, marked "T.O. Buss. Hatton Garden, London," England, very good condition (very light yellowing) ...... **115**

**Protractor,** iron blade w/wood handle, marked "Brown & Sharpe Mfg. Co. No. 510," in original fitted case, very good condition ................................. **110**

**Rolling rule,** ebony & brass, marked "Newman & Sons. Square London.," clean w/good edges, good condition, 15 1/4" l. ..................................... **66**

**Rolling rule,** mahogany, marked "A. West & Partners. London S.W.," rule near new, retains much of original luster, cased in original mahogany box, fine condition .................................. **116**

**Rope caliper,** boxwood & brass, marked "Rabone No. 1207," tables & scales, very good condition, 6" l. ........................ **61**

**Rope caliper,** boxwood w/brass caliper, marked "The Trenton Iron Company. Trenton, N.J. M'F'R'S of Wire Rope, Aerial Tramways," extra wide, traces of original finish, fine condition, 2 1/2" w., 6 1/2" l. (two cracks on top pins) ............................. **135**

**Rope caliper,** hardwood w/brass caliper slide & tips, marked "John A. Roebling's Sons Co. Mfr's of Wire Rope. Trenton, N.J.," w/tables for breaking strength, Roebling was builder of Brooklyn Bridge & supplied wire rope for Golden Gate Bridge, rare, good condition, 1 7/8 x 4 5/8" (minor staining)........ **130**

**Rope caliper,** ivory w/German silver trim, marked "Coulsell & Son. Makers. Salmons Lane, Linehouse," w/tables for strength & weight, fully readable, rare, very good condition, 1 3/4" w., 4 1/2" l. (one 1/4" crack in ivory)................... **550**

**Rope caliper rule,** boxwood, marked "Stout Bros. Linehouse.," brass slide & tables for calculating various particulars about rope, good condition ................................. **65**

**Rule,** aluminum, Stanley No. 413, zig zag-type, w/original box, one of the rare 'Schade' Sweet Hart rules remaining, original box w/full label, fine condition (box w/two bad corner)...................... **330**

**Rule,** bone, graduated w/lines only, good condition, 12" l. (light yellowing)....................................... **85**

**Rule,** boxwood, A. Stanley & Co. No. 76, four-fold, bound, early & rare, great color, very good condition, 24" l............................ **935**

**Rule,** boxwood, marked "E.A. Stearns & Co. Brattleboro, VT. No. 32," four-fold, broad w/square joint & scales, fine condition, 24" l. (missing the pins)............................................... **523**

*Boxwood Rule*

**Rule,** boxwood, marked "E.A. Sterns & Co. - Makers - Brattleboro, Vt - Warranted Box Wood" and "No. 5," two-fold w/arch joint, slide w/scales & tables, fine condition, 24" l. (ILLUS. of part)............................ **468**

**Rule,** boxwood, marked "E. Preston & Sons. T. Wilkinson's Improved Engineers," Routledge pattern, two-fold, arch joint, full bound, steel tips, much original finish, early & clean, fine condition, 24" l. ....................................... **187**

**Rule,** boxwood, marked "H. Chapin. Union-Factory.," twofold, w/slide, arch joint & scales from 1" to 12", honey-brown patina, early, very good condition, 24" l............................ **132**

**Rule,** boxwood, marked "Hatter's," slide & tables, very clean, fine condition, 5" l.................... **50**

**Rule,** boxwood, marked "J. & G. Walker. Makers. New York.," two-fold, decorative joint

w/screw adjustment, steel tips, very thin, near new, rare, fine condition, 24" l........................................ **440**

**Rule,** boxwood, marked "Kerby & Bros. 51 Fulton St. N.Y.," twofold & slide inside measure, opens to 26", slides to 50", uncommon, very good condition.... **182**

**Rule,** boxwood,marked "No. 56 1/2," four-fold, half bound, arch joint, made by Biddle Hardware Co., traces of original finish, rare, very good condition, 12" l................................................ **175**

**Rule,** boxwood, marked "Stanley No. 31 1/2 E 1/8 inch to the foot," two-fold, like new, 24" l. ...... **248**

**Rule,** boxwood, marked "Stephens & Co. No. 16 Engineer's.," two-fold, scales, tables & slide, edge markings, arch joint, like-new, fine condition, 24" l................................................ **193**

**Rule,** boxwood, marked "The C-S Co. No. 7," four-fold, blindman's-type w/red figures, nearly like new, 24" l. ............... **50**

**Rule,** boxwood, marked "The C-S Co. No. 75 1/2 Architect's," four-fold, scales, beveled edges, much original finish, fine condition, 24" l........................... **369**

**Rule,** boxwood, Stanley No. 1, two-fold, arch joint, traces of finish, fine condition, 24" l................ **303**

**Rule,** boxwood, Stanley No. 1, w/S.R. & L. logo, two-fold, clean & near mint, 24" l................................ **330**

**Rule,** boxwood, Stanley No. 14, two-fold caliper, clean w/block letter logo, very good condition, 12" l. ............................................... **688**

**Rule,** boxwood, Stanley No. 18 E & M, Sweet Hart logo, two-fold, English measures on one side, metric on other, very good condition, ca. 1920s, 24" l. (stain on one edge)......................... **495**

**Rule,** boxwood, Stanley No. 18, two-fold , marked w/the "NY CITY APP. TYPE 352 SERIAL F.2" markings that show up on

No. 62 rules & some Stanley yardsticks but not usually on No. 18, traces of original finish, fine condition, 24" l. ............................ **55**

**Rule,** boxwood, Stanley No. 29, S.R. & L. trademark, two-fold, very clean, near mint, 24" l. ............ **550**

**Rule,** boxwood, Stanley No. 3, four-fold caliper, traces of original finish, very good condition, 112" l. ............................ **193**

**Rule,** boxwood, Stanley No. 31 1/2   1/16   In.   per   Ft. Shrinkage, folding-type, very fine condition ........................ **468**

**Rule,** boxwood, Stanley No. 31 1/2, two-fold shrinkage type, 1/10 per foot, uncommon, very good condition, 24" l. (some staining & paint spots) ..................... **190**

**Rule,** boxwood, Stanley No. 4, two-fold, thin-type, good color, little wear, very good condition, 24" l. .......................................... **264**

**Rule,** boxwood, Stanley No. 54 Special, Sweet Hart logo, two-fold, tenths of a foot on the outside, light use, good condition, ca. 1920s, 24" l. ............. **116**

**Rule,** boxwood, Stanley No. 58 1/2, six-fold, bound, unmarked except for number, very good condition, 24" l. ............. **550**

**Rule,** boxwood, Stanley No. 58, six-fold, not marked Stanley but clearly made by them, arch joint, fully readable, very hard to find, very good condition, 24" l. ..... **450**

**Rule,** boxwood, Stanley No. 6, two-fold, w/engineer's scales, tables & slide, brass arch joint, like-new, fine condition (two very small holes near each end)... **275**

**Rule,** boxwood, Stanley No. 61 1/2, four-fold, traces of finish, very good condition, 24" l. ............................................ **83**

**Rule,** boxwood, Stanley No. 66 1/2 Special, four-fold, outside marked as standard No. 66 1/2 in inches to 36, inside laid out in "Chair Measurements" of about 1" from 11 to 17 & "Desk Measurements" from 22 to 18 in approximately 1 1/2" gradations, all markings in red (a first for Stanley rules), all marks laid out in quarters, extremely unusual & rare, good condition, 36" l. ............................... **1,000**

**Rule,** boxwood, Stanley No. 66, four-fold, inside laid out in fractions of a yard, brass arch joint, clean, good condition, 36" l. ........................................... **300**

**Rule,** boxwood, Stanley No. 7, Sweet Hart vintage, blindman's type, fine condition............... **83**

**Rule,** boxwood, Stanley No. 78 1/2, four-fold, bound, arch joint, much original finish, fine condition, 24" l. ............................ **220**

**Rule,** boxwood, Stanley No. 79, four-fold, w/board scales, much original finish, fine condition, 24" l. ............................................ **303**

**Rule,** boxwood, Stanley No. 83 w/slide, four-fold, arch joint & 6" slide, edge markings, fine condition, 24" l. ............................ **660**

**Rule,** boxwood, Stanley No. 83C, four-fold, w/caliper, arch joint, traces of finish, very good condition, 24" l. ............................ **220**

**Rule,** boxwood, Stanley Rule & Level Co. No. 83C, four-fold caliper-type, new-old stock, 24" l. (only spotting on brass from years of storage) ..................... **525**

**Rule,** boxwood, two-fold, both ends beveled & tipped, unusual, good condition, 12" l. ........................... **39**

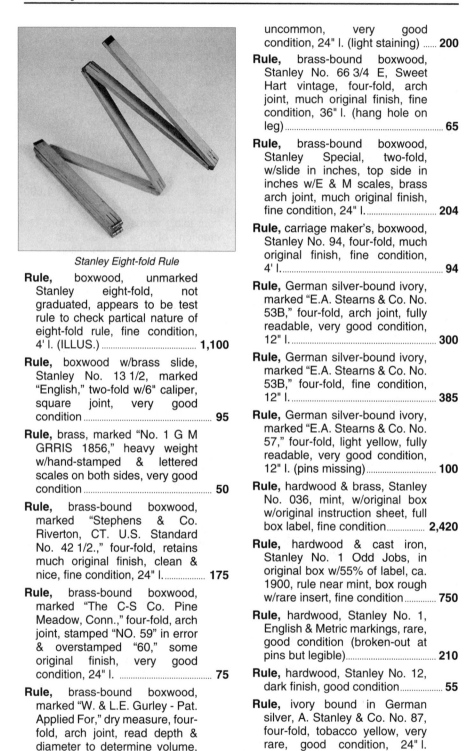

*Stanley Eight-fold Rule*

**Rule,** boxwood, unmarked Stanley eight-fold, not graduated, appears to be test rule to check partical nature of eight-fold rule, fine condition, 4' l. (ILLUS.) .................. **1,100**

**Rule,** boxwood w/brass slide, Stanley No. 13 1/2, marked "English," two-fold w/6" caliper, square joint, very good condition ....................................... **95**

**Rule,** brass, marked "No. 1 G M GRRIS 1856," heavy weight w/hand-stamped & lettered scales on both sides, very good condition ....................................... **50**

**Rule,** brass-bound boxwood, marked "Stephens & Co. Riverton, CT. U.S. Standard No. 42 1/2.," four-fold, retains much original finish, clean & nice, fine condition, 24" l. .............. **175**

**Rule,** brass-bound boxwood, marked "The C-S Co. Pine Meadow, Conn.," four-fold, arch joint, stamped "NO. 59" in error & overstamped "60," some original finish, very good condition, 24" l. ..................................... **75**

**Rule,** brass-bound boxwood, marked "W. & L.E. Gurley - Pat. Applied For," dry measure, four-fold, arch joint, read depth & diameter to determine volume, looks to be Stanley-made, uncommon, very good condition, 24" l. (light staining) ...... **200**

**Rule,** brass-bound boxwood, Stanley No. 66 3/4 E, Sweet Hart vintage, four-fold, arch joint, much original finish, fine condition, 36" l. (hang hole on leg) ................................................. **65**

**Rule,** brass-bound boxwood, Stanley Special, two-fold, w/slide in inches, top side in inches w/E & M scales, brass arch joint, much original finish, fine condition, 24" l. ............................ **204**

**Rule,** carriage maker's, boxwood, Stanley No. 94, four-fold, much original finish, fine condition, 4' l. ................................................. **94**

**Rule,** German silver-bound ivory, marked "E.A. Stearns & Co. No. 53B," four-fold, arch joint, fully readable, very good condition, 12" l. ................................................. **300**

**Rule,** German silver-bound ivory, marked "E.A. Stearns & Co. No. 53B," four-fold, fine condition, 12" l. ................................................. **385**

**Rule,** German silver-bound ivory, marked "E.A. Stearns & Co. No. 57," four-fold, light yellow, fully readable, very good condition, 12" l. (pins missing) ........................... **100**

**Rule,** hardwood & brass, Stanley No. 036, mint, w/original box w/original instruction sheet, full box label, fine condition .............. **2,420**

**Rule,** hardwood & cast iron, Stanley No. 1 Odd Jobs, in original box w/55% of label, ca. 1900, rule near mint, box rough w/rare insert, fine condition ............ **750**

**Rule,** hardwood, Stanley No. 1, English & Metric markings, rare, good condition (broken-out at pins but legible) .................................... **210**

**Rule,** hardwood, Stanley No. 12, dark finish, good condition ................ **55**

**Rule,** ivory bound in German silver, A. Stanley & Co. No. 87, four-fold, tobacco yellow, very rare, good condition, 24" l. (crack at joint on one leg) ................ **935**

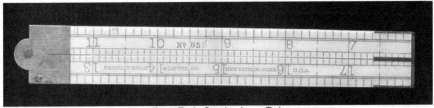

*Rare Early Stanley Ivory Rule*

**Rule,** ivory bound in German silver, Stanley No. 87, four-fold, arch joint, very light yellowing, rare, very good condition, 24" l. .... **633**

**Rule,** ivory, four-fold, round joint, brass trimmings, light yellowing, very good condition, 12" l. ............ **176**

**Rule,** ivory, marked "H. Chapin.," two-fold, uncommon size for American maker, 12" l. (ivory only lightly yellowed) ...................... **525**

**Rule,** ivory, marked "John Renshaw," four-fold, brass arch joint & steel tips, scales, slightest yellowing, extra wide, very good condition, 24" l. ............. **468**

**Rule,** ivory, Stanley No. 0, two-fold, marked w/company name & number, light yellowing, very good condition, 6" l. ............. **963**

**Rule,** ivory, Stanley No. 0, two-fold, narrow, small rules made as samples from leftover ivory scraps, very good condition, 6" l. (minor hinge crack) .................. **450**

**Rule,** ivory, Stanley No. 24 Button Gauge Caliper, marked w/Stanley name but no number, brass caliper slide, light yellowing, extremely rare, ca. 1857, very good condition .......... **3,520**

**Rule,** ivory, Stanley No. 38 Caliper, two-fold, light yellowing, legible, very good condition, 6" l. ...................... **149**

**Rule,** ivory, Stanley No. 38, two-fold, w/caliper, light yellowing, very good condition, 6" l. ................. **330**

**Rule,** ivory, Stanley No. 39 Caliper, four-fold, well yellowed, good condition 12" l. (worn) ............. **72**

**Rule,** ivory, Stanley No. 39, four-fold, w/caliper, hint of yellowing, fine condition, 12" l. ........................... **523**

**Rule,** ivory, Stanley No. 40 1/2, two-fold w/caliper, hard to find, fine condition, 6" l. (slight yellowing, light wear) ........................ **798**

**Rule,** ivory, Stanley No. 40 1/2, two-fold, w/caliper, light yellowing, very good condition, 6" l. ............................................ **385**

**Rule,** ivory, Stanley No. 40, four-fold, w/caliper, very good condition, 12" l. (some moderate staining) ............................... **171**

**Rule,** ivory, Stanley No. 85, four-fold, strong lettering, medium yellow patina, good condition, 24" l. ............................................ **248**

**Rule,** ivory, Stanley No. 85B, four-fold, marked w/Stanley name, number & letter "B" for brass fittings, brass joints, light yellowing, slight spring to board legs, rare version, ca. 1858, very good condition, 24" l. (ILLUS. above) ................................ **3,300**

**Rule,** ivory, Stanley No. 88, four-fold, narrow, German silver-bound, medium yellowing, good condition, 12" l. (worn) ........................ **55**

**Rule,** ivory, Stanley No. 90, four-fold, brass joints, light yellowing, very good condition, 12" l. ............................................ **193**

**Rule,** ivory, Stanley No. 95, four-fold, bound, extra wide, very rare, good condition, 24" l. (worn & moderately yellow, two small cracks) ............................... **605**

**Rule,** ivory, Stanley No. 97, Type 2, four-fold, broad, bound, arch joint, medium yellow, good condition, 24" l. (minor stress checks on one outside face)...... **1,980**

**Rule,** ivory w/brass fittings, marked "J. Rabone & Sons. Makers.," four-fold, round joint, ivory white & bright w/only slightest hint of yellowing, maker's mark on edge, 12" l.......... **290**

**Rule,** ivory w/German silver fittings, Stanley Rule & Level Co. New Britain, Conn. No. 38, two-fold, caliper-type, good condition, 6" l. (some wear but fully readable w/light yellowing).... **160**

**Rule,** ivory w/German silver hinges, Stanley No. 86, four-fold w/arch joint, tenth scales on edges (indicating pre-1862 production), fine condition, 24" l. (very light yellowing)....... **1,430**

**Rule,** ivory w/German silver tips & joints, zig zag-type, fine condition, 1 meter (light yellowing to ivory).............................. **120**

**Rule,** ivory w/German silver trimmings, marked "Stephen & Co. U.S. Standard No. 83.," four-fold, w/drafting scales, numbers crisp, very good condition, 24" l. (ivory w/light yellowing).............................. **750**

**Rule,** maple, marked "W. Quinton. Make. Prov. R.I.," two-fold, square rule joint at fold, brass tips, numbers faint but readable, unusual rule by very rare maker, good condition, 4' l. (broken out at the pin) ..................... **775**

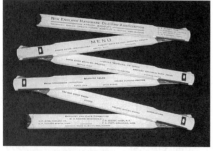

*Rare Zig Zag Rule Banquet Souvenir*

**Rule,** painted hardwood, Stanley No. 103, zig zag folding type, white finish, commemorative w/back printed w/"New England Hardward Dealers' Association Annual Banquet, Thursday, March 23, 1911, Pat'd 10/22/07," menu printed inside w/names of officers & committee members, extremely rare, very good condition, 36" l. (ILLUS.)................................**575**

**Rule,** painted hardwood, Stanley No. 593F, zig zag folding-type, white finish, direction arrows & "ZZ" in shield border, made only from 1911-14, extremely rare, fine condition, 36" l. (slight use wear)................................**190**

**Rule,** painted wood, Stanley No. 593F, zig zag folding-type, white finish, direction arrows & "ZZ" in shield border, unusual rule, extremely rare, ca. 1911-1914, fine/w tight joints, fine condition, 36" l. (very little use except for some minor wear) ........**270**

*Stanley No. 68 Rule*

**Rule,** walnut, Stanley No. 68, four-fold, round joint, marked & numbered, dark wood, mint condition, 24" l. (ILLUS.)..............**1,430**

**Rule,** white-painted wood, marked "S.R. & L. Club. Ladies Night. Feb. 21, 1919," & w/"ZZ" mark, two-fold zig zag-type, limited production made for one-night event just for the women of Stanley, made for Stanley only on special order, very good condition, 12" l. (minor wear, light edge staining) .... **400**

**Rule counter display case,** upright curved glass case front on rectangular metal base, Stanley Zig Zag Rule display, holds six rules, top w/upright rectangular bold orange & blue metal Stanley sign, price card still in back, complete w/all six proper zig zag rules, ca. 1935, mint & rare condition ...................... **1,350**

**Rules,** aluminum, Stanley No. 413, Sweet Hart trademark, patented "December 12, 1922" by William Hart, zig zag type, in original box for six rules, two rules remain, fine condition, box w/full label, minor corner wear & light stain on top, 36" l., the set (ILLUS. on p. 205 right w/various measuring tools) ......................... **605**

**Rules,** boxwood, Stanley No. 62 1/2, set of two, near new condition, in original labeled box, fine condition, the pair ........... **176**

**Rules,** painted wood, Stanley No. 66 1/2, yellow w/red numbering, half dozen near new condition in original box w/full label & rates, fine condition .......................... **350**

**Sector rule,** ivory, two-fold, unusual short size, early, 5 1/4" l. (light yellowing, stress cracks at pins) .............................. **70**

**Sewing rule,** boxwood, marked "E. M. Chapin. Pine Meadow, Conn. No. 84 1/2 *Mrs. Elisha Johnson* *Hartford, Conn.* *Dec. 25, 1858*.," four-fold, gift to Mrs. Johnson, fractions of yard on outside, inches on inside, retains much of original finish, fine condition, 36" l. ............. **500**

*Ship Carpenter's Bevel*

**Ship carpenter's bevel,** brass blade w/rosewood body, marked "Stanley Rule & Level Co. No. 42 1/2," rare, fine condition (ILLUS.) .......................... **1,320**

**Ship carpenter's bevel rule,** boxwood, Stanley No. 42, square block form, ca. 1915, crisp almost new condition ............. **100**

**Shoe rule,** boxwood w/rosewood jaws, marked "F.B. Cox. Makers.," bone stop keeps lower jaw from sliding off end, worn but legible, good condition ....... **83**

**Shoe rule,** maple, Stanley, caliper-type, not in catalogs, very rare, fine condition .................... **358**

**Shoe rule,** maple w/ivory-inlaid graduated slide plates, marked "Kerby & Bros. Makers. 51 Fulton St. N.Y.," measures width & height, sizes 17 in U.S. Standard & 53 in Paris, very good condition ................................. **231**

**Slide rule,** German silver, marked "Kerr & Co. Aarau.," unusual scales, all-metal cursor, w/original case, like new, fine condition ................................. **375**

**Slide rule,** hardwood, marked "Keuffel & Esser Co. NY. Pat. June 5, 1900. Model 100," point-of-sale wall-mounted display-type, w/six scales, very good condition, 7+' l. (cursor missing) ................................. **150**

**Slide rule,** hardwood, marked "Thatcher's Patent by K&E.," numerous scales revolve around sliding cylinder, appears to be model #4012, original mahogany box, good condition (some scales missing about one inch of numbers on the outside ring) .......................... **500**

**Slide rule,** mahogany, marked "Keuffel & Esser Co. No. 4096," DF, CF, CI & two D scales on front, for merchants, importers, accountants, etc., w/hinged case, appears unused, very fine condition, 21 1/2" l. ............................. **300**

**Sliding tailor's T- square & caliper,** boxwood w/brass trim, marked "The Jno. J. Mitchell Co. N.Y.," legs graduated to 6", beam to 14", clip for cloth tape, beam w/strip rule attached to back, appears to be for setting top edge of hem, unusual rule by rare maker, fine condition ............. **70**

**Slip stick,** maple w/brass ends, marked "N.C. Dunn. 6 & 8 N. 6th st. Phila. Pa.," some original finish, unlisted maker, very good condition, 8' l. .................... **70**

**Slip stick,** maple w/brass fittings, marked "Belcher Bros. Co. N.Y.," used for inside measurement as in sash work, much original finish, very good condition, 4' l. ............................ **105**

**Slitting gauge,** beech, marked "E. W. Carpenter. Lancaster.," 14" beam & wedge lock, clean & nice w/classic carpenter thumb-screw, very good condition ............. **130**

**Slitting gauge,** beech, Stanley No. 70 1/2, knob on beam, made only between 1911 & 1923, very good condition ............... **275**

**Slitting gauge,** burl wood head locked w/a wrought-iron wingnut nearly 2" d., wooden roller, very good condition.... **99**

**Slitting gauge,** ebony, brass wedge for cutter, beam w/full brass wear plate, screw lock head, good condition ............................ **70**

**Slitting gauge,** hardwood, Stanley No. 70 1/2, knob handle on beam, very legible, very rare, good condition ..................................... **220**

**Slitting gauge,** hardwood w/brass roller, wedge & screw-lock head, graduated beam, perfect 18th c. handle, dated 1846, mint & perfect............................ **105**

*Slitting Gauge*

**Slitting gauge,** rosewood & brass, marked "Thomas Rice

Patent Sept. 8, 1873," round cutter rotates as cut is made, wooden handle, extremely rare, very good condition (ILLUS.) ......... **880**

**Slitting gauge,** rosewood & brass, marked "Thomas Rice Patent Sept. 8, 1873.," round cutter rotates as cut is made, extremely rare, fine condition..... **1,155**

**Slitting gauge,** tiger stripe maple, unusual design w/a roller the full length of the beam, beam graduated in Roman numerals, very good condition ............................. **413**

**Splitting gauge,** highly figured hardwood perhaps rosewood, brass tip w/wedged cutters, very good condition, overall 16" l. ................ **72**

*Two Squares*

**Square,** brass handle w/steel blade, marked "M' Daniel Voster. Corke. Facit. 1726.," blade w/decorative nib at end & handle ends in ogee, swing-away handle support, an early instrument maker from Corke, Ireland, very early & rare, 'facit' area of mark drilled & part of 'Fac' letters missing, good condition (ILLUS. left w/folding square) ...................................................... **240**

**Square,** burl handle w/brass plate & support, marked "B. Roth," logo etched into blade, good condition, handle 5 1/2" l., blade 23" l. (blade needs cleaning)......... **138**

**Square,** cast iron w/brass-fitted rosewood handle, Stanley No.

24, handle marked, good condition, 9" l. ............................................ **99**

**Square,** cast iron w/wooden handle, marked "Houle Try Square & Bevel. Pat'd Dec. 11, 84," blade graduated in inches & degrees, bright & shiny, very good condition, blade 8" l. .............. **220**

**Square,** galvanized iron, marked "Eagle Galvanized Rust Proof Square," early full-eagle trademark, sample or give-away, very good condition, 4 x 6". .............................................. **65**

**Square,** iron, marked "Pat. July 24, 94. Sep. 12, 99," framing type that folds up, hinge joint slides to lock at 90 degrees, fairly rare, very good condition ..... **105**

**Square,** iron w/rosewood-infilled handle, Stanley No. 10, very clean, very good condition, 12" l. .................................................. **100**

**Square,** iron & wood, Stanley No. 24, patented try & bevel, early type w/long slot & wing-nut locking, good condition, 5" l. (screw stripped) .............................. **121**

**Square,** ivory & brass, folding-type, w/drafting scales, brass plate joint, ivory w/minimum of yellowing, tight shrinkage cracks at hinge pins, legs 4 7/8", very good condition (ILLUS. previous page right w/Voster square) .......... **400**

**Square,** maple & brass, marked "The Nonpareil System. J.A. Glass. Patented 1892. Patented & Improved 1897.," layout square in form of 90 degree triangle, perhaps for tailor's system, could be some other trade, very well made tool w/dozens of scales & markings, wooden storage box ca. 1890s, near new w/original finish, fine condition ...................................................... **200**

**Square,** maple w/brass plates, carved mark "Elizabeth Buzzed Strafford 1845" on one leg, brass plates held in place w/handmade screws that typically date from about 1810 or earlier, so date may have been carved later, numbers hand stamped, good condition (shrinkage checks at screws) ......... **65**

**Square,** steel, marked "Original Blue Brand. E.C. Simmons. B:B Extra Steel, Celebrated. No.

*Point of Sale Tape Measure Display*

**Tape measure display case,** Stanley Push Pull Rule Display Rule Case No. 291, six retractable rules in round cases displayed in wooden point of sale display case w/clear celluloid cover & "Stanley" sign at top, w/original store card, mint ... **2,090**

BB10.," white lettering, fine condition, size 8 x 12"............ **60**

**Square,** steel, marked "The Ideal Square," bright & shiny.......... **55**

**Square,** steel, Stanley No. R-100-B Steel, bright & new in original wrappings, large L-shaped original box w/clear full label, fine condition (box w/some water stains)............... **440**

**Square & protractor,** cast iron, marked "Goodell-Pratt Co. Pat. Jan. 17, 93.," combination protractor w/adjustable square blades, dark finish, good condition............... **110**

**Tape measure,** steel, Stanley No. 1166 Four Square model, round case marked "Nickerson Lumber Co.," mint............... **65**

**Tape measure,** steel, Stanley No. 1166, round case marked "Compliments of F. Bowie Smith. The Lumberman. Baltimore," mint............... **110**

**Tape measure,** steel, Stanley No. 1266A, round case, metric & English, unlisted in metric, mint.... **285**

**Tape measure,** steel, Stanley No. 348W, arched metal case, new in plastic case............... **65**

**Tape measure,** steel, Stanley No. 7886, round red case, mint............. **160**

**Tape measure,** steel w/brushed satin finish, Stanley No. 1166 Four Square model, round case, mint............... **210**

**Tape rule,** steel, marked "The Original Farrand Rapid Rule - Compliments of M.A. Coe - MGR. S.R. & L. Plant," open-case type w/clip on each side, no case, rarest style of Farrand rules, in original red box, fine condition (box faded but fully readable)............... **525**

**Timber scribe,** wrought iron, all-iron w/loop end, unusual form, 18th c., good condition.......... **72**

**Trammel points,** plated iron, unmarked, in style of L.S. Starrett, fine adjustment on one point, good condition, wood beam 21 1/2" l. ............... **45**

*Stanley No. 6 Trammels*

**Trammels,** cast iron w/97% japanning, Stanley No. 6, original wooden keeper marked "Pat. Apld. For," fine condition w/very minor stain on plating of some legs (ILLUS.) ............... **963**

**Trammels,** gunmetal, brass adjuster nut & pressure plates, for heavy construction, good condition (fine adjustment on one, brass adjuster nut a replacement)............... **90**

**Trammels,** maple, good form w/walnut diamond inlays on both heads, one head fixed, one w/wedge lock head, fine condition, 38" beam............... **132**

**Trammels,** rosewood w/brass trim, steel tips, nuts w/fancy knurl turning, fine condition............. **110**

*Brass Traveler*

**Traveler,** brass w/walnut handle, marked "Patent," graphite marker, wheel graduated in inches to 24, pointer can be set to desired starting point, body ends w/spring-loaded holder for graphite lead, fine condition (ILLUS.)............ **325**

**Traveler,** brass wheel w/ebonized wood handle, graduated circle, delicate & perhaps used for tailoring, fine condition...................... **374**

**Traveler,** cast brass wheel w/iron handle & brass pointer, marked "Maxheider," graduated to 24", very good condition............................. **60**

**Traveler,** cast-iron wheel & handle w/65% finish, graduated wheel w/pointer, good condition....... **61**

**Traveler,** clockmaker's, wrought iron w/turned wooden handle, large cut-out star in center of wheel, brass ferrule, well-made, good condition, wheel 4" d.............. **374**

**Try square,** rosewood handle, marked "Disston & Morss," w/level & scribe, blade w/92% original finish, fine condition, blade 18" l................................... **770**

**Try square,** rosewood w/handle support, marked "Stanley. Pat. 3, 16, 97," blade graduated &

*Stanley No. 37 Wantage Rod*

*Try Square*

fully legible, good condition, 18" l. ........................................... **220**

**Try square,** steel, Stanley 150th Anniversary model, tool & box new ....................................... **72**

**Try square,** steel w/whalebone handle, dated "1937" but appear much earlier, well made, fine condition (ILLUS. above)........ **330**

**Try square,** steel w/wooden handle inlaid w/brass diamonds, marked "David Flather Universally Celebrated Joiners Tools Made Especially for America," blade etched w/Lady Liberty, sailing ship & a steam locomotive, rare & seldom seen, very good condition, blade 12" l. ......................... **605**

**Try square w/level,** steel w/rosewood handle, marked "CS Co.," graduated blade, level adjustable by removing plate, very good condition, blade 15" l. .............................. **413**

**Twist drill gauge,** cast iron w/90% plating, marked "Morse Twist Drill & Mch. Co. Pat. Nov. 7, 1911," clean, very good condition .................. **26**

**Wagon gauging rod,** wrought iron, heart-shaped screw-on sliding section, gauging rods not common & should not be confused w/gauges used for setting wheel camber, early, good condition ...................................... **100**

**Wantage rod,** cast iron & hardwood, marked "Ellis Prime - Pat'd. July 23, 1878," sliding section allows measuring both the amount of liquid in vessel & amount needed to fill same, thus combining function of two sticks into one, w/locking device for sliding rod, fine condition (edge chip)............................................... **600**

**Wantage rod,** hardwood, Stanley No. 37, marked "No. 37 - Stanley - New Britain, Conn. U.S.A.," rare, unused condition (ILLUS. bottom of previous page) ...................................... **1,210**

**Wantage rod,** long slender maple rule w/brass sliding head, marked "Dring & Fage Ltd. makers. 56 Stamford St. London," scales on all four sides, England, excellent condition, 48" l. ...................................... **231**

*South Union Wantage Rod*

**Wantage rod,** wooden w/mushroom brass knob w/copper-plated tip, marked "South Union - 1820," handstamped w/single wine scale on one side, inches & feet on other two sides, fourth side blank, designed for single-size barrel, believed to be from the South Union Kentucky Shakers, good condition (ILLUS. of part) ... **880**

**Wantage rule,** hardwood w/brass stop, Stanley, marked "No. 44," double scales on all sides, very good condition ....................................... **50**

**Wantage tool,** maple & brass, marked "Belcher Bros. & Co. NY. US Standard.," barrel gauging caliper for measuring length of a barrel or cask, scales from 0 to 42", brass trim & interlocking slide, very well made, fine condition.......................... **310**

**Wine case wantage rod & barrel caliper,** cast iron, marked "Stanley Rule & Level Co. - Prime & McKeen. Pat'd. March 2 & July 12, 1870. Washington, D.C.," fancy filigree decoration includes letters "USS" & "US Standard," only made on special order, probably limited to U.S. government customs office, never shown in any Stanley catalogs, worn plating, rare (ILLUS. bottom of page) .... **1,000**

**Wine cask wantage rod & caliper,** cast iron w/97% plating, marked "Mf'd by Stanley Rule & Level Co. New Britain, Conn. Prime & McKeen. Pat'd. March 2 & July 12, 1870.," combination wantage rule barrel & caliper, rod very clear & readable from tip to tip, fancy filigree perfect w/letters "USS, US Standard," extremely rare gauge instrument made only on special order & considered one of top three Stanley collector rules, production limited to U.S. government customs office, rod never shown in any Stanley catalogs, finest to surface, very fine condition ..................................... **3,200**

**Wire rope gauge,** boxwood w/brass trim, marked "Hazard Manufacturing Co. Iron Steel and Wire Rope. Conestoga Building. Pittsburgh, PA.," large size rule w/98% original finish made by Kerby & Bro. Makers, New York, marked along edge, caliper gauge for circumference, tables for weight per foot, fine condition, 2 1/2 x 6 1/2" ........ **300**

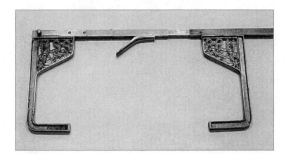

*Wine Case Wantage Rod & Barrel Caliper*

# Saws

Saws, with their distinctive serrated teeth, probably have their origins in specialized stone tools of Neolithic times. The ancient Greeks are credited with the development of hand-hammered iron saw blades, but the ancient Egyptians also made use of this tool.

The earliest saw blades were fitted in a wooden framework for supports, and saws of this style are still in use today. By the late 17th century wider blades of hardened steel could be operated using only a cutout handle at one end. The saw became ever more refined during the 18th and 19th centuries, and blades of all shapes and sizes were available as the Industrial Revolution progressed. Today the basic hand saw has not changed greatly from its 18th century ancestors.

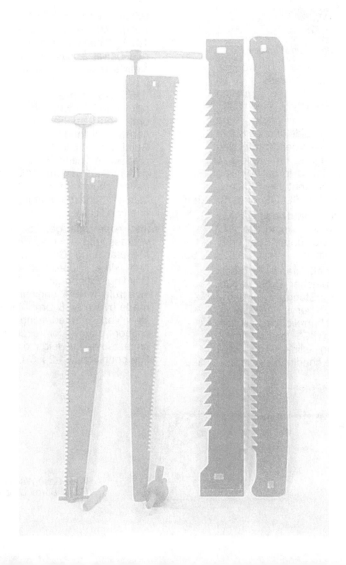

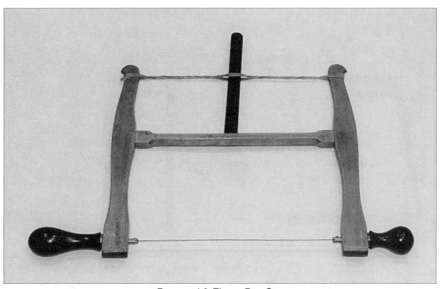

*Boxwood & Ebony Box Saw*

**Backsaw,** brass-backed steel w/mahogany handle, marked "Cortlandt-Wood. NYC, NY," carcass-type, near perfect condition, blade 10" l. ........................ **75**

**Backsaw,** iron, marked "Fenn," ornate scroll-cut open handle w/hanging hole, good condition, 8" l. ............................................. **77**

**Backsaw,** steel blade, marked "Disston No. 4," wooden handle, in original box, fine condition ................................... **138**

**Backsaw,** steel, marked "Henry Disston & Sons," handle w/grooves for fingers & marked w/1874 patent date, rare, very good condition, 14" l. ..................... **260**

**Bench saw set,** cast iron & brass, marked "J. Wignall.," hand- cut thumbscrews, hammer struck, ca. 1810 or earlier, early & choice, good condition...................... **100**

**Bow saw,** boxwood & beech, small size, good condition, blade 9" l. ...................................... **83**

**Bow saw,** steel blade in boxwood frame w/ebony handles & tensioner, marked "Heanshaw Bros. & Nurse - London," England, showy, very good condition (ILLUS. above) ................. **743**

**Dovetail saw,** steel blade w/brass back w/rosewood handle, marked "C.E. Jennings," very good condition, blade 4" l. .............. **187**

**Drive saw,** steel w/wood handle, marked "Shepley's Patent - Feb. 19, 1889," made by Lewis E. Williams, West Groton, Massachusetts, 95% finishes, fine condition ............................................. **94**

**Four square saw set,** steel, Stanley No. 1142, original grey & red paint 100%, in original box w/top & end labels, tool mint, ca. 1930s.................................... **660**

**Frame saw,** wooden frame & ram's-horn nut for blade tightening, flat chamfered stretchers, found in Pennsylvania, 18th c., fine condition, 37" h. .............................. **77**

**Frame saw,** wooden frame w/fancy carving & decoration, inscribed "To R.T. Black, Bellville, Ohio 1915. At Old School Shop. Bellville, Ohio. Richland, Co....," double-mortise frame, fine Scandinavian influence, fine condition .................................................. **660**

**Framed turning saw,** rosewood, fancy rosewood frame w/carved tensioning block, captive slide

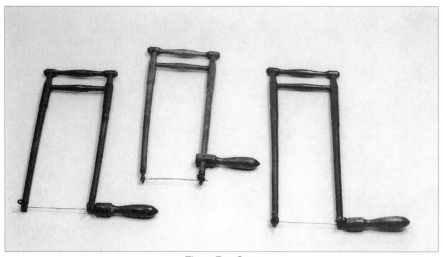

*Three Fret Saws*

in tension block slides up or down allows tightening of bow, deep throat w/nearly 8" of clearance, fine condition, blade 10" l., overall 16"l. ............................ **300**

**Fret saw,** beech & steel, 5" maximum blade length, 12" throat, good condition (ILLUS. above, center) ........................................ **85**

**Fret saw,** rosewood & steel, 12" throat, fine condition (ILLUS. above, left w/fret saws) ................... **100**

**Fret saw,** rosewood & steel, maximum 5" blade, 14" throat, fine condition (ILLUS. above, right w/fret saws) ............................. **230**

**Hand rip saw,** steel blade, marked "Winchester No. 10," carved applewood handle, brass saw nuts, six point, good condition ................................................ **80**

**Hand saw,** cast steel w/applewood handle, marked "Our Saw. Warranted Cast Steel," extra small panel saw w/six points, Disston-made, clear etching on blade, very good condition ..................................... **150**

**Hand saw,** hand-hammered steel blade w/hand-cut teeth, wooden handle, rare hand protector & grip w/nice turned tip, bolt threads are early & hand-cut, 18th c. or possibly earlier, good condition ................................................... **264**

**Hand saw,** steel blade & ornate wood handle, marked "Henry Disston No. 43" in early stamped arched mark, combination-type w/saw, rule, square, level & scribe, very good condition (blade cleaned, chip off both handle tangs) ......... **1,815**

**Hand saw,** steel blade w/fancy hardwood handle w/a carved panther head on each edge over the blade, made by Woodrough & McParlin, blade w/even brown patina, rare, good condition (small chip on one handle tang) ............................. **1,650**

*Woodrough & McParlin Hand Saw*

*Detail of Presentation Saw*

**Hand saw,** steel blade w/wooden handle, marked "Woodrough & McParlin," ink stamped patent date "Jnr'y 13, 1880" on handle, logo w/panther on blade, handle decorated w/carved panther head on each side, Cincinnati, Ohio, very good condition (ILLUS. on previous page) .......... **3,300**

**Hand saw,** steel & hardwood, marked "Henry Disston & Sons Acme 120," perfect handle w/99% original finish, clean & near mint, fine condition (ILLUS. below) .................................... **231**

**Hand saw,** steel & hardwood, marked "Henry Disston & Sons," made from spent war materials found on the battlefields of World War I & presented to F.P. Kelley of the Savage Arms Corp. on March 22, 1920 as outlined in accompanying letter from Horace Disston, saw engraved w/eagle hand-enameled in color w/"Victory" above & "Proclaim Liberty Throughout the World" below, handle laminated in several sections like the biplane propellers that supplied the wood, like new, letter on Disston stationery clear & legible but part of righthand side missing (ILLUS. of part of saw, above) .. **3,600**

**Hand saw,** steel, marked "H.H. Woodrough 66.," patented blade-clamping device marked

*"Henry Disston & Sons Acme 120"*

*"H.H. Woodrough 66" Hand Saw*

"Jan. 25, 1881 James R. Woodrough," one split nut, wooden handle fine, company later joined w/McParlin to make Panther saw, early & rare, good condition (ILLUS. bottom of previous page) ........................................................................ **935**

*Henry Disston
Special-Order Saw*

**Hand saw,** steel, marked "Henry Disston. Philada."(in Old English font), presentation or special-order saw, blade marked "Pappenheimf & Defyfoos Cincinnati," wooden handle deeply carved w/wheat design, split-net screws w/steel inlaid plate marked w/Disston name & three eagles, earliest known "special Disston," ca. 1860, very good condition (ILLUS.) ........................ ........................................................ **2,860**

*Henry Disston & Son Hand Saw*

**Hand saw,** steel, marked "Henry Disston & Son.", triple medallion label screws w/split nuts, near perfect handle & most of original blade depth, most unusual saw, very good condition (ILLUS.) ........................................................................................**1,210**

*"Henry Disston & Sons 7" Hand Saw*

**Hand saw,** steel, marked "Henry Disston & Sons 7.," wooden handle perfect w/93% of original labels, blade w/minor stain, overall fine & unused (ILLUS.) ............. **165**

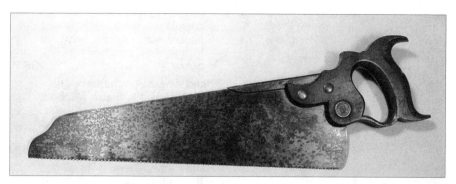

*"Henry Disston & Sons 8 Half Back" Hand Saw*

**Hand saw,** steel, marked "Henry Disston & Sons 8 Half Back.," stamped logo, perfect handle, rare, very good condition (ILLUS.) ........................................................ **605**

*Hand Saw by American Saw Co.*

**Hand saw,** steel, marked "The American Saw Co. Patented tooth of July 16, 1867.," many small holes act as cleaners, carved applewood handle, very tip w/mouse bite, legible logo, good condition (ILLUS.) ................................................................. **495**

*"Wm. Marples. & Sons." Hand Saw*

**Hand saw,** steel, marked "Wm. Marples. & Sons. Taylor Bros. Patent.," blade w/three rows of holes & deep gullets, split nuts, full length w/nib, panel size only 20" l., good condition (ILLUS.) ........................................................................................ **330**

*Brown Patent Saw by Disston*

**Hand saw,** steel w/applewood handle, marked "Brown's Patent Ground No. 3 Keystone Saw Works," 8-point Disston-made (probably made by Disston after Henry Disston bought out Brown Saw Co.), Disston stopped producing the Brown Patent Ground saw just after 1900, mint condition (ILLUS.) ....... **275**

**Hand saw,** steel w/applewood handle, marked "Disston D-12.," seven point rip, straight back, original price tag is a small fold-out catalog showing tool line, new-old stock & near new, wood perfect, blade bright & shiny, very fine condition (quarter-sized stain on blade) ....... **240**

*Disston Combination Handsaw, Rule, Square, Scribe & Level*

**Hand saw,** steel w/applewood handle, marked "Disston -

Patented May 25," No. 43 combination-type w/rule, square, scribe & level, very hard to find, fine condition (ILLUS. below left) ............................................. **3,410**

**Hand saw,** steel w/hardwood handle, marked "Lame & McNiece Saw Works. Philada.," split nuts, strong stamps on both blade & saw nut, early Philadelphia maker, very good condition ...................... **190**

**Hand saw,** steel w/hardwood handle, marked "Spear & Jackson. Sheffield," split nuts, nib, handle w/owner stamp "T. Judd" (Judd family connected w/manufacture of Miller's 1872 patent plow plane), England, very good condition ............................. **205**

**Hand saw,** steel w/rosewood handle, marked "Disston D-15 Victory," logo good, very good condition ................................................ **55**

**Hand saw,** steel & wood, marked "Disston D-76 Centennial No. 0221," manufactured only in 1976, new & mint ................................. **275**

**Hand saw,** steel & wood, marked "Henry Disston & Sons No. 42," combination-type w/saw, rule, square & scribe, rule on blade faint, good condition (tip off tote tang) ................................................. **138**

*"Myatt's Patent" Hand Saw*

**Hand saw,** steel & wood, marked "Myatt's Patent," combination saw, rule, degree finder, level & square, early w/split nuts, good condition (ILLUS.) ........................... **1,018**

*"Henry Disston & Sons" Ice Saw*

**Household saw,** steel w/95% plating, marked "Christy Household Saw. The Christy Knife Co. Fremont, O. Patented Nov. 12, 1889," rule on back side, w/original pasteboard mailing cover, very good condition (spots on blade) ............ **35**

**Ice saw,** steel, crescent moon design w/wooden end handles, rare variation, about 6' long tip to tip (some minor pitting, one tooth missing) ............................ **468**

**Ice saw,** steel w/single wooden rod handle, teeth more like a marking saw, used at the Holyoke Ice Co., Holyoke, Massachusetts, good condition, blade 4' 7" l. (blade pitted) ............... **61**

**Ice saw,** steel w/wooden handle, marked "Henry Disston & Sons," long blade w/full logo & most original finish, T-shaped handle original & in good condition, near-new condition (ILLUS. above) ....................... **132**

**Ice saw,** steel & wood, marked "Woodrough & McParlin," rare wooden handle w/a panther head carved where handle joins the blade, also carved w/wheat stalks, blade w/even brown patina, ink stamp visible but faint, early, good condition (ILLUS. of part, below) ...................... **990**

**Jeweler's saw,** gold-finished iron w/60% plating, miniature, turned wooden end handle, blade length adjustable, tiny saw perfect in all details, very good condition, 4" l. .............................. **260**

**Keyhole saw,** wooden scroll-cut handle w/slender steel blade, marked "C.E. Mitchell. Lowell, Mass. Pat. Oct. 24, 1865," brass ring twist to lock & hold blade, good condition ......................... **127**

*"Woodrough & McParlin"*
*Ice Saw*

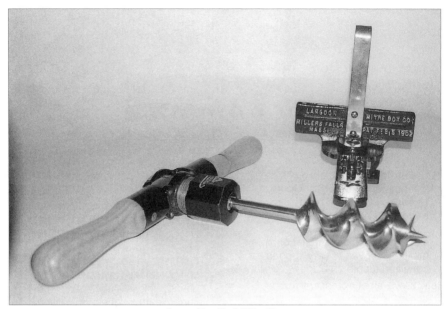

*Auger Handle & Mitre Box*

**Mitre box,** cast iron w/100% japanning, gold stars & lettering reading "Landon Mitre Box Co. Pat. Feb. 5, 1902," type used w/handsaw, fine condition w/new plating (ILLUS. right w/auger handle) .................................. **121**

**Mitre box saw,** cast aluminum, Stanley No. A358, Sweet Hart vintage, w/brass plate on end, wooden table, saw by Henry Disston w/second Sweet Hart logo, rarest of Stanley aluminum tools, very good condition ................................. **225**

**Mitre saw,** steel, Stanley No. 100, combination mitre saw & vise for picture-frame work, complete w/two rules, one w/stop & a No. 39 24 x 4" backsaw, mounted on oak base, like new, fine condition (ILLUS. below)........................ **275**

**Mitre saw & box,** steel, Stanley No. 360, Made in Canada, Disston saw marked "The Stanley Tool Co. of Canada, Limited," like-new, very scarce Canadian Stanley set........................ **132**

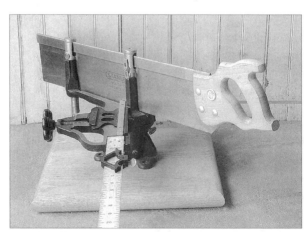

*Stanley No. 100 Mitre Saw*

**Pit saw,** steel w/wooden handle, w/box & tiller, early, good condition (tiller w/replaced handle, old repair in box, crack in saw at eye)...................................... **198**

**Pit saw,** wrought iron, early w/hand wrought tiller & box, wooden handles, good condition, w/few worm holes, blade 59" l. (ILLUS. below, far left w/various saws)............................ **75**

*Early Handmade Saw*

**Saw,** wrought iron & hardwood, possibly for stair work, flat board w/long arched end handles, crude saw blade inserted along the bottom, dated 1808, very good condition (ILLUS.).................... **193**

**Saw set,** hand wrought iron, pliers type w/screw to adjust amount of set, very well made, unmarked, very good condition....... **65**

**Stair or related hand saw,** D-form cherry handle, fixed blade, very good condition............................. **149**

**Stair saw,** steel blade w/applewood handle, marked "Geo. H. Bishop.," adjustable depth of cut, uncommon Bishop saw, good condition............................. **250**

**Surgeon's bone saw,** cast iron & ebony, cast & hand finished, ebony handle, very fancy w/lots of detail, rare, good condition, 19" l. (handle w/age check)............. **775**

**Tenon saw,** brass-backed steel, marked "E.C. Atkins & Co. Silver Steel. No. 2., Indianapolis, Ind.," applewood handle, excellent condition (handle w/few scuffs)......................... **340**

*Turning Saw*

**Turning saw,** rosewood & steel, arched H-form frame w/slender blades & turned handles, pocket mortise for tensioner,

*Various Saws*

**Pit saw,** wrought iron & wood, early saw w/wrought iron tiller, wooden box, very good condition, blade 77" l. (ILLUS. above, second from left w/various saws).................................. **325**

**Plane saw,** steel, marked "Reliance Saw Co. Philada.," split nuts, near perfect wood handle, very good condition, blade 18" l. .................................................. **80**

small size, great form, very good condition, blade 8" l. (ILLUS. bottom of previous page)............................................. **275**

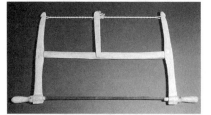

*Turning Saw made of Whale Bone*

**Turning saw,** whale bone, six piece construction w/all parts except tension cord made of whale bone, beautifully done, first half of 19th c., very fine condition (ILLUS.)............................. **2,600**

**Up and down saw,** cast steel, marked "Roe & Co. New York. Cast Steel. Warranted. Patent Ground. [with Eagle trademark].," large saw w/six teeth per foot, huge old blades contained lot of great steel quickly remade when no longer in use, blades extremely rare & seldom found, ca. 1850, three chipped teeth, very good condition, 6 foot 10" tall (ILLUS. previous page, second from right w/various saws)............................. **75**

**Up and down saw,** wrought iron, taper hammered front to back edge, all hand-wrought, seven teeth per foot, ca. 1800, very good condition, 6' 11" (ILLUS.previous page, far right w/various saws)......... **325**

*Veneer or Resaw Saw*

**Veneer or resaw saw,** wood & steel, frame-type w/long rectangular wooden frame w/side handles at each end & blade down the center, very good condition, blade 2 1/2" deep, blade 36" l., overall 48" l.......... **105**

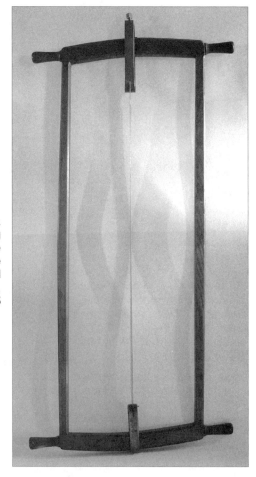

# Special Use & Miscellaneous Tools

In this section we are including a wide variety of tools that don't fit neatly into broad categories included earlier. Often these will be tools of a very specialized nature used by specific craftsmen or in certain trades. You may see tools listed here that are not easily recognized by the non-specialist collector. With luck you may find out what that mysterious "what's-it" is that you've found during your collecting forays.

**Aircraft splicing tool,** steel w/98% japanning, Stanley, used to clamp the loop in aircraft cable for crimping, rare .......... **$50**

**Anvil,** cast iron, miniature, marked "Amos Seamans. Nov. 1899.," anvil w/one hardy, very well made, fine condition, 3 1/2" h., 9 1/2" l. .................................. **325**

**Anvil,** cast iron, stake-type designed to sit on wooden base, shield decoration on either side marked w/nine touchmarks, 18th c. or earlier, good condition, 20" l., 15 1/2" h. ......................... **175**

**Balance scales,** wrought-iron base w/cooper pans, 18th c., good condition, beam 18" l., overall 21" h. ......................................... **193**

**Barn door hinges,** hand-wrought iron, complete w/wall brackets & pins, early & nice, very good condition, 38" l., pr. ............................... **88**

**Bench anvil,** hand-wrought iron, square & round horns, clamps to bench, round hardy on end projects from bench for special shaping, early & unusual, very good condition ...................................... **110**

**Bench vise,** hardwood, hand-carved front post features full face carving decorated w/vines & chip carving, 2 1/2" jaws covered w/heavy felt pad, vise clearly intended for one of the finer trades, very good condition (ILLUS. right) ......................................... **900**

**Blade holder,** cast iron w/85% japanning, Stanley No. 198, hard to find, very good condition ............... **77**

**Blind nailing tool,** cast iron w/99% plating, Stanley No. 96, original cutter, fine condition .......... **132**

**Blind nailing tool,** metal w/90% plating, Stanley No. 96, Type 1 w/patent date, Witherby chisel, very good condition ............................ **248**

**Blind nailing tool,** steel w/99% plating, Stanley No. 96, original cutter, small size, fine condition ... **303**

**Blubber cutter,** wrought-iron curved spade-form blade w/long wooden handle, good condition, blade 7" deep, edge 9" w., overall 70" l. .................................... **39**

**Boat building tool,** hardwood, boat building industry plane-style device, engine lapstrake end beveler, lapstrakes slide in slot on side & planned to taper, two tapered ends overlap to maintain constant thickness, used in Loon Lake region of Maine on Rangeley guide boats, good condition, board 4" w., 2 9/16" thick, 24 1/2" l. ......... **425**

**Brace wrench,** cast iron, marked "P. Lowentraut," Schultz 55, all the proper parts including the

*Hand Carved Bench Vise*

crank & screwdriver bit, good condition ....................................................... **70**

**Buggy wrench,** cast iron, marked "Pat. April 14, 1896," Schultz 224, clean w/good spring, good condition (ILLUS. on next page middle row, third from left with other wrenches) ...... **90**

**Butcher's hanging hook and saw rack,** wrought iron, attaches to wall, cutout design shows tools of trade including saws, knives & cleavers, good condition, nearly 2 feet long ...................... **165**

**Cabinet maker's bench,** cast iron w/laminated top, marked "Emmert's," w/small pattern maker's adjustable vise at one end, a 3 1/2" bench vise on other end, six drawers in base, fine condition, top 22 x 57" l. (ILLUS. below) ....................................... **770**

**Carpet stretcher & auto tacker,** iron w/wooden handle, teeth grab carpet, lever action stretches, a pound to the head drives the nail, track feed moves next nail in line, good condition ............................................... **25**

**Carriage wrenches,** cast iron, marked "Joy's Carriage Wrench. No. 1," Schultz 220, one w/90% plating but replacement handle, other w/good handle but rusted, good & better condition, pr. (two ILLUS. next page, middle row far left with other wrenches) .......................... **55**

**Chute board,** cast iron w/99% japanning, Stanley No. 52, all hold-downs & pins, mint (no plane) ..................................................... **825**

**Combination wrench,** cast iron, marked "Bonny Tomhawk," combines wrench, hatchet, hammer, staple puller, etc., rare combination, very good condition (ILLUS. next page, top row second from left with other wrenches) ..................................... **41**

*Cabinet Maker's Bench*

*A Variety of Older Wrenches*

**Combination wrench,** cast iron w/45% plating, marked "Thomas Mfg. Co. Dayton, Ohio," combines wrench, hatchet, hammer, etc., good condition (ILLUS. above, top row far left with other wrenches) ............................ **45**

**Compass,** brass case w/engraved & silvered dial, level vial set into dial, unmarked but heavy & high quality, 3 1/4" l. needle, very good condition, 4" d. ......................... **135**

**Compass,** silvered iron, mahogany & brass, marked "E.A. Kutz. New York.," silvered dial, two level vials, compass center engraved w/vine & leaf design, Kutz worked 1862 & earlier, 6 1/4" l. detachable vanes, mahogany box w/brass cover, very good condition, dial 5 3/4" d. w/5" needle, overall 14" w. (brass finish as found w/an even patina, one hasp on box replacement)..................................... **1,450**

*Cooper's Barrel Forms*

**Cooper's barrel form,** wood, sets up barrels w/approximately 13" heads, good condition, hard to find, 24" h. (ILLUS. left w/other barrel form)............................................... **358**

**Cooper's barrel form,** wood w/stone ring at center, sets up barrels w/approximately 8" heads, foot pedal tightens form, semi-mechanical, good condition (ILLUS. right w/other barrel form)............................................... **248**

*Corn Sheller*

**Cooper's dividers,** carved elm, single-piece bent arch w/double-acting screw, good condition (points pitted, missing a sliver on one side) .............. **121**

**Cooper's dog,** wrought iron, early, good condition.................... **55**

**Cooper's jointer,** beech w/cast iron screw caps, unmarked but cast iron caps very similar to Seigley bench plane cap, double throated, sweep for stave radius, good condition, 5" w., 47" l. ...................................... **160**

**Cooper's jointer,** yellow birch, w/double irons & wedges, both sides w/applied fence, good condition, 4" thick, 8 1/2" w.,

4'4" l. (measurements include fences)................................. **150**

**Corn sheller,** cast iron, marked "Golden Corn Sheller - Gray & Bros. - Pat. 1870 - Louisville, Ky.," double-sided hinge type, near perfect (ILLUS. above) .......... **275**

**Corn sheller,** cast iron & wood, marked "Little Giant," double-jaw type w/wooden handle, finishes fine, shows little use, very good condition.......................... **248**

**Dinglestock,** wrought iron, large pointed spike w/a heavy ring loop at one side opposite a large flat round projecting tab, fine condition, 9" l.................................. **72**

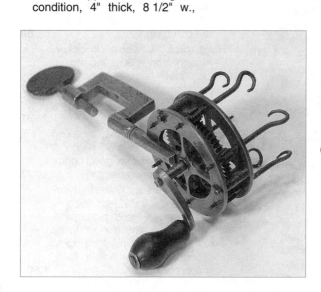

*Cord Winder*

**Cord winder,** brass frame, geared wheel interfaces w/six others, each connected to rotating hook, all mounted in frame that clamps on tabletop, possibly early 19th c., good condition, thumbscrew & one post are pitted (ILLUS.) . **330**

*Wooden Dividers*

**Dividers,** hardwood w/hand-wrought iron tips, marked "PG 1879," quarter arc w/decorative carving, good condition, 11" h. (ILLUS.)............................................ **330**

**Dividers,** wrought iron, early, good condition, 23" h. ...................... **60**

**Dowel maker,** cast iron w/95% japanning, Stanley No. 77, w/hand crank, nine cutter heads, eight w/original boxes, rare w/cutter heads, good condition (cutter heads purchased over time & three box styles exist, geared wheel has been drilled around outside edge, two boxes missing bottoms).............. **1,210**

**Dowel maker,** steel w/90% japanning, Stanley No. 77, w/nine cutter heads, all in original boxes w/some wear, ca. 1915, the set..... **770**

**Drafting set,** brass & ivory, two-tiered box w/instruments above & ivory sector & parallel rule below, walnut box, all but one instrument original to the case, good condition (crack on corner of rule)............................................ **77**

**Drafting set,** German silver & ivory, includes two ivory-handled inking pens, an ivory-handled bow compass, two sizes of Ger-

man silver dividers, 6" compass w/many pencil & inking attachments, complete set of quality tools, fitted mahogany case w/both bottom & cover compartments, fine condition .......................... **190**

**Drafting set,** ivory scale rule, three ivory-handled pens, two ivory-handled compasses, proportional dividers & several plain dividers w/attachments in fitted rosewood case; case w/lift-out tray & compartment in lid, outside inlaid w/mother-of-pearl & brass, fine condition, set of 13 tools w/case .......................... **1,100**

**Firing pin tool,** steel factory-modified screwdriver for working on firearms at the Springfield Armory, Stanley, wooden handle ...... **193**

**Glass cutters,** diamond points & rosewood handles, marked "Bush & Chipper. Makers," stored in fitted box w/inlaid diamond design on top, good condition, pr. ...................................... **72**

**Graining combs,** wood, marked "Henry Taylor," set in tin box w/original label, label 60%, combs like new, very good condition, the set........................... **66**

**Hay knife,** steel w/wooden handles, marked "The Welland Vale Manufacturing Co. Ltd. St. Catharines, Ont.," 95% of original paint, perfect label, Canada, fine condition ............................ **39**

**Hoof pick & snow knocker,** wrought iron w/30% japanning, long loop handle, very good condition........................................ **22**

**Jamb tap,** wrought iron, large, early, good condition............................ **31**

**Jeweler's turn,** brass, indexing cutter head, owner's name & 1900 date on base, good condition (one crank replaced)................. **127**

**Jeweler's vise,** pedestal-type, cast iron w/95% japanning & 90+% red & gold pinstriping, swivel base allows work to be rotated in full circle, clamping action holds removable jaws, fine condition ................................. **1,500**

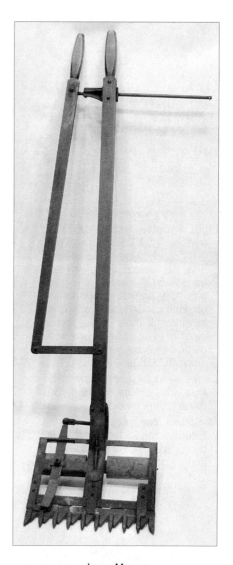

*Lawn Mower*

**Lawn mower,** cast iron, hand-powered, w/sickle bar-type cutter that chops grass as two handles are pushed & worked, ca. 1900, good condition (ILLUS.) ...... **248**

**Leather creaser,** lignum vitae, Stanley Rule & Level Co., clearly marked, like-new w/most original finish............................................. **83**

*Adjustable Leg Ladder*

**Ladder,** hardwood, salesman's sample marked "Ladder.," adjustable leg on one side adjusts downward to allow for sloping ground, very well made, fine condition (ILLUS.)................................ **275**

*Early Gurley Mountain Transit*

**Light mountain transit,** cast iron, marked "W. & L.E. Gurley. Troy, NY.," early type w/Gradienter only, no vertical arc, green leveling vials, 8" l. scope, 4" l. needle, 95% original brown finish, original wooden case w/leather covering & tripod, case holds most original tools & two non-original plumbs, very good condition (ILLUS.)............................ **770**

**Lock,** wrought iron, early slide type, w/key, 18th c., good condition (some pitting)................................ **77**

**Miniature can,** copper w/brass fixtures, marked "K" on side, pump type, 1 1/2" tank, Meccano, good condition w/working

pump (ILLUS. bottom of page, right w/pencil sharpener & miniature "rabbit" plane)............................ **170**

**Miniature "rabbit" plane,** cast brass, in the form of a rabbit, 3/16" cutter, fine condition, overall 1" l. (ILLUS. bottom of page, center w/pencil sharpener & miniature oil can)....................... **210**

*Rare Reed & Co. Mining Compass*

**Mining compass,** iron & brass, marked "James R. Reed & Co. Pittsburgh, PA. No. 318.," vernier scale for horizontal swing & 180-degree arc for vertical swing, 3 1/2" l. removable vanes, 4 1/2" l. compass nee-

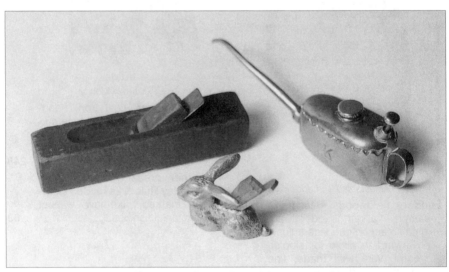

*Pencil Sharpener, "Rabbit" Plane & Miniature Oil Can*

*Nail Maker's Bench and Anvil*

dle, 5 3/4" d. dial w/original brass cover marked w/serial number, original dovetailed wooden case w/paper label on top, instrument fine w/much original finish, case needs restoration, rare, very good condition (ILLUS. previous page) ....... **3,740**

**Mitre jack,** oak & maple, screwtype w/7" jaws, good condition ........ **39**

**Monkey wrench,** cast iron, marked "Winchester No. 1007," adjustable, rare, fine condition, 21" l. (small chips) ............................ **110**

**Nail maker's bench & anvil,** wood, three-legged, pegged construction throughout, late 18th or early 19th c., extremely rare, very good condition, anvil 1 1/2" by 1 3/4", seat 20" h., anvil surface 29" h. (ILLUS. above) ....... **475**

**Nail puller,** cast iron, compound leverage-type, early but unmarked, long turned wood handle, very good condition (ILLUS.

om p. 242 bottom row right, with wrenches) ................................................ **120**

**Nut wrench,** cast iron, revolving-type, unmarked, similar to Schultz 556, good condition, 9" l. (even surface rust) ..................... **110**

**Padlock,** cast brass, marked "Amos Sword. Patent Sept. 19, 1882," w/original key, very good condition ...................................................... **88**

**Paint-bucket holder,** cast iron, beam slides under clapboard & prongs stick to wall below, rare & unusual, fine condition ..................... **39**

**Painter's pot,** copper w/domed cover so that it can hold the brush, bright but not polished, w/old brush, fine condition ................. **83**

**Pargetting tool,** hand-wrought iron, incised "EE 1845," wide flat half-round blade w/dentil-notched edge, long slender handle extends from center back & ends in acorn finial, good condition ...................................... **105**

*Early Patent Model*

**Patent model,** brass & steel, marked "G.W. and T. Parker. Saw Gummer. Dec. 14th, 1875," very mechanical, original tags, fine condition (ILLUS.) .......... **440**

**Patent model,** brass & steel w/dovetailed wooden frame, marked "Chars. W. Hubbard. Machine for Grinding Saws. Patented July 1866.," very mechanical, original tag torn & taped, may be missing one adjustment arm, very good condition (ILLUS. below) ............................ **440**

**Patent model,** mahogany, marked "H.R. Packard. Machine for Affixing Caps to Nails and Tacks. Patented Apl. 5, 1881.," very complex, two parts w/small broken sections, good condition ................................................... **385**

**Patent model,** wood & brass, marked "Joseph Thomas. Brooklyn, New York. Machinery for Felting Hat-Bodies.," bowl-like reservoir moves back & forth while two paddle-like arms apply the felt, patent issued July 1, 1856, w/original Patent Office

*Saw Grinding Patent Model*

tag & photocopies of patent, mint condition .................................... **750**

*Carriage Hinge Patent Model*

**Patent model,** wood, brass & steel, marked "George A. Royce. Carriage Hinge. Patented Oct. 1st. 1889.," fancy working model w/swing-down & swing-out hinge for carriage, original papers, fine condition (ILLUS.)................................... **495**

**Patent model,** wood & metal, marked "E. Hechler. Patented Dec. 22, 1874. Reading, PA.," machine for stretching hat bodies, complete & working, original ribbon & fragment of original Patent Office tag, fine condition ... **625**

**Patent model,** wood & steel, marked "J.T. Jenkins. Wedge Cutter. Patented May 26, 1885," lever arm action, original tags, very good condition (ILLUS. below).......... **330**

**Pencil sharpener plane,** hardwood & cast iron, promotional model, marked "Advertising Results Co. Chicago. Pat. Applied for," good condition, 5/8" w., 3 1/8" l. (ILLUS. on p. 246 left w/miniature "rabbit" plane & miniature oil can) ............................. **120**

**Pharmacist's pill-rolling table,** mahogany & brass, consists of pill-forming plate & accompanying sliding portion that together form rounded pills, very good condition............................................. **132**

**Pipe & nut wrench,** cast iron, combination stubby model, similar to Schultz 580, works well, good wooden handle, good condition, 10" l. .............................. **46**

**Pipe & nut wrench,** cast iron, marked only "1869," lever lock & screw adjusts, clean & working, very good condition, 15" l. ................ **210**

**Pipe wrench,** cast iron, marked "H.B. Smith Perfect Handle," wooden handle, good condition, 18" l. ................................................. **55**

*Wedge Cutter Patent Model*

**Pipe wrench,** cast iron, marked "Porter Mfg. Co. Revere, Mass.," Schultz 708, bolt for spring may not be original good condition, 13" l. (ILLUS. on p. 242 top row, third from left, with other wrenches) ...................................... **60**

**Pipe wrench,** cast iron, marked "Sheffy," Schultz 338, clean, good condition, 12" l. ........................... **65**

**Pitcher adjuster,** cast iron w/70% plating, Stanley No. 7, for metal levels, very hard to find, good condition .............................................. **330**

**Pitcher adjuster,** steel w/98% plating, Stanley No. 5, for wood levels, original wooden block, like-new ................................................. **440**

**Plain compass,** brass & silvered metal, marked "Bleuler. London.," 6" silvered dial w/5 1/8" needle, round top w/detachable vanes, in wooden box w/very early "H. Gattey" of London name & sporting New York address, very good condition, tripod, 15" h., compass 5 1/2" h. ...... **900**

**Plain sighting compass,** mahogany w/brass vanes, marked "H.S. Pearson. Portland.," compass card w/fleur-de-lis at north & full eagle w/breast shield at east, card is signed "Wightman Sculpt.," brass ring dial w/one-degree gradations, dovetailed wood case finished in old red paint, original Jacob's staff w/all-wood locking joint & ball, staff w/what appears to be bone ring just below top, Henry Sleeper Pearson made watches, rules & mathematical instruments in Portland, Maine, from at least 1823 until 1875, 6" vanes, 4 3/4" needle, 6" dial, rare, fine condition, overall 15" l. (wood body a transitional piece, staff ball & joint sock cracked & need restoring, one brass vane bolt a replacement) ................................................. **2,000**

*Plumb Bobs*

**Plumb bob,** brass ball shape w/steel tip & top, 2 lbs., 7 oz., 4 1/2" l. (ILLUS. above, right) .......... **55**

**Plumb bob,** brass & cast iron w/90% plating, marked "Goodell Pratt Company. Toolsmith No. 782.," reversible-type in four pieces, internal shaft & point can be reversed in body, sleeve & cap screw to hold items in place, uncommon, good condition ..................................... **110**

*Various Plumb Bobs*

**Plumb bob,** brass, experimental, similar in design to Stanley reel bob, 5" h. (ILLUS. above, left w/other plumb bobs) ........................... **450**

**Plumb bob,** brass, needle-type, 1/2" diameter, 8" l. .................... **165**

**Plumb bob,** brass, round w/steel tip, 3 lbs., 12 oz.., very early, unusual design, good condition, 5" l. (ILLUS. top of page, left) ........ **165**

**Plumb bob,** brass, Stanley No. 1, reel-type, fine condition (a few nicks) ............................................. **253**

**Plumb bob,** brass, Stanley No. 2, reel-type, mid-size, very good condition (some dings) ..................... **187**

**Plumb bob,** brass, turnip-shaped, almost 5 lbs., like new, 8" l. (ILLUS. below, right w/other plumb bobs)............................. **242**

**Plumb bob,** brass, turnip-shaped w/steel tip, wooden line reel, very good condition .............................. **55**

**Plumb bob,** brass w/fixed reel, unusual cylindrical shape w/turned steel tip, fine condition, 6" l. ........................................ **165**

**Plumb bob,** brass w/reversible steel center & point, egg & band w/a cove design, 3 lbs., 5 oz.., very clean w/good age, fine condition, 6 3/4" l. (ILLUS. top of p. 250, center)............................ **264**

**Plumb bob,** brass w/steel tip, marked "A.L. Thompson. Lowell, Mass.," very small, very good condition, 2 1/4" l. .............................. **165**

**Plumb bob,** brass w/steel tip, tapered cone w/acorn cap, good condition, 5" l. ............................... **110**

*Four Plumb Bobs*

**Plumb bob,** brass w/steel tip, turnip-shaped, w/part of original wooden box & line reel, very good condition, 7" l. (ILLUS. left w/other plumb bobs)............................. **176**

**Plumb bob,** bronze, Stanley No. 1, w/original finish & finger loop, in original box, ca. 1925, fine condition, box near mint (ILLUS. p. 250, center w/various plumb bobs).......... **850**

**Plumb bob,** bronze, Stanley No. 2, in original box, ca. 1915, unused condition but finish worn, box in fine condition w/full label & good color (ILLUS. p. 250, right w/various plumb bobs)........... **425**

**Plumb bob,** bronze w/85% nickel plating, detachable steel tip, turnip-shaped, very good condition (ILLUS. below, center bottom w/other plumb bobs)......................... **193**

**Plumb bob,** cast iron, cast-in mark "Roberts Duplex Gauge Cock," marked w/illegible patent date on back side (appears to be Apr. 25, 87), flat sides, good condition w/traces of original finish, 5" l. (ILLUS. below, center top w/other plumb bobs) ............................... **165**

**Plumb bob,** cast iron, marked "W. & L.E. Gurley," engineer's type w/extra long neck, steel tip, leather case, good condition, 14 oz.......... **61**

**Plumb bob,** cast iron, Stanley No. 1, early unmarked version, good condition (some nicks & bangs) ..... **130**

**Plumb bob,** cast iron, Stanley No. 1, reel-type, marked on reel w/SR&L logo, good condition (some dings) ................................. **155**

**Plumb bob,** cast iron, Stanley, reel-type, never listed in catalogs, orange paint & decal, ca. 1930, paint fine, 85% decal dinged a bit, very good condition, 4 1/4" lbs., 7 1/2" h. ............ **1,500**

**Plumb bob,** cast iron w/95% plating, Stanley No. 5, reel-type, original string & ring, largest size, fine condition .......................... **352**

**Plumb bob,** cast metal, internal reel type, unmarked but appears to be K&E design, hard to find, working, very good condition.............................................. **264**

*Stanley Plumb Bob*

**Plumb bob,** cast-iron w/built-in reel, Stanley, orange paint w/95% of decal, never listed in catalogs, 2 lbs., 10 oz., fine condition (ILLUS.) .................................. **2,310**

**Plumb bob,** mercury-filled hollow brass w/brass screw cap/string holder, rare in that it hasn't been emptied of its mercury, fine condition, 2 3/4" d., 3 1/2" h. ............. **180**

**Plumb bob,** metal w/65% plating, Stanley No. 5, marked on reel, good condition.............................. **190**

**Ratchet wrench set,** cast iron, marked "Allen Universal 41 Wrench Set," tools in good condition & ratchet w/most original finish, complete in original wooden box, very good condition, 22 pcs. ...................... **75**

**Ratchet wrench set,** cast iron, marked "Starrett No. 443," 36 pieces in good condition in original wooden box w/labels, the set (not complete)..................... **110**

**Rope maker & perforator,** cast iron, marked "Monark," complete w/swivel, key & four-hook head, clamps onto a board, cast-iron perforator w/original japanning & yellow & blue pinstriping, very good condition ....... **165**

**Rosette punch,** cast iron, oval open ring w/serrated edges, very good condition, 3" l. ................. **20**

**Rounder over tool,** cast iron, marked "C.H. Reid," material rolls in & is rolled over to make a 180-degree turn, good condition............................................... **20**

**S-wrench,** cast iron, Baxter's Patent-type, adjustable, good condition (even coat of rust)............. **26**

**S-wrench,** cast iron, marked "W. Baxter. Pat. Dec. 1, 1868," Schultz 305, clean & nice, very good condition, 8" l. (ILLUS. p. 242, middle row, second from right with other wrenches) ................ **25**

**Salesman's sample cutting apparatus for mowers,** cast iron, tin & wood construction, marked "L. Rundell. Patented August 4, 1885.," cutting apparatus for mowers & reapers, cutting bar appears to be design that became standard on thousands of farms, cutter bar teeth move as wheels rotate, some minor damage, New Baltimore, New York, retains 70% of original red wheel paint........................... **760**

**Scales,** brass & steel hanging-type, often called a buffalo hide scale, uncommon, German, very good condition............................. **105**

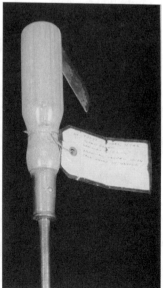

*Rare Stanley No. 1022 Screwdriver*

**Screwdriver,** cast iron & hardwood, Stanley No. 1022 Jack Knife Screwdriver, original

*Stake Anvil*

**Stake anvil,** cast iron, unmarked, w/round & square horns, 18th c., good condition, some pitting, 15" tip to tip, 11" h (ILLUS.). .............................................................. **190**

Stanley Model Shop tag reads "9-17-37 - Model 11741 - Screw Driver - Stanley #1022-6 - Original model with jack knife in handle," & is dated two years before tool showed up in catalogs, rare, fine condition (ILLUS. on previous page) ..................................... **495**

**Screwdriver,** cast iron, unusual style w/a side tip for screws w/a filled center as in saw nuts, very odd, turned wood handle, good condition (ILLUS. p. 242, top row second from right with wrenches).... **120**

**Screwdriver,** iron, marked "Yankee No. 90-10" - North Bros.,"in original box, tool like new, box w/edge wear but good label .............. **44**

**Screwdriver,** steel, marked "H.H. Mayhew Co. Interchangeable Screw Driver," in original box w/good color & label, includes three bits, very good condition (light use, three box flaps missing)...... **72**

**Screwdriver,** steel, marked "Mann's Holdfast Screw Driver," in original box w/full picture label, fine condition (slight tool use, box worn)........................................ **55**

**Screwdriver-flashlight combination,** steel w/95% finishes, Stanley No. 1021, clean & rare, batteries not included, fine condition .............................................. **220**

**Screwdrivers,** cast iron, Stanley No. 86, rare first Sweet Hart logo, in original box, tools like new, box fine, 5" l., full box of 6..... **242**

**Screwdrivers,** iron, marked "Yankee North Brothers," No. 95-1 1/2" & No. 90-2", in original boxes, tools still unwrapped, boxes fine, two full boxes of 6....... **198**

**Screwdrivers,** steel, Stanley Yankee No. 4595, new set in original box, only one unwrapped, box w/70% labels, early 20th c., the set .......................... **193**

**Seam rubber,** lignum vitae, Stanley Rule & Level Co. New Britain, Conn. USA., clearly marked by Stanley, shape offers two rounded working edges, fine condition, 4 x 5 1/2" (very minor chip on one edge, otherwise near new) .................................. **300**

**Shingle thief,** wrought iron, early, good condition ......................... **21**

**Sighting device,** cast metal, marked "Palmer," head rotates in a full circle, adjustable weight swings in an arc graduated from 5 to 50, very good condition ............. **50**

**Slater's tool set,** hammer w/leather handle by Belden Machine Co., large anvil w/illegible mark, hand-wrought iron shingle their w/ram's-horn end, a scarce roofer's seat or jack having a wooden seat w/chisel-like legs, rare set, very good condition, the set .......................... **187**

**Stone holder,** cow horn, early tapering funnel-form clipped to the belt & worn into the fields during hay-mowing time, could be filled w/water to keep the stone damp ............................... **33**

**String winder,** bentwood, hard-carved, bent long arch on slender center post, old red paint, quite early, good condition ............. **83**

**Surveyor's chain,** cast iron w/cast iron handles & brass swivels, brass tags at quarters, two rods, good condition (even coat of rust) ............................ **160**

**Surveyor's chain,** iron w/brass handles & tags, marked "K & E Tested. 130 ft. No. 12," welded links, swivels, rare, very good condition ............................... **130**

**Surveyor's chain,** wrought iron, marked "Chesterman, Sheffield England.," brass handles & tags, quality chain, no surface rust, good condition, 100' l. .......... **160**

**Surveyor's chain,** wrought iron, marked "Keuffel & Esser Co. 7736D.," brass handles & tags, very minor surface rust, good condition ................................. **200**

**Surveyor's cross with sighting scope,** brass, marked "C.G. King (1841-1858).," label in lid of box, drum-type design w/two sections rotating independently,

meeting point of two sections silvered degree scale, two level vials, sections can lock, upper section rotated by thumbscrew at base, Jacob staff socket, original box, instrument unmarked, very unusual, silvered compass dial, 3 1/2" w., needle 2 3/4" l., fine condition, slide focus scope 8" l., overall 9" h. .......... **725**

**Surveyor's vernier compass,** brass & silvered metal, marked "Stackpole & Brothers. New York.," silvered face 5 1/2" w/5" needle, screw adjust vernier, tee plate vials, vanes 6 1/2" l., Stackpoles worked in New York last half 19th c., screw type base, mahogany box, very good condition, 15"l. ............................... **1,250**

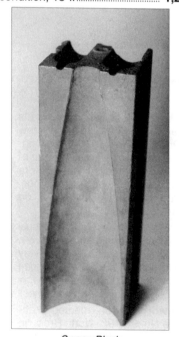

*Swage Block*

**Swage block,** cast iron, tapered reamers, forms for six sizes including two small hook reamers from 4" to 1 1/8", two reamers included as examples of the work produced by this swage, extremely rare, museum quality, 4 1/4 x 4 3/8", 12 7/8" l. (ILLUS.) ............................... **225**

*Tap Box*

**Tap box,** hardwood, two wooden bolts w/turn heads & tips hold box together, good condition, approximately 2" (ILLUS.) .............. **165**

**Tap box & screw,** boxwood, marked "Marples & Son," size marked "4" (looks to be about 1/4"), threads wooden bolts smaller than 3/8" in diameter, these small bolts very weak & seldom used, boxes extremely rare in this small size, fine condition ......... **75**

**Tape repair kit,** iron tools, marked "Lufkin," includes hammer, snips, anvil & replacement tips, in original leatherette case, very good condition, the set ........................ **41**

**Tar bucket,** wood, Conestoga wagon-type, hand-carved from a single piece of wood in an upright stepped form, cover slides on leather strap, early & proper, very good condition ........................... **110**

**Thatcher's comb,** wood, early wooden tool for laying thatch roofs, clean & rare, very good condition ...................................... **94**

**Tinsmith's creaser,** wrought iron, double curl ram's horn nuts, very rare, good condition ................. **280**

**Tinsmith's tool,** wrought iron, creaser or swage, hammer-type, straight poll, hand-wrought & early, very rare, fine condition ...................................... **300**

**Tinsmithing beading tool,** cast iron, unmarked, w/crank adjuster, wooden post wedge locks into hole in bench, clean & working condition (ILLUS. below, left w/other tinsmithing tools) ................. **150**

**Tinsmithing burring tool,** brass bearings, steel rollers, marked "Peck, Stow & Wilcox Co.," hand crank adjusts to work size, good condition (ILLUS. below, right w/other tinsmithing tools) ......... **90**

**Tinsmithing burring tool,** cast iron, marked "A.W. Whitney. Woodstock, VT.," adjustable, post can be mounted on block, w/interchangeable collar that fits other machine, good condition (ILLUS. below, center w/other tinsmithing tools) ................. **220**

*Tinsmithing Tools*

**Tool box,** cobbler's, wooden, signed "Capt. Spates Tool Box," rectangular, rustic construction, includes about 17 tools & a vise, some marked "T.D.S.," name carved in top, good condition (tools well-used) ...................................... **88**

*Keen Kutter Tool Cabinet with Tools*

**Tool cabinet,** oak, marked "Keen Kutter Korner Kabinet No. K-11-C," w/double front doors, three drawers inside, 27 Keen Kutter tools, rare, good condition, 14 x 27", 32" h. (ILLUS.) .............. **1,700**

**Tool caddy,** maple, Stanley No. 801 Tool Caddy, lift-top lids, brass Sweet Hart tag on top of lid, Sweet Hart strap hinges, very good condition ............................ **550**

*Fine Stanley No. H892 Tool Kit*

**Tool kit,** cast iron, Stanley No. H892, new & mint, most tools never unwrapped, purchased in 1959, original metal box & outside cardboard shipping box, very fine condition, the set (ILLUS.)................................................. **440**

**Tool set,** cast iron & oak, inside label reads "'Yankee' Tool Set No. 100," set includes three screwdrivers w/14 bits, North Brothers Mfg. Co., Philadelphia, abel 97%, w/original box, good condition, the set................................. **286**

**Tool set,** cast iron, original wood box w/green cardboard covering & label reading "Yankee Tool Set No. 100," tools mint & unwrapped, early 20th c., fine condition, the set................................ **385**

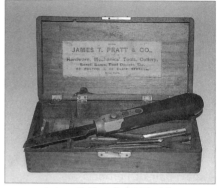

*James T. Pratt & Co. Tool Set*

**Tool set,** mahogany fitted box w/label inside lid reading "James T. Pratt & Co.," square shank as used on braces, includes about 24 tools, many marked, good condition, the set (ILLUS.) ....................................... **495**

**Tool tote,** mahogany, rectangular w/turned center handle, fine condition (ILLUS. p. 264, front, w/tool tote & tool chest).................... **198**

**Tool tote,** maple, ebony & mahogany, rectangular w/turned center handle, three drawers at bottom w/spring-load friction clips to keep them from falling out when tote is moved, inlaid design of five-pointed star at one end, cross on other end, both of contrasting woods w/inlaid borders, very good condition (ILLUS. p. 264, top, w/tool tote & tool chest)............................... **550**

**Transit compass,** brass & silvered metal, marked "Transit. B. Pike & Sons. 518 Broadway, New York.," compass dial engraved & silvered, 5" d. vertical circle, darkened finish accented w/90% original brass highlights,

*Huge Emmert's Patternmaker's Vise*

original mahogany box & tripod, ca. 1860s, very good condition, tripod 13 1/2" h., 9" l. scope w/working optics, 5 3/4" d. compass w/5" l. needle.................. **1,025**

**Vernier transit compass,** brass, marked "William T. Gregg. New York.," 10" l. telescope w/working optics, 4" d. vertical circle, 5" d. compass dial w/4 3/8" l. needle, two plate leveling vials, darkened brass w/95% finish, tripod 10 1/2" h. without detachable leveling base, very good condition (walnut case missing leather strap)................................... **1,550**

**Vise,** cast iron, marked "Emmert's Patternmaker's," face 7 x 18" rotates so four different surfaces can be worked, outer face tilts to handle different shapes of wood, entire front & rear face can be tilted upward, jaws open to hold a 14" piece & have dogs to facilitate holding irregular shaped pieces, huge 70 lb. size, good condition (ILLUS. above) ..... **303**

**Vise,** cast iron, marked "Stephen's Patent," quick action type for jeweler or pattern maker, pressure applied to work via lever arm, good condition, jaws 2" w. overall 5" l. ...................................... **85**

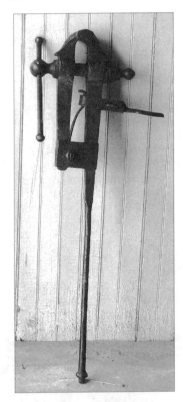

*Blacksmith Leg-type Vise*

**Vise,** wrought iron, blacksmith leg-type, good condition, 4" w. jaws, 40" l. (ILLUS.) ............................ **110**

**Wagon brake or slipper,** wood & iron, hand-wrought, Conestogatype, placed under the wheel, early .................................................. **50**

**Wagon jack,** wood & iron, Conestoga wagon-type, decorated wood post w/iron crank, carved date unclear, ca. 1871, very good condition ................................. **121**

**Wagon jack,** wrought iron & wood, Conestoga wagon-type, hand-forged crank & iron works enclosed in a wooden frame, vertical iron stem decorated w/white smithing & date "1818," good condition ............................... **248**

**Wagon wrench,** iron, marked "Joy's Wagon Wrench No. 3," old long wood handle, working, large, 20" l. ..................................... **80**

**Washer cutter,** all-wood construction, wedge-locked center section w/removable dowel plug that probably originally came w/interchangeable sizes, two-handled cutter arm slides through center section, wedge lock cutter can be set for maximum of about 11" d., unique, good condition ............................... **90**

**Washer cutter for brace,** cast iron, adjustable to about 4", good condition ................................. **20**

**Water pipe rounder tool,** probably maple, two-handled for 4 1/2" d. pipe, very good condition ............................................. **110**

**Woodworker's bench,** hardwood, marked "E.W. Carpenter. Lancaster.," massive size w/side & dovetailed tail vise, tool till on backside of bench, two iron dogs, one of only three of this type by this maker, good condition, 6' 8" l. (ILLUS. below) ........ **4,290**

**Woodworker's gluing furnace,** copper double-boiler style, tin cone stove w/burner, rare, good condition ............................... **116**

**Wrench,** cast iron, marked "Bay State Tool Co. Pat. June 7, 1904," Schultz 476, quick adjusts w/the flip of a lever, works well, good condition .......................... **130**

**Wrench,** cast iron, marked "Boyton's Patent Pat'd Jun. 14, 1887," Schultz 28, rare adjustable-type, fine condition (ILLUS. p. 242, top row, third from right with other wrenches) ..... **180**

**Wrench,** cast iron, marked " Gordon Automatic," Schultz 493, works slowly, good condition, 7" l. (ILLUS. p. 242, middle row, far right, with other wrenches) .......... **31**

**Wrench,** cast iron, marked "Hande," quick-adjust-type, slide adjusts work well, very good condition, 10" l. ............................. **41**

**Wrench,** cast iron, marked "Kibbon Katchkwick 18 Inch - Pat. Pend," Schultz 693, rare

*Early Woodworker's Bench*

Nashville, Tennessee wrench, good condition (ILLUS. p. 242, top row, far right, with other wrenches) ............................................. **100**

**Wrench,** cast iron, marked "Pollock's Automatic Quick Adjuster," Schultz 521, spring-loaded jaw closes w/press of lever, retains original removable pipe jaw clip, very good condition .......... **175**

**Wrench,** cast iron, marked "Vadegrift Mg. Co.," quick adjuster, wedge slides to adjust, wooden handle, rare, good condition (some pitting) ...................................... **130**

**Wrench,** cast iron, marked "Yoke Wrench. Patent Pending. Chandler Co. Cedar Rapids, Iowa.," unlisted, lever arm-type, very good condition, 12" l. (ILLUS. p. 242, bottom row left, with other wrenches) .............................................. **21**

**Wrench,** cast iron, quick adjuster, as handle rotates jaws tighten on nut, good condition, 12" l. ............. **95**

**Wrench,** cast iron w/100% japanning, Stanley No. 1 Tire Bolt Wrench, polished surfaces bright, tight to shank wooden handle, ca. 1905-20, very fine condition ...................................... **425**

# Tool Chests

This section includes listings and illustrations of a number of chests that were crafted specifically to hold either a set of tools or a general collection of tools in general use in the past. Most of these chests were hand-crafted in wood and can range from fairly primitive pine examples to finely detailed and carefully crafted works of art built with pride by a craftsman of the past.

*Cabinet Maker's
Tool Chest*

**Cabinet maker's tool chest,** bird's-eye & crotch flame walnut, dovetailed construction, lid design laid out in eight-segment oval w/center circle & star, bird's-eye band circles outer edge, w/four tills, top two w/inlaid lids, outside stripped & waxed, very good condition, 23 x 38", 22" h. (ILLUS. above)..... **990**

**Cabinet maker's tool chest,** mahogany & burl & bird's-eye maple, dovetailed inside & out, w/six tills, contrasting woods in lid bookmatched w/fancy-edge molding, very good condition,

*Mahogany Cabinet Maker's
Tool Chest*

one till professionally replaced, 25 x 40", 23" h. (ILLUS. bottom of previous page) ................................ **715**

**Cabinet maker's tool chest,** walnut burl, inside of lid inlaid w/maple & mahogany wood in geometrics, pinwheels, stars & diamonds, two till covers inlaid w/design of leaves & vines, dovetailed inside & out, w/seven tills, one for saws, two w/covers, sliding cover at base of till tier, good condition, 38" w., 23 1/2" h. (missing lock, minor inlay damage) .............................. **2,000**

**Jointer's traveling tool chest & tools,** wood, deep rectangular sides w/deep moldings, pull-out side handles for ease in carrying, includes a good selection of tools including framing chisels, corner chisels, backsaws, etc., very good condition (ILLUS. below) .......................................................... **385**

**Machinist's tool chest,** walnut, rectangular w/lift top w/two sliding trays, storage compartment in the top w/sliding cover, drawer below, brass Victorian Eastlake-style hardware, w/keys, clean & very good condition, 11 x 20", 9" h. ........................................ **440**

*Maple & Mahogany Tool Chest*

*Old Jointer's Traveling Tool Chest*

**Tool chest,** bird's-eye maple frame w/mahogany panels, w/eight dovetailed covered tills for planes, saws & other tools, "GEM" inlaid on front center, fine condition, center plane till in style but not original, 24 x 39", 24" h. (ILLUS. on previous page) .......... **1,458**

**Tool chest,** bird's-eye maple, inside top & lid in top till accented w/bird's-eye maple, three tills all w/fitted compartments, top till w/a small lift-out tray, saws kept in a slide in till that may be a unique feature, hard-to-find middle size, good condition, 36" w., 20" deep, 17" h. .................... **925**

*Chestnut & Mahogany Tool Chest*

**Tool chest,** chestnut & mahogany, dovetailed construction, w/two mahogany drawers w/two bale handles each, top compartment w/lift lid w/raised panel, good condition, one handle is replacement, 10 x 15 1/2 x 23 1/2" (ILLUS.) ................................................. **275**

**Tool chest,** hardwood w/oak interior, Stanley No. 851, w/roll-up lid & holders for various tools, full decal inside & label outside, good condition (no tools included, some hooks missing) ................. **425**

**Tool chest,** machinist's, walnut, rectangular lift top opens to till, two drawers below, original finish, 13 x 20", 12" h. ........................... **187**

**Tool chest,** mahogany crotch grain burl w/bird's-eye maple quadrants in the corners & a wide ebony border, silver nameplate in center of top inscribed "Wm. T. Jones. Rome, NY. 1856," six sliding tills & a saw till, dovetailed construction, refinished, w/key, 24 x 37", 25" h. .... **660**

*Mahogany Tool Chest*

**Tool chest,** mahogany, raised-panel lids on top & inside tills, five compartmented sliding tills, dovetailed, completely refinished & well done, small size, fine condition, 19" h x 18 d., 36" l., (ILLUS.) ................................... **1,210**

*Mahogany Tool Chest*

**Tool chest,** mahogany w/crotch burl inlaid on inside lid, four sliding tills, saw till & sliding front till, tills dovetailed & top ones w/lids, outside refinished in tan & natural wood, 25 x 38", 24" h. (ILLUS. bottom of previous pg.) ... **413**

*Tool Chest & Two Tool Totes*

**Tool chest,** maple & walnut, dovetailed construction, rectangular, w/six tills, the top till covered w/alternating strips of light & dark wood, finger-jointed inside & out, good condition, 23 x 37", 17" h. (ILLUS. at left, center w/tool totes) .............................. **330**

**Tool chest,** milk-painted wood, dovetailed inside & out, rope handles, four sliding tills inside painted red & w/cockbead edges, outside painted soldier blue, ca. 1800, very good condition ................. **300**

**Tool chest,** mixed soft & hard woods, combination wooden bench & chest, oversized top acts as bench, inside a large array of tool holders & bins, top 22 x 49" (ILLUS. below) .................... **330**

**Tool chest,** oak, marked "Keen Kutter," tool holders include cast-iron screwdriver holder, drawer in base, brass tag outside & two large decals inside,

*Mixed Wood Tool Chest*

*Pattern Maker's Tool Chest*

fine condition, 17 1/2 x 26", 9" h. ............................................... **300**

**Tool chest,** pattern maker's, wooden, marked "G. Ralphs," wide rectangular hinged top overhanging & opening to a rectangular base w/two drawers, flat base, includes full complement of tools including plane sets, brace w/bit, gouges & chisels, w/key, very good condition, chest 17 x 31", 16" h., the set (ILLUS. above).......................... **2,420**

**Tool chest,** pine, signed "George M. Beatty. Phila, PA.," dovetailed inside & out, w/sliding tills, saw box, original key, owner's name handpainted on inside of lid, miscellaneous tools include five planes, two hammers & Stanley No. 93 level among oth-

ers, very good condition, 23 x 39", 21" h. ..................................... **225**

*Walnut Burl Tool Chest*

**Tool chest,** walnut burl w/crotch burl on top both inside & out, dovetailed construction, opens to six tills, old red paint, 24 x 37", 22" h. (ILLUS. bottom of previous page) .................................. **330**

**Tool chest,** walnut w/rectangular mahogany panels, dovetailed construction, five inside trays & saw till w/cockbead edges, paneled covers over both tiers, top divided into two panels w/edge molding, w/key, very good condition, 25 x 35", 24" h. ...................... **633**

**Tool chest,** wood & leather, steamer trunk style w/five drawers, lid latches completely to protect contents to be safely shipped town to town or across seas, very good condition, 29" l., 15 1/2" deep, 16" h.

(leather handles broken out, otherwise clean & nice) ..................... **275**

**Tool chest,** wood, signed "J.C. Hockenbury," w/lift-out tray, name painted on top w/pinstripe decoration, fine condition, 11 x 23", 8" h. ............................... **110**

**Tool chest,** wood w/nearly 100% finishes, Stanley Four Square No. 861, retains 95% decal, fine condition (no tools) ............................. **200**

**Tool chest with tools,** oak, marked "Wm. Marples & Sons," wall-mounted style, double-hinged front doors, inside w/hooks, hangers, & fixed tray in base, includes about 20 tools, saws, shaves, rules, & chisels (ILLUS. below) ....................................... **358**

*Wall-Mounted Oak Tool Chest*

# Books & Paper Ephemera

An interesting adjunct to the collecting of tools themselves is the gathering of old books, catalogs, flyers and advertisements that help tell the story of tools. Since there are so many types of tools to collect, there is obviously a huge volume of published material to choose from. As you will see below, some old literature can sell for a few dollars, with rarer items bringing several hundred.

**Book,** "Peter Nicholson, Nicolson's New Carpenter's Guide. Being a Complete Book of Lines" ca. 1825, pages of finely engraved plates for hand railing, church work, roofs, domes, etc., 240 pages, 8 1/2 x 11" format (some staining, & cover loose), early & rare book, good condition ........................ **$230**

**Book,** "Tools of the Nation Maker," Henry C. Mercer, 1897, signed by author, "With Compliments of Henry C. Mercer," inventory of 761 tools in Mercer Museum 103 years ago, rebound, 87 pages, good condition ........................ **150**

**Catalog,** "Keen Kutter Complete Catalog. 1935.," 2118 pages, 8 x 11" format, good condition ...... **200**

**Catalog,** "Plomb Hand-Forged Tools for the Automotive Industry," ca. 1930, 64 pp., very good condition, 4 x 9" ..................... **70**

**Catalog,** "Stanley How-To Hints for Good Gardening with Lawn and Garden Tools," printed in black & yellow, rare, very good condition, 16 pp. ..................... **55**

**Catalog,** "The F.W. Loll Mfg. Co.," 1908-09, shows screwdrivers, mincing knives, tack pullers, can openers & other kitchen utensils, very good condition, 22 pp. ............... **25**

**Catalog,** "The West Haven Manufacturing Company," 1918, shows hacksaws & related items, used, good condition, 6 x 9" ..................... **47**

**Framed certificate,** paper, marked "United and Industrious Amalgamated Society of Engineers, Machinists, Millwrights, Smiths and Pattern Makers," certificate for Smith Slingsby of Boston, Mr. Slingsby admitted to society on January 15, 1881, full color lithograph w/tradesmen at work, great color, oak & plaster frame w/minor chipping, frame inside measures 22" x 28," overall 30 x 36," (ILLUS. below) ............. **150**

**Newspaper,** "Newspaper And Daily Advertiser. Dec. 16, 1799," four pages of original paper w/ad by Thomas Napier, plane maker of Philadelphia, Napier offered full line at competitive prices, details of location & outlet in Baltimore, framed in two sided frame w/reading on both sides, very good condition ........................ **230**

**Pamphlet,** "Stanley Tools in Sets," 1934, six-fold, shows eleven tool sets including No. 850, very good condition ..................... **46**

**Poster,** "Stanley Four Square," shows full line of Four Square tools, printed in red & black, rare, fine condition, 18 x 24" ........... **200**

*Framed Certificate*

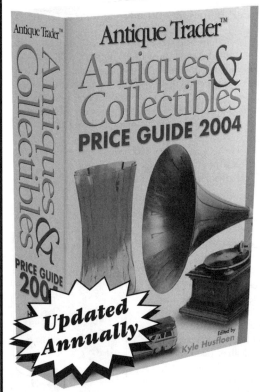

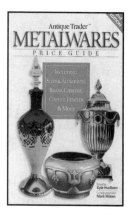
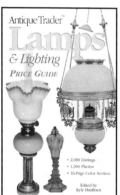

### Antique Trader® Oriental Antiques & Art
*An Identification and Price Guide, 2nd Edition*
by Mark F. Moran & Sandra Andacht

Explore the Far East and lose yourself in the mysterious allure of the Oriental culture with this guide to Asian treasures. This new identification and price guide provides the information you need to catalog and evaluate your collectibles. Historical backgrounds, current values, and detailed descriptions are included for unique treasures ranging from apparel and textiles, jewelry, rugs and carpets, Chinese porcelain and pottery, to furniture, paintings, and Japanese porcelain and pottery.

Softcover • 6 x 9 • 528 pages
650+ b&w photos • 16-page color section
**Item# WORA • $24.99**

### Antique Trader® Book Collector's Price Guide
by Richard Russell

This comprehensive book collecting reference explains which books and authors are truly collectible and why. More than 5,000 collectible books written in English are identified, priced, and organized into 12 categories, including Americana, banned, fantasy, horror & science fiction, mystery, occult & paranormal, and philosophy & religion. Also discusses the world of book collecting and how to identify first editions and grade books.

Softcover • 6 x 9 • 448 pages
1,500 b&w photos • 16-page color section
**Item# ATBK1 • $24.99**

### Antique Trader® Clocks Price Guide
edited by Kyle Husfloen, Contributing Editor Mark Moran

Clocks are among the most sought after antiques and collectibles, and can be found in almost every American home. This comprehensive, compact price guide offers you the opportunity to learn about all the major types of large timepieces from the 17th century through the 20th. Crisp photographs highlight the more than 1,400 detailed listings.

Softcover • 6 x 9 • 280 pages
600+ b&w photos • 16-page color section
**Item# ATCL1 • $17.95**